How Advertising Works

Merry Christmas 2000!

Nadia, I hope this book, which I give you from the bottom of my heart will have a cherished place in your office – next to your Nancy Drew books!

Ccause I know it will probably have to stay on that shelf for quite some time!) Please read it with thoughts of me.... maybe you'll one day become obsessed with advertising as much as me! OK. well, stick with Barbie!

Love Ba

How Advertising Works

The Role of Research

EDITED BY

JOHN PHILIP JONES

SAGE Publications
International Educational and Professional Publisher
Thousand Oaks   London   New Delhi

For information:

SAGE Publications, Inc.
2455 Teller Road
Thousand Oaks, California 91320
E-mail: order@sagepub.com

SAGE Publications Ltd.
6 Bonhill Street
London EC2A 4PU
United Kingdom

SAGE Publications India Pvt. Ltd.
M-32 Market
Greater Kailash I
New Delhi 110 048 India

Printed in the United States of America

Library of Congress Cataloging-in-Publication Data

Main entry under title:

How advertising works: The role of research/edited by
John Philip Jones.
    p. cm.
  Includes bibliographical references and index.
  ISBN 0-7619-1240-1 (acid-free paper)
  ISBN 0-7619-1241-X (pbk.: acid-free paper)
  1. Advertising. 2. Advertising—Research. I. Jones, John Philip.
  HF5823.H58   1998
  659.1—dc21   98-8871

This book is printed on acid-free paper.

00   01   02   03   10   9   8   7   6   5   4   3

Acquiring Editor:	Harry M. Briggs
Editorial Assistant:	Anna Howland
Production Editor:	Michèle Lingre
Editorial Assistant:	Karen Wiley
Designer/Typesetter:	Janelle LeMaster
Cover Designer:	Ravi Balasuriya

This series of handbooks is dedicated to David Ogilvy

The quality of research will improve, and this will generate a bigger corpus of knowledge as to what works and what doesn't. Creative people will learn to exploit this knowledge, thereby improving their strike rate at the cash register.

—David Ogilvy, 1983
(the first of 13 predictions about advertising)

Contents

Part II
Research Before the Advertising Runs

Part III
Research After the Advertising Has Run

Part IV
Advertising Effects, Including Some Unexpected Ones

Introduction

John Philip Jones

This handbook is the first in a planned series of five. The individual volumes are to come off the press in sequence and with minimal delays between them. The titles of the five volumes are as follows:

1. *How Advertising Works: The Role of Research*
2. *Advertising Procedures and Operations*
3. *How to Use Advertising to Build Strong Brands*
4. *Multinational Advertising: Realities and Myths*
5. *Advertising Organizations and Publications: A Resource Guide*

This rather ambitious project, which I have been planning for many years, comprises a collection of separate articles by advertising specialists—many of them world-renowned figures—all of their contributions focused on the topics covered by the five volumes. Each volume is designed to cover its subject area fairly comprehensively. The large majority of individual chapters were written specially for this series, although a relatively small number are adaptations of articles that have appeared in the professional press. These are the pieces that I consider to be the classics: the cornerstones of an edifice of knowledge about advertising and how it works. Notes accompanying the previously published chapters detail where they originally appeared.

Most of the individual chapters include endnotes that contain carefully selected references to further published sources, with an emphasis on the empirical rather than the theoretical. It is my ambition to make the battery of references represented here the best possible knowledge bank relating to advertising available anywhere.

Each of the five volumes in this series covers a relatively self-contained field, and I have tried to minimize the overlap between volumes (although I fear that some will inevitably remain—but perhaps this does not matter much). Each of the individual chapters can also stand on its own, although in many cases different contributors, using different types of analysis, come to similar conclusions about advertising.

This volume is the work of 20 authors; 15 are practitioners and 5 are academics. Of these, 13 are American and 7 are British (of whom 6 have lived and worked in the United States). The contributions of the British analysts signal the importance of the British intellectual contribution both to our understanding of how advertising works and to those developments in methods that were pioneered in the United Kingdom.

The Advertising Business

Advertising is carried out by three main groups of participants: clients, the media, and agencies (including agencies' outside suppliers). Some analysts think that researchers should be included as a fourth group. However, I believe research to be so important that I prefer to consider it as a component part—a strong basic element—of each of the three main groups.

Clients and agencies carry out work that overlaps to a considerable degree. They are both involved in strategy, budgeting, media planning, media buying, and the evaluation of campaign effects. The specific expertise of agencies lies in their flair for developing creative ideas and their craft skills in supervising how these are executed as finished commercials and print advertisements. This supervision calls for intimate knowledge of the talent market as well as negotiating ability.

Agencies to some extent resent clients' attempts to trespass on the agencies' creative territory, but this does not prevent most clients from expressing robust views about their agencies' creative efforts. Some clients go further and try to become a (not totally welcome) part of the creative team. It is a refined art for a client to develop sensitivity in exercising informed and constructive creative judgment while at the same time not interfering in the creative process itself. Some client organizations are cleverer than others in this regard, and within the better client companies there are wide differences among individuals.

The division of responsibilities between clients and agencies highlights the fact that advertising is partly a scientific and partly an artistic activity. The "science" is the concern of both clients and agencies; the "art" is the responsibility of the agencies alone. *Science* is rather a flattering word to use in this context. Nevertheless, there is (or should be) a good statistical foundation to advertising strategy, media planning, and much advertising evaluation. Also, agencies carry out on a routine basis a good deal of qualitative research to help develop strategy and to evaluate creative ideas.

This duality in the advertising process is the reason advertising agencies (and clients, to a smaller degree) recruit two types of people—those with analytic skills and those with creative skills. The combination of these two types of talent working closely together is a source of much excitement, but at the same time considerable tension. To use a reasonably appropriate metaphor, this tension acts like the grit in an oyster necessary to produce a pearl.

Advertising Agencies

A striking characteristic of the advertising agency business is its fragmented nature. Individual agencies may appear prima facie to be large. However, in comparison with the aggregate size of the advertising business, they are in fact small. In most years, the top six individual agencies in the United States account for a total of only about 20% of all advertising in measured media—an extremely low concentration ratio in comparison with the fields in which their clients operate. The six-firm concentration ratio in most consumer goods industries is at least 60%, and in many cases it is much higher than that. The figure for breakfast cereals is more than 90%.

There are two reasons for this fragmentation. First, clients are very restrictive about their agencies' accepting competitive business—a narrowness that often goes to extreme lengths. A client employing an agency in one product field but in no others will often require that the agency not accept competitive business in other fields in which the client operates but the agency does not. This attitude on the part of clients has grown stricter over time, and it inevitably inhibits agency growth. Interestingly, the only important country that does not put sanctions on agencies' handling competitive business is Japan. As a result, Japan is a country of many large agencies. This does not mean, however, that the large Japanese agencies are better than the smaller American ones. There is in fact a limit to growth.

The second reason for the relatively small size of agencies is that economies of scale are less apparent in the agency business than in capital-intensive enterprises, such as most manufacturing businesses. It is true that in advertising, large clients will normally generate slightly higher relative profits than small clients, as a result of lower operating costs per million dollars of billing, because the costs are more widely spread. But clients are aware of this and frequently impose sliding scales on their agencies' remuneration, with the rates going down as the volume of business increases—a procedure that pinches out the agencies' financial rewards from their scale economies.

A related point regarding scale is that *diseconomies* of scale set in fairly early in an agency's initial growth phase. An individual agency is invariably dominated professionally by a small number of people at the top—sometimes by only one key figure. The larger an agency grows, the thinner becomes the contribution of the top talent to each individual client. This naturally tends to slow growth; in the words of a notable contemporary practitioner, Jay Chiat, founder of Chiat/Day (now TBWA Chiat/Day), "How big must we grow before we get bad?"

These characteristics of the advertising agency business have contributed to the ferocious nature of the competition among agencies.

Secular Difficulties for Advertising

This volume is concerned with the research needed to understand the advertising process. The problems afflicting the industry that are discussed in this section would be solved by the wider exposure of *effective* advertising.

Perhaps not surprisingly, advertising agencies have always put great emphasis on generating powerful ideas. The trouble is that we do not know enough about which ideas are powerful before advertising is exposed; and we are also not very good at evaluating the effectiveness of ideas after the event. Hence the stress I am placing on research.

The strong growth that was such a remarkable feature of the advertising business during the period after World War II came to an end during the mid-1980s. Although 1996 and 1997 saw a cyclical upturn, advertising is no longer making large strides in real terms, and the earlier rate of growth is unlikely to be renewed. The reasons are complex, but they ultimately stem from the fact that in developed economies most consumer goods categories have stopped growing significantly. What has made the situation worse is a factor already mentioned: the weakness of agencies in providing account-ability for their campaigns. *Demonstrably* effective work is still the exception and not the rule.

Clients have contributed to the lack of advertising growth in two ways. First, they have hugely increased their expenditure on sales promotions, mainly direct price-cutting to consumers and the retail trade. This is described as "below-the-line" activity. Clients have done this because they judge pro-motions to have greater immediate sales effects than advertising does. (The cruel paradox is that most promotions are unprofitable.) This trend toward promotions has of course decelerated the long-term growth in advertising. Second, clients have put downward pressure on their agencies' incomes (e.g., through the imposition of sliding scales, as mentioned above) so that agency income has not kept pace with increases in the absolute size of the business.

Advertising agencies, although engaged in an apparently vibrant activity, are in reality extremely conservative. Their first response to the lack of aggregate growth, the pressure on agency incomes, and the move of funds below the line demonstrated an astonishing lack of imagination. Agencies tried to maintain their profits by reducing their costs. They did this by cutting savagely into their payrolls, which had a predictable effect on their ability to produce superior work and to prove its effectiveness—the very things that might have started billings growing again.

Until the present temporary revival in their fortunes, agencies floundered in a sea of difficulties. At the same time they were cutting into their numbers of employees, they also made a strong move toward amalgamation. This was done with the aim of generating scale economies that could in some way compensate for the downward pressure on their income. As already discussed, scale economies are relatively unimportant in the agency field; the opportunities for these economies appeared more tempting than their performance has demonstrated. A number of "multiagencies"—unwieldy conglomerates—were also assembled, the most important being interpublic Omnicom, Saatchi & Saatchi (which subsequently fragmented), and WPP. The reasons for these super-amalgamations were mixed, and went beyond simple scale economies; and they certainly did not have much to do with generating superior advertising. Perhaps predictably, the marketplace performance of these bulky organizations has proven disappointing, as judged by the market value of their stock.

What it all comes down to is that most agencies have been too narrow in their thinking to realize that size alone—being a large unit with a traditional framework and conventional professional capability—is not enough for success in the future, a future that may continue to be both troubled and volatile. What is needed is some sort of radical restructuring:

1. Agencies must provide greater accountability for their work, so that they can separate the efficient campaigns from the inefficient ones and dump the latter. *This key recommendation has caused me to devote the first volume of these handbooks to the basic and applied research that, if suitably developed, will provide such accountability.*

2. Agencies must apply their skills—which they have up to now applied only to a small number of main media—to all media, including nontraditional ones, such as direct mail, cable television, interactive television, and point-of-sale consumer promotions. The synergistic use of all such media—which has been called *integrated marketing communications* (IMC)—has been a source of much spoken and written chatter, but there has been very little definite movement in the agency world toward implementing it.

3. Agencies must adapt their expertise in their familiar product fields (e.g., repeat-purchase packaged goods) to a situation in which aggregate growth is no longer possible in these fields and where the most important task is the protection of existing brand franchises.

4. At the same time, agencies must develop the capability to sell new types of goods and services that have good prospects for growth, such as direct-response business, financial and many other types of services, retail operations, and new concepts in the field of consumer durables. Given that many of the latter may not yet be discovered, let alone exploited, agencies should be playing a major role in product development in cooperation with their clients.

5. Following the above points, agencies must learn to operate in a more flexible, responsive, uninhibited, and entrepreneurial fashion than they have in the past. An astonishing feature of advertising agencies is that for such small and skilled organizations, they have always had essentially bureaucratic corporate cultures.

6. Agencies must abandon the anachronistic system of remuneration by commission. In the way in which it has been used since the introduction of reduced rates and sliding scales, commission has had two pernicious effects: It undernourishes agencies, and at the same time it grossly impedes organizational change in the industry. It discourages experimentation with new systems and structures because these will cost the agencies money that, under the commission system, clients will not underwrite. (Small, vigorous agencies invariably begin operations remunerated by fees.)

7. Most important, agencies need to equip themselves to produce more highly effective advertising—and more often—than they do at present.

The traditional inflexibility of the advertising agency business helps to explain why it has suffered a most significant loss of esteem over the course of the past 30 years. My feeling about the decline in the prestige of advertising is not unsupported. The two meticulous investigations of the business conducted by the eminent journalist Martin Mayer (*Madison Avenue, USA,* published in 1958, and *Whatever Happened to Madison Avenue?* published in 1991) make this point with considerable force. In fact, Mayer's work reveals the sharpest single change that has taken place in the advertising industry since the late 1950s. Whether or not this change will prove irreversible is totally within the control of today's agency practitioners.

Part I

Markets and Advertising

2

The Advertising Process

Timothy Joyce

In 1967, at a seminar on advertising research organized by the European Society for Opinion and Marketing Research (ESOMAR), I gave an invited paper titled, "What Do We Know About How Advertising Works?"[1] For some reason, at that time this paper appeared to strike a chord. It came to be frequently quoted and was several times reprinted—including in a somewhat revised form in Simon Broadbent's collection of ESOMAR papers, *Market Researchers Look at Advertising.*[2] It was also, in the year of the original seminar, picked up by *Advertising Age* in the United States and published by them in three parts. On my first visit to the United States, in 1967, I was surprised to find that many of the research and advertising people I met were familiar with it.

NOTE: The paper on which this chapter is based was first published in *Marketing and Research Today,* Volume 19, Number 4, November 1991. Permission for using this material has been granted by ESOMAR, the European Society for Opinion and Marketing Research, J.J. Viottastraat 29, 1071 JP Amsterdam, The Netherlands.

In the early 1990s, it was suggested that I should attempt to update that paper, which was by then almost 25 years old. In one key respect, however, I am handicapped. When I wrote the 1967 paper, I had the good fortune to have had considerable hands-on experience of advertising research in the 1960s, principally for clients of J. Walter Thompson (JWT), encompassing scores of tracking and brand image studies and hundreds of copy tests, both quantitative and qualitative. I could call upon practical examples and generalizations based on them to make my points. For the past 20 years, however, I have been laboring in the vineyards of media and media research. What I know about recent trends in advertising research is necessarily therefore secondhand rather than firsthand, informed largely by reading journal articles such as many in the *Journal of Advertising Research* and *Admap*.

Recalling advertising research in the 1960s evokes nostalgia. Research budgets were sizable; many clients were keen to fund research that was primarily developmental; everything was new; we had the feeling that we were writing the book on the subject, not just applying it. "Bliss was it in that dawn to be alive, but to be young was very heaven!" Not only the clients but the agency itself, JWT, were generous patrons of research. As to the latter, for example, JWT sponsored the development of a tracking service called the Advertising Planning Index, a pioneering venture that was a precursor of the studies Millward Brown has so successfully exploited in Europe and more recently in the United States. JWT put much more money into development of copy research methods. Perhaps most important, they sponsored, based on my proposal, the experimental "single-source" diary work of 1966, which justly became famous when Colin McDonald published his analysis of the data with respect to the short-term effects of advertising.[3]

What We Thought We Knew

What did we, or more correctly what did I, think we knew back in 1967 about how advertising works? I shall start by recapitulating some of the main themes of my 1967 paper. I queried certain quite common assumptions about the advertising process, and substituted conclusions based to the extent possible on actual data and experience. An explicit limitation of the paper was that it was restricted to advertising for what the Americans call repeat-purchase packaged goods and the British call fast-moving consumer goods (fmcg).

The first assumption that was queried related to purchasing itself, in terms of what advertising would achieve if it was effective. This assumption was that advertising achieved "conversion," in the sense of converting loyal users of the other brands to loyal users of the brand advertised. I pointed out that this pattern, although it could on occasion be found in actual purchasing sequences, was actually quite rare. Far more common was a situation in which the consumer had a repertoire of brands within the category that were purchased with varying frequency. Those familiar with consumer panel data know this very well. It came out particularly clearly from the single-source diary work referred to above, because the diary was a "journal," recording purchases day by day, so that an actual time sequence of brands purchased within a given category could be established for each panelist.

Clearly, therefore, if advertising is to "work," in most cases it will do so by causing the brand to be added to the consumer's repertoire (or at least preventing it from being dropped) or causing it to be purchased more frequently (or at least preventing it from being purchased less frequently). Conversion in the sense of "I have always bought brand B, but now the advertising for brand A has persuaded me that it is better, so in future I'll buy brand A" just never occurs—well, hardly ever.

The second assumption that was queried related to the advertising communication process—to the effect that the consumer was merely a passive receiver of messages. It was pointed out that this was not supported by actual experience of copy testing, and indeed that by that time there was a considerable body of evidence in the field of social psychology showing that communication is a far more dynamic and interactive process than this would suggest. People took away from communications, including advertising, what they chose to and, indeed, brought existing preconceptions to them. To cite a classic example, people in theater test audiences exposed to commercials for Persil and Kellogg's Corn Flakes guessed the ages of the same eight different presenters (16 tests in all) as considerably older when they were advertising Persil than when they were advertising Kellogg's Corn Flakes—Persil mostly being thought of as "used by older housewives" and Kellogg's as "used by younger housewives." The preexisting images of the brands influenced the perceptions of the presenters; and, at least in the context of these single-exposure tests, the actual ages of the presenters (which were of course varied in the design) did not affect the images of the brands one little bit!

The third set of assumptions that was queried had to do with models of the advertising process that were then rather conventional—models described variously as step-by-step, hierarchical, or transmissional—all, in any event, implying a rational consumer being moved by advertising through a sequence of steps to purchase of the product. There were a number of models, but at that time perhaps the best known was DAGMAR (Defining Advertising Goals for Measured Advertising Results), which had been devised for the Association of National Advertisers in the United States. The stages in this model were as follows: Awareness–Comprehension–Conviction–Action.

To quote again from Russell Colley, who was incidentally another one of the invited speakers at the 1967 ESOMAR seminar:

> All commercial communications that aim at the ultimate objective of a sale must carry a prospect through four levels of understanding: from unawareness to *Awareness*—The prospect must first be aware of the existence of a brand or company; *Comprehension*—He must have a comprehension of what the product is and what it will do for him; *Conviction*—He must arrive at a mental disposition or conviction to buy the product; *Action*—Finally, he must stir himself to action.[4]

DAGMAR had the great merit of proposing that there could be quantifiable objectives for advertising (in terms of awareness levels, brand ratings, and so on) over and above sales objectives. Indeed, independently JWT had developed the Advertising Planning Index to provide just such measurements on a continuing basis—what would now be called tracking studies.

However, at the outset we had had the belief—which would seem to be supported by DAGMAR and similar models—that such measures as brand awareness and ratings would be leading indicators of sales; that they would go up ahead of sales if a campaign were successful, and helpfully decline ahead of sales if there were a problem—for example, the campaign was proving ineffective or was encountering superior competition.

In real life, we found nothing of the kind. On a static basis, it was found that awareness and ratings (or intentions to buy) were very closely associated with usage. On a dynamic basis, in general we found that sales (use) moved *first*. This was noticed anecdotally a number of times, and then documented systematically by Andrew Ehrenberg and Michael Bird in several published papers.[5]

In the mid-1960s, several major U.S. studies were reported that were portrayed as demonstrating that "attitude change causes behavior change." My late colleague Jack Fothergill, in an ESOMAR conference paper, demonstrated most ingeniously that the data in these studies proved nothing of the sort.[6] He showed that they would follow directly from the assumption that one was looking at static markets in which probabilities of purchasing bear a constant relationship to probabilities of making specific ratings or intentions-to-buy claims.

In a dynamic situation, the finding that attitude changes may be found to follow behavior changes—and may therefore at least in part be caused by them—has turned up in a considerable amount of more recent research and is now generally accepted.

To summarize the main point of my 1967 paper, I portrayed the consumer as being far-from-passive advertising fodder. There is a continual tug-of-war between perception of advertising and brand attitudes, and between brand attitudes and behavior. Further, advertising evidently can affect behavior "directly" without affecting attitudes as an intermediate variable in any measurable sense.

I believe that most of the above reasoning would now be generally accepted. An important development of the late 1960s/early 1970s, however, was the "multiattribute attitude model," which with hindsight was somewhat against the spirit of the 1967 paper and also of then current thinking about advertising. The best-known model was that of Fishbein.[7]

But let us now move to the present time, noting before we do so that there still are two important sets of benefits to be had from advancing our knowledge of how advertising works. First, with respect to advertising itself, knowledge of how it works can help with decisions about what to say, how to say it, and where to say it, as well as how many times to say it. This is the old question of "How much is enough?"—and, therefore, "How much to spend on it?" with implications for profitability. Second, with respect to advertising research, knowledge of how advertising works potentially can help determine what measures are relevant both in pretests of copy and in tracking research, and also help target group definition (with direct implications, therefore, for media research).

What Has Happened Since?

Over the past 25 years or so, many things have changed. I shall list four major changes in the advertising environment that seem worth noting, and also four major changes in the advertising research environment. Of course, I am referring primarily to the U.S. market, with which I am most familiar, secondarily to the U.K. market, and less so to other European markets.

As to *advertising,* the first thing to be noted is that the consumer has become exposed to still more advertising messages. Any meaningful quantification will support this conclusion. In part, it is due to the growth in importance of shorter-length (and therefore more) TV commercials, but also to more magazines read, which are thicker magazines with more ads. In European countries that are experiencing the deregulation of TV, of course audiences will enjoy (if that is the right word) the same experience—more ads.

Second, advertising messages in every respect have on average become briefer. In the case of TV, this again can be quantified. Fifteen-second commercials now account for more than 35% of all network spots in the United States. In the case of print, general observation and some quantitative work show that ads have become more visual, less wordy, and more like billboards—whatever the product advertised. It is generally understood that in the case of print, to use Herb Krugman's telling phrase, "advertising works as quick as a wink."

Third—and now I am referring principally to TV, and this is a more subjective comment—there is more emphasis on creativity and on likeability. It used to be thought that there was a great gulf fixed between U.S. and U.K. commercials in these terms, with U.K. commercials being highly creative and enjoyable, even if in some cases not too relevant to the product, and U.S. commercials often being intrusive, strident, and loaded with copy points ("Tell more—sell more"). I don't now, myself, see a big difference. There is some quantitative support for the conclusion about the trend to likeability. In work referred to again below, Biel reports on consumers' recent evaluations of a large representative number of U.S. commercials, and notes as an interesting finding in itself that only 4% on average disliked the commercial either a little or a lot.[8] (See also Biel, Chapter 10, this volume.)

Fourth, the most dramatic change affecting advertising has undoubtedly been the growth in importance in promotions, both consumer and trade. Most promotional expenditure does, indeed, lead to a price reduction, whether directly or through a coupon, or money back, or whatever. It is beyond the scope of this chapter to discuss how this should be looked at from an accounting point of view; certainly in an important sense, much promotional "expenditure" can be properly regarded as income forgone rather than as an active line item in the marketing budget—but the fact is that from the marketer's point of view, advertising and promotional expenditures can be seen as competitive, and the latter have grown enormously, to the disquiet of the traditional full-service advertising agencies and of the traditional media.

Turning to *advertising research*, the most important development of the past few years has undoubtedly been the availability of bar code/scanner data. In the United States this has become important in at least three respects. First, the availability of store scanner data on a weekly basis, when a retail field such as supermarkets is sufficiently highly penetrated, can replace manual store audit data. The mere existence of weekly rather than bimonthly data, with all the variability shown in response to price changes and other promotional activity, undeniably has enhanced the use of promotions. Next, test markets such as the Behaviorscan system from Information Resources Inc. (IRI), which link addressable cable TV systems to household panel members who bring identification cards to local scanner stores, have greatly improved our ability to compare, experimentally, alternative campaigns and weight levels. Most recently, such household panels have gone national—IRI's Infoscan and Nielsen's Scantrack household panel being the research products (the last employing in-home scanner wands rather than store scanner data). Now we have electronic "single-source data," links with TV viewing, and prospectively other media exposure data being forged. In terms of applications and knowledge, the surface has been only scratched.

The second way in which advertising research has advanced is in the routine use of tracking studies—"usage and attitude" (U&A) studies from a less sophisticated point of view, or a Millward Brown bag of tricks from a more sophisticated one. Gordon Brown in particular must be commended for wringing useful generalizations about how advertising works out of his extensive databases and for publishing them.[9]

Third, we now have more analytic tools in the kit than we had before. I refer especially to econometrics, and will deal with this in a little more detail below.

Fourth, there have been basic research and basic studies within the industry that inform us considerably on the matter. In some cases these have been so important that they are worth dealing with in separate sections of the remainder of this chapter.

	THINK	*FEEL*
HIGH *INVOLVEMENT*	*1* *Life Insurance* *35mm Camera* *Motor Oil*	*2 Family Car* *Perfume* *Complexion Soap*
LOW *INVOLVEMENT*	*3* *Liquid* *Household* *Cleaner* *Clothes Pins*	*4* *Greeting Card* *Popsicle*

Figure 2.1. Psychological Processes in Advertising

The Different Advertising Tasks

In what follows, incidentally, I shall talk generally about all advertising (at least for consumer products and services) and not restrict myself to repeat-purchase packaged goods.

Seminal work was reported some years ago by Krugman on the topic of low involvement versus high involvement. He made the obvious but necessary-to-be-stated point that consumers are not greatly "involved" with many of the products they buy. They do not view television or read magazines with a view to making decisions about which brand of toothpaste or dog food to buy next. If they do learn from such advertising, it is learning with low involvement.[10]

Other seminal work has been done on thinking versus feeling, with the physiological underpinning of left-brain versus right-brain information processing. It happens that these two strands of work have been pulled together in what I think is a most clear and compelling manner by researchers Dave Berger and Dick Vaughn at Foote, Cone & Belding.[11] The "FCB grid" involves four quadrants, which are illustrated in Figure 2.1.

- Quadrant 1 would apply to big-ticket items, such as cars, appliances, and insurance.
- Quadrant 2 would apply to products such as cosmetics, jewelry, and fashion clothing.

TABLE 2.1 Psychological Processes in Advertising

	Think	*Feel*
High involvement	informative (economic)	affective (psychological)
Low involvement	habitual (responsive)	satisfaction (social)

TABLE 2.2 Psychological Processes in Advertising

	Think	*Feel*
High involvement	learn–feel–do	feel–learn–do
Low involvement	do–learn–feel	do–feel–learn

- Quadrant 3 would apply to fmcg and to other categories that essentially require commodity decisions, such as gasoline/petrol.
- Quadrant 4 would apply to "life's little pleasures," such as beer, cigarettes, and candy/sweets.

For each of these types of products, a particular type of advertising strategy is suggested as appropriate, as shown in Table 2.1. It is even suggested that different sequential models of the advertising process may be appropriate to each quadrant, as Table 2.2 illustrates.

It is claimed that the grid has been validated in the United States by "operationalizing" involvement and thinking in terms of scales, and obtaining ratings of some 250 product categories, which are shown in Figure 2.1.

This grid is most elegant, and has had the benefit of input and experience of applications from real-life advertising practitioners. I believe it concentrates our minds extremely well on the different types of products—and the different models of advertising that may accordingly be appropriate.

Effective Advertising Communication

An important breakthrough in advertising research is reported by Russell Haley in the final report of the Advertising Research Foundation (ARF) Copy Research Validity Project.[12] Quoting from the ARF Executive Research Digest, Haley states that the objective of the study was to determine the predictive validity of various typical types of measures used in copy research. Five products were included. Each submitted pairs of commercials that had demonstrated significantly different levels of sales response in 1-year split-cable sales tests. These were then tested across six different copy-testing methods. The objective was to determine how successfully each of the various copy-testing methods and measures predicted sales "winners."

The copy-testing methods included all major types of measures but did not necessarily reflect the proprietary differences in measures used by specific copy-testing firms. Moreover, as Haley notes, "it is always possible that with other commercials, other brands, other markets or other question phrasing, or in other time periods, different relationships would be found between sales and the measures used in this experiment. On the other hand, the measures that do show strong relationships to sales performance are certainly worth your attention." Analyses were conducted on differences between on-air versus post-only, and single exposure versus reexposure. All the brands were packaged goods and established brand names.

The results of the project indicated that copy testing works. No set of measures was perfectly predictive, but all types of measures (e.g., recall, persuasion, communication) included at least one reasonably predictive measure. The most surprising result was that the overall reaction to the commercial—likeability—proved to be the most predictive measure within the experiment. Haley observes that "commercials that are liked sell better than those that are not liked." Put another way, "Commercials that sell are commercials that are liked (as measured by the liking measure) and commercials that lead people to believe that you have an excellent product (as measured by the highest scoring persuasion measure)." Each could be considered an aspect of liking.

In terms of the interactions of various elements, the study indicated that "interactions improve predictability. Different approaches yield different combinations of measures. Likeability can interact with three factors: persuasion, recall, and diagnostics." According to Haley, the study further indicates that "likeable advertising is an asset to established brands. Therefore, likeability deserves a lot more attention than it has been given in the past."

At the same ARF workshop, Alex Biel presented two prior studies that point in the same direction.[13] (His contribution to this volume, Chapter 10, is derived from this presentation.)

Also at the ARF workshop, Jim Donius pointed out that in recent years advertising has become more visual and more entertaining. This has been in response to changes in the consumer, who is better educated, has less time, and leads a more complete life. This has been combined with media proliferation, increased clutter, and remote controls that zip, zap, and mute unwanted messages. Much work has been done developing research batteries to tap emotional elements of advertising, largely by the agencies for whom the creative "is our end product." Donius noted that he was not at all surprised "that measures other than recall or persuasion, measures of affect—both overall liking and commercial reaction—might also have a strong relationship to sales of packaged goods products in the 1980s and 1990s."

Yet another speaker at the ARF workshop, Jim Spaeth, then working for ViewFacts Inc. and referring to that company's experience, noted that the company's validation results paralleled the ARF study and extended the findings beyond packaged goods. Among the products tested, magazine sales via a toll-free telephone number, a soft drink, and an automobile all showed that the most effective commercials, when measured on a moment-by-moment scale, were those for which the likeability factor remained high during the presentation of product attributes: "Just a few seconds, and just a simple reaction like 'I like it' to those few seconds, make all the difference between whether a commercial sells more product or doesn't sell more product." ViewFacts's research also indicates that likeability increases over the first four exposures to a commercial, then tends to fall back and flatten out.

Notwithstanding the qualifications stated by several of the speakers, and the admittedly very small number of cases on which the ARF study was based—five pairs of commercials—I wonder who would have thought that a strong correlation between likeability and communications effectiveness would be found and recognized as plausible by many experienced practitioners. But it does make sense. Perhaps the most telling supporting argument is that of Biel, to the effect that likable ads stand less chance of being "switched out," literally or figuratively, and therefore get more effective exposure.

Long-Term Versus Short-Term Effects

Whether advertising works both in the short term and in the long term, and to what relative extents, has continued to be a major topic of discussion throughout the past several decades. But more recently, it has been illuminated by analysis of scanner test data and by econometric analysis of sales in relation to advertising and other "causal" data.

For example, recent work based on cumulation of IRI's Behaviorscan tests shows that in cases where "heavy-up" of advertising in years produced a significant improvement in sales, this was followed by more sales in years 2 and 3 as well as after the test had ceased (i.e., the two matched subpanels were then receiving the same levels of exposure).

As to long-term effects revealed by econometric analysis, the work of Broadbent in particular with the adstock model and its decay rates is especially relevant. So from another point of view is the Millward Brown work, concentrating especially on advertising awareness.

I should say, however, that I have some reservations about the results, and about econometric models as they exist today in particular. First, the results seem to be uncomfortably dependent on the models used. This seems to my nonmathematical eye to arise from the controversy between Broadbent and Stewart in recent issues of the *Journal of the Market Research Society*.[14]

Recently, Dennis Bender of the Nielsen company in the United States referred to the results of alternative econometric analyses of advertising, promotional, and sales time series data.[15] His point is that if the analysis is not executed correctly, the effects of advertising will be grossly understated. But how can one know what type of analysis is correct? This seems to be a situation in which the results of econometric analysis should be carefully checked against experimental data.

However, even with the data that are experimental in the strict sense—such as Behaviorscan data—I have a problem concerning the inference of long-term effects that I believe is not a mere quibble. It is this: Much purchasing, especially of repeat-purchase packaged goods, is habitual—in the sense that having purchased brand A on a given occasion, one is more likely to purchase it on another occasion, thus increasing sales in the long term. In a sense, this is a long-term effect—but in another sense it may not be. It might be true, in some cases, that advertising operates, directly, causally, only on the next purchase. After that, everything in the memory store is set to zero, so to speak, except that that particular purchase will influence the next one with respect to brand choice—and so on. In terms of advertising effectiveness, it would all be short-term effect.

To be sure, even with repeat-purchase packaged goods, there are clear long-term effects. The memory store carries on with awareness of past advertising and impressions of the brand. But those who have seen, as I have, "live" data of the type analyzed by McDonald from the single-source diary work, cannot fail to be impressed by the fact that short-term effects do exist and can potentially be estimated—which was a surprising finding when it first appeared.

Pulling It Together

Ruminating on short-term and long-term effects, and returning for emphasis to repeat-purchase packaged goods, it occurred to me that one could propose two ways in which advertising works. In the short term, advertising works by establishing *presence*—a useful term, developed in an article by Moran.[16] Another term for this is, of course, *salience*. If the brand is present and salient, it is more likely to be purchased next time.

We must also remember that presence derives from other factors that are not media advertising—display being an obvious example. Also, though some advertising agency people may not like to hear this, *coupons are advertising!* Almost every coupon, in the United States at any rate, carries an illustration of the package. It is a well-attested fact that coupon drops increase sales even among those who do not redeem them.

Turning to the long term, in this case the advertising is essentially an extension of the product—its physical form and appearance, its packaging, and so on. From this point of view, advertising is part of the *presentation* of the product. It should be consonant with the functions and aura of the product. A recent publication of the American Association of Advertising Agencies put this rather well:

> Consumer perceptions and all the communications it takes to build and nurture them can no longer be looked at as mere costs of doing business. They should no longer be treated merely as variable, flexible, up-for-grabs distribution expenses. They are a fundamental part of manufacturing the product—as much as size, shape, color, flavor, design, or raw materials. To short-change a product's perception-building communications can be as devastating to its market value as short-changing the most tangible product attributes.[17]

So there we have two suggestions as to how advertising (at least for repeat-purchase packaged goods) works, which I believe are consistent with the rest of this chapter:

- *Short-term:* Advertising is presence.
- *Long-term:* Advertising is presentation.

At least they're alliterative!

Conclusions

I believe the main conclusions of the paper I gave in 1967 should not be changed—presenting a more complex and, perhaps, more human view of the consumer than the rational/conversion models that had previously been largely accepted without question. However, much *has* changed since then. In the advertising environment, there is an ever-greater quantity of advertising exposures, but they tend to be briefer and to rely more upon creativity and likeability, and promotions have in some senses raced ahead of advertising in terms of importance.

In advertising research, we now have scanner data, established tracking studies, econometric analysis, and basic research results. We are also perhaps clearer now about the appropriateness of different models of advertising for different products—low versus high involvement, reason versus emotions.

Basic research on effective advertising communications has, surprisingly perhaps, shown the evident importance of attitudes toward ads, specifically likeability—though it is important to be clear just what this means.

Finally, I believe that the jury is still out—or should be—on the relative importance of short-term and long-term effects. However, both clearly exist.

In this context, two ways in which advertising "works"—at least for repeat-purchase packaged goods—are proposed:

- *Short-term:* Presence.
- *Long-term:* Presentation.

Notes

1. Timothy Joyce, *What Do We Know About How Advertising Works?* (Amsterdam: European Society for Opinion and Marketing Research, 1967).

2. Simon Broadbent (ed.), *Market Researchers Look at Advertising* (Amsterdam: European Society for Opinion and Marketing Research, 1980).

3. Colin McDonald, "What Is the Short-Term Effect of Advertising?" in *Proceedings of the ESOMAR Congress, Barcelona* (Amsterdam: ESOMAR, 1970); reprinted in Broadbent, *Market Researchers Look at Advertising.*

4. Russell Colley, *Defining Advertising Goals for Measured Advertising Results* (New York: Association of National Advertisers, 1961), 37-38.

5. Michael Bird and Andrew S. C. Ehrenberg, "Consumer Attitudes and Brand Usage," *Journal of the Market Research Society,* vol. 12, no. 4, October 1970.

6. Jack E. Fothergill, "Do Attitudes Change Before Behavior?" in *Proceedings of the ESOMAR Conference, Opitija* (Amsterdam: ESOMAR, 1968), Book 2, 875-900.

7. Mary Tuck, *Practical Frameworks for Advertising and Research* (Amsterdam: European Society for Opinion and Marketing Research, 1971); reprinted in Broadbent, *Market Researchers Look at Advertising.*

8. Alexander L. Biel, "Love the Ad. Buy the Product?" *Admap,* September 1990.

9. Gordon Brown, "Facts From Tracking Studies: An Old Advertising Chestnut?" *Admap,* June 1988.

10. Herbert Krugman, "The Impact of Television Advertising: Learning Without Involvement," *Public Opinion Quarterly,* vol. 29, no. 3, 1965.

11. Richard Vaughn, "How Advertising Works: A Planning Model," *Journal of Advertising Research,* vol. 20, no. 5, September/October 1980.

12. Russell J. Haley, *Final Report of the ARF Copy Research Validity Project* (New York: Advertising Research Foundation Copy Research Workshop, July 1990).

13. Biel, "Love the Ad."

14. Broadbent, *Market Researchers Look at Advertising.*

15. J. Dennis Bender, *Byte by Byte Through the Aisles of Life* (Chicago: Marketing Modelers' Group, January 1991).

16. William T. Moran, "Presence and the Perceptual Frame," *Journal of Advertising Research,* vol. 30, no. 5, October/November 1990.

17. American Association of Advertising Agencies, *The Value Side of Productivity* (New York: American Association of Advertising Agencies, 1989).

The Turbulent Depths
of Marketing

Leo Bogart

The typical packaged goods marketer looks out on a calm sea of national sales statistics. In this chapter, we are going to descend into the turbulent depths.

There was a time when a manufacturer's best intelligence about what was going on in the marketplace came from sales statistics and from the impressions gathered by sales representatives. This meant that any assessment of the effects of marketing actions had to rely on the manufacturer's record of sales as they rose and fell in response to product and packaging changes, pricing, dealing, and promotion. All this changed with the advent of market research that looked at the sum total of consumption and purchasing and positioned the manufacturer's own brands within the context of the total market. From consumer surveys and from store audits, it became possible to track those factors that affected sales but over which the manufacturer had no control: seasonality, general changes in the economy, and long-term changes in consumer habits.

Manufacturers' attention thus shifted from unit sales and dollar sales volume to market share as an indication of their competitive position and as a basis for evaluating their marketing programs. Their own records or orders received and factory shipments began to carry less weight than the records of sell-through, as measured in syndicated store-audit or warehouse withdrawal reports. The fortunes of brands and of brand managers reflected the oscillations of their market shares, plotted in endless series of symmetrical bar charts.

The result is expressed in a number of premises that are generally accepted in packaged goods marketing:

1. Changes in market size and brand position usually occur slowly over time.
2. Price cuts for a brand generally build market share; price increases reduce it.
3. Because most major packaged goods brands compete nationally, they must analyze their markets and plan their marketing strategies on a national or broad regional scale.
4. Big packaged goods advertisers expose their messages to the public in major media most of the time.
5. Any substantial advertiser in any major medium should be able to see its advertising's immediate sales effects.

Some of these principles may require some qualification, but a great many working marketers take them for granted because they are constantly being reinforced by the standard sources of data that guide them in their work.

This chapter will demonstrate the following:

1. Packaged goods markets are much more complex and much more volatile than they are often thought to be.
2. The real action takes place at the local level.
3. Newspaper advertising spurs that action in a unique way.
4. Packaged goods advertising often lacks the consistent visibility that newspapers can provide.

Let's start with the ripples on the surface, the changes in total category sales and in brand share. We will look first at the patterns of product movement, then at pricing, and finally at the role of advertising.

a. Sales Volume, for Total Category and
   Leading Brand—Major HBA Item
   (from National Syndicated Service)

b. Total Paper Towel Sales, and Bounty's
   Share (six markets)

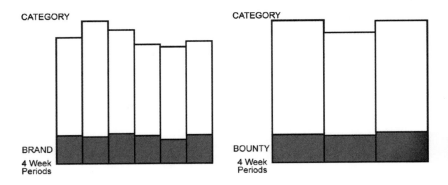

Figure 3.1.   Sales Tracking at One-Month Intervals

Retail Tracking

Up to the mid-1980s, marketers tracking the positions of their brands commonly used national product movement data on sell-through, as represented either by Nielsen Food Index (NFI) store audits or by SAMI warehouse withdrawal reports. Customarily, these data showed rather small changes from a given 2-month or 1-month reporting period to the next, either in total industry sales volume or in the position of any given brand (see Figure 3.1).

The 1980s saw the introduction of scanner data, which automatically report purchases at the checkout counter, and which provide the most accurate and sensitive measurement of actual consumer purchasing and provide it week by week. *The analysis presented in Figure 3.2 and subsequent tables and figures uses data from Nabscan (the first scanner data service) for five different packaged goods items in six markets (New York, Chicago, Los Angeles, Detroit, Kansas City, and Raleigh) with six stores in each. Sales have been standardized to reflect unit sales per hundred stores, to compensate for the differences in the sizes of the markets.*[1]

On a 4-week aggregate basis for all six markets, total category sales for each product class show the same familiar picture as NFI and SAMI, with very little change from one period to the next. As an example, Figure 3.1b shows the sales of paper towels and Bounty's share. In contrast, the analysis in Figure 3.2 will look below the surface of these apparently stable figures to examine the dynamics of the packaged goods market.

Because we are looking at the composite for just six markets, we would expect to find much more variability than if we had a sample of stores distributed throughout the entire United States. With a broader sample, local sales variations would be even more likely to cancel each other out when one reporting period is compared against the next.

The five categories under study are all quite different, but they cover the range of packaged goods sold in supermarkets: dry cereals, instant coffee, margarine, paper towels, and dishwashing detergent. With such a variety of products, one would expect great disparities in marketing philosophies, seasonality of consumption, brand share distribution, and consumer action. Indeed, such disparities are reflected in our findings.

Weekly Variations in Total Category Sales

This analysis covers 12 weekly reports, from April 21 through July 13, 1983. (The measured week runs from Thursday through Wednesday.) Overall, sales (per hundred stores) for any product category are never identical from one week to the next (see Figure 3.2a).

- *Dry cereals:* In this case there is hardly any variation of more than a few percentage points from one week to the next (see Figure 3.2a).
- *Instant coffee:* Weekly sales range from 14% above the average to 15% below, only partly reflecting a seasonal change (See Figure 3.2b).

Are these ups and downs related? Do extra sales in a given week come at the expense of future sales, or are they a net gain at the expense of other consumer purchases? There is no clear common pattern that cuts across categories.

- *Margarine:* In all six markets, total sales show a seasonal decline with the onset of summer, and the downward trend continues after exceptionally strong weeks. In individual markets, a sales increase may be sustained for 2 successive weeks at almost the same level, but then sales fall below the 12-week average (see Figure 3.3a).

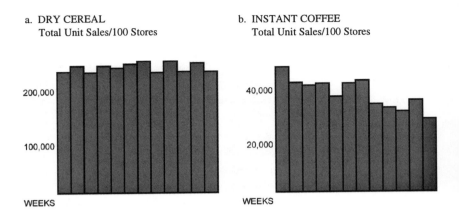

a. DRY CEREAL
   Total Unit Sales/100 Stores

b. INSTANT COFFEE
   Total Unit Sales/100 Stores

Figure 3.2.   Weekly Tracking of Dry Cereal and Instant Coffee

- *Paper towels:* A rise in sales seems to be followed by a drop, suggesting that the market compensates for unusual gains or losses and then returns to equilibrium. In general, this happens in most of the product categories, but one model does not fit all (see Figure 3.3b).

Total Category Sales and Leading Brand Activity

Do changes in the total market result from activity by just a few leaders? Market share was tracked for the major brands in each category, and significant retail price changes were noted, as well as magazine, newspaper, and television advertising for each. For the given product classes over the 12 weeks of analysis, no instance was found in any category of a brand that steadily built its market position.

- *Paper towels:* When leading brands increase their share, there is no increase of sales for the total category.
- *Margarine:* A large gain in a major brand's market share in any given week (following a price cut) does add to aggregate sales.
- *Dishwashing detergent:* A rise in a major brand's share in individual markets goes along with a jump in total category sales in some instances and with a drop in other cases.

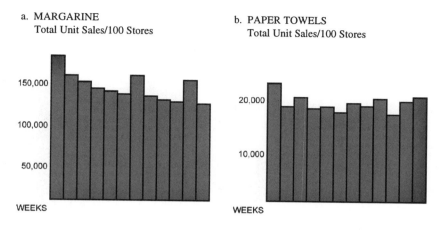

a. MARGARINE
Total Unit Sales/100 Stores

b. PAPER TOWELS
Total Unit Sales/100 Stores

Figure 3.3. Weekly Tracking of Margarine and Paper Towels

Again, no uniform rule seems to apply. Evidently, it is not easy even for a top brand to change the total size of a product category, at least for the five products analyzed here. For categories with greater brand distinctiveness, overall demand may be more responsive to what the leader does.

Category Sales Variations by Market and by Week

In comparing the weekly unit sales per 100 stores for individual markets, we find variability in local consumption patterns, even when we control for the differences in all-commodity store volume for the stores in our sample.

- *Dishwashing detergent:* Chicago outsells Raleigh by 27 percentage points.
- *Paper towels:* Kansas City outsells Chicago by 11 percentage points.

Such volume differences in part probably reflect the character and location of the store samples in the various cities, though local preferences and product usage may also be a factor. However, brand share differences cannot be explained so easily.

a. MARGARINE
   High and Low Weekly Unit Sales/
   100 Stores

b. INSTANT COFFEE
   High and Low Brand Share,
   Six Market Total

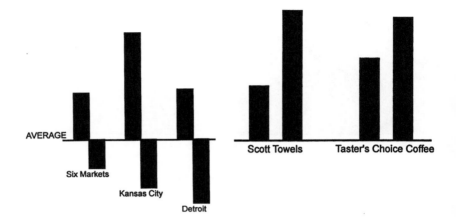

Figure 3.4. Variations by Regions and by Weeks—Category and Brands

I have already noted the weekly variations in overall sales, but these variations are even more striking in individual markets, as Figure 3.4a illustrates. For all five products, the increases caused by promotions result in far greater deviations from the average than do the decreases, which are spread out over a longer period.

Variations in Brands

If category sales vary weekly within markets and also from market to market within the same week, it is not surprising to find that individual brand shares show comparable variability, as seen in Figure 3.4b.

Individual brand shares also vary greatly within the same week from market to market, as Figure 3.5a shows for Parkay, Ajax, and Scott. The differences become even more dramatic when we look at the fluctuations in brand share week by week, not only overall but in individual markets. Figure 3.5b provides an example.

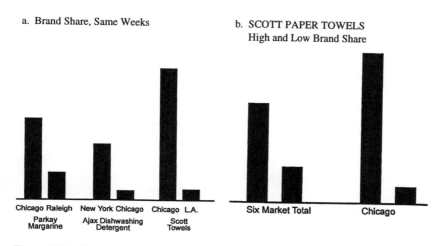

a. Brand Share, Same Weeks

b. SCOTT PAPER TOWELS
High and Low Brand Share

Chicago Raleigh New York Chicago Chicago L.A.
Parkay Ajax Dishwashing Scott
Margarine Detergent Towels

Six Market Total Chicago

Figure 3.5. Variations by Regions and by Weeks—Brands

One reason for the market-by-market variability in sales is the role played by local or regional brands. But their position is not constant. In paper towels, for example, even Jewel generic, which had no price changes during the period of the study, had a weekly share in Chicago that ranged from 55.2% to 34.7% in Jewel stores. In Los Angeles, Alpha Beta paper towels, which did have price changes, ranged from 29.6% to 5.5%.

Pricing Changes

The effects of retail price changes for a given brand cannot be evaluated except in relation to the brand's own price-off promotions and to the concurrent pricing and promotional activities of its competitors. A price reduction cannot be expected to produce added sales or market share points unless it is communicated to consumers.

A previous analysis of Nabscan data for 479 items in 17 stores found that dollar sales volume tripled for price-cut items supported by newspaper supermarket advertising and merely doubled for advertised items with unchanged prices.[2] Table 3.1 shows the results of a comparison of average sales for the 2 weeks before the ads ran with those for the week of the ad.

TABLE 3.1 Sales Increase in Ad Week: 479 Advertised Items in 17 Stores

Index, previous weeks	100
Items with no price cut	101
Items with price cut	195

Price changes may result either directly from a manufacturer deal that is passed on by the retailer or from the retailer's own initiative. (The scanner data provide information on the current price for every package size.) Pricing changes were tracked week by week, store by store, and market by market, as were average prices for all six markets. Because a given brand is usually sold in a variety of package sizes, a pricing change may take place in one or more items of the same brand and not in others. In a given week, some package sizes may increase in price while others decrease.

The importance of pricing as a marketing force varies among the five different products tracked:[3]

- *Dry cereals:* Prices were steady week by week and item by item. Dry cereals made up a particularly troublesome category to analyze, because of the many dozens of varieties on the market, each with a small share. For purposes of this study, the varieties sold under a given brand label, such as Kellogg's, have been lumped together throughout the analysis.
- *Margarine:* There was pricing action among major brands overall in 10 weeks out of 12.
- *Paper towels:* Some brands showed considerable price volatility, whereas others showed none.
- *Instant coffee:* In one week, in Kansas City, five out of the seven leading brands raised prices. (Incidentally, this had little effect on sales for the total product category.) The case of instant coffee shows the difficulty of detecting a pattern in pricing if one looks only at the six-city averages. Two brands were up in price in the same week, but that was a unique instance. In another week, one was down; the following week one went up and one went down; the next week one went up and two went down; one of these went back up the following week.

Summing up, although there are some instances in which several brands of a product had price reductions or increases within the same weeks, there was little uniformity of price changes by more than one brand within a market or by individual brands across markets.

Price Changes and Brand Share

The comparative pricing of grocery brands reflects not only the posted retail price of each item but also the effects of whatever coupon or price-off offer is currently being merchandised and promoted. (The scanner record provides only the actual cash register price of the merchandise.)

Consumers look at pricing in a competitive context. They see a brand's comparative price position not merely in terms of whether it costs more or less than it did the previous week, but relative to its competitors' prices from one week to the next. As we have seen, changes in price rarely coincide for competitive brands.

Perhaps because of the ubiquitous use of coupon promotions, there appears to be no universal rule regarding the sales effects of posted price changes.

- *Instant coffee:* Price cuts sometimes lead to share increases and price increases to share decreases, but the opposite effects can also be found. In New York, Nescafé's share doubled with a price cut, but in another week it stayed relatively level after a price cut, and then went up the following week. On the other hand, share sometimes increased without a change in price. In Chicago, with a price cut, Sanka's share declined from 20.8% to 17.8%.

- *Paper towels:* Some price decreases in individual markets are associated with dramatic jumps in market share, but others are not. Price increases sometimes lead to noticeable losses of share and in other cases do not. Here again, some dramatic shifts in brand share occurred without visible changes in pricing, either by a brand itself or by its competitors.

- *Dishwashing detergent:* Large shifts in share were sometimes found unrelated to price changes, and the total sales volume did not appear to relate directly to pricing action (or, for that matter, to total advertising activity). For example, Palmolive in Chicago had no price action during 4 consecutive weeks, nor afterward. In other instances, share rose with a price decrease and dropped with an increase, as might be expected. In still other cases, a price increase was associated with an increased share.

- *Margarine:* In some cases a dramatic increase followed a price reduction, with no advertising (Land O'Lakes in Detroit). In other cases, also with no advertising, as for Parkay in New York, a price change was not followed by a shift in the brand's position (see Figure 3.6).

In sum, posted price changes in themselves do not guarantee changes in market share, because of the unpredictable force of competitive activity. For

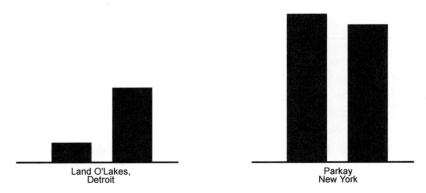

Figure 3.6. Margarine Brand Shares—Price Reduction

consumers to perceive a price cut as a benefit, they have to know about it. And that brings us to the subject of advertising.

Advertising and Its Visibility

In all six markets, for all 12 weeks, newspaper advertising was measured brand by brand for both national and retail ads. Brand appearances in retail ads were designated as "featured items" (with 4 square inches or more), "promotional items" (less space), or "liners" (simply one line). All the national run of paper (ROP) ads (i.e., those not placed in special positions) measured for these product classes during this period turned out to include price-off coupons. Freestanding inserts (FSIs) printed in color also contained coupon advertising in every case, all but two of the coupons directly redeemable for price rebates at the point of sale. Magazine ads were also measured for the 4 months that overlapped the study's 12-week period. Both network and spot television were tracked for the individual 12 weeks—network in all six markets and spot in New York, Chicago, and Los Angeles (the only cities where weekly sales data were available).

Does increased advertising pressure add to total sales of a product? In those weeks when, by chance or for a combination of reasons, a number of competing brands happened to step up their advertising volume, this is not clearly reflected in increased product movement.

In five such heavily advertised product fields, a layperson might suppose that every major brand maintains a continuous and ubiquitous presence through all the media. This turns out to be far from the case. Some brands used magazines and network or spot television in every one of the 12 weeks; other brands made no use of magazines or network television at all or used no spot TV in at least one of the three markets for which we have data.

Magazines

In two of the five product classes—paper towels and dishwashing detergent—no magazine advertising at all ran for the measured brands during the 12-week period.

- *Instant coffee:* One advertiser, Taster's Choice, used magazines in 3 out of the 4 months. The others used them in only 1 or 2 of the 4 months.
- *Margarine:* Magazines were used by only three of the eight measured brands, and then on an inconsistent basis.
- *Dry cereals:* Kellogg's used magazines in all 4 months; General Mills did not use them at all.

Altogether, there were eight instances where a brand ran magazine ads during only 1 or 2 months of the measured period. Share was higher for those months in four cases and lower in the other four.[4] Thus the scanner data show no consistent short-run effects from magazine advertising on market share.

Network Television

Television gets more than half of all national consumer advertising dollars, and in the case of most packaged goods its share of the media budget ranges from 80% to 90%. But network television use was by no means universal.

- *Dry cereals:* All brands except Ralston's made heavy use of network television. Ralston began using some network television halfway through the 12-week period, and also started using spot TV; its share went up from 4.8 in the pre-TV period to 5.9%.[5]

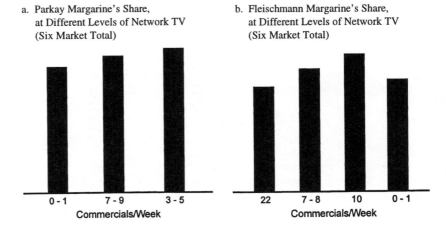

a. Parkay Margarine's Share,
   at Different Levels of Network TV
   (Six Market Total)

b. Fleischmann Margarine's Share,
   at Different Levels of Network TV
   (Six Market Total)

Figure 3.7. Margarine Brand Shares

- *Instant coffee:* Only two of the eight brands used network television. In addition, High Point had one commercial, obviously a "make-good" (a spot given in compensation for a missed or spoiled transmission), in the course of the 12 weeks studied. There was no indication of market share effects when network TV dollars went down or up for a brand.
- *Paper towels:* Of the three main brands, only Bounty used network television. Coronet had one commercial a week in just two of the measured weeks.
- *Margarine:* Two of the five brands tracked used network television, as Figure 3.7a shows. Parkay's share rose after its network schedule was heavied up to a level of 7 to 9 commercials a week, in combination with a price cut, but its share went up further after network TV was reduced to a level of 3 to 5 commercials a week. Figure 3.7b shows that Fleischmann's share grew after its network television schedule was cut back from 22 commercials a week, but fell in the two weeks after it was eliminated.
- *Dishwashing detergent:* There was a strong, consistent use of television by all brands measured except Dove. Ajax's share fell after its network television started, but built up when the schedule was heavied up to a rate of 7 to 9 commercials a week (Figure 3.8a). Ivory's share grew when its network advertising diminished (Figure 3.8b). And Palmolive lost share after increasing its network TV dollars (Figure 3.8c).

Altogether, there were 14 instances where network TV expenditures were either present or markedly higher in certain weeks. In six cases brand share was higher, in six lower.

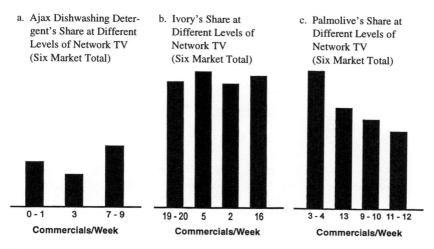

Figure 3.8. Liquid Detergent Brand Shares

To sum up, the evidence shows network television producing no consistent short-run effects on market share.

Spot Television

Strong use was made of spot television in all five measured categories:

- *Dry cereals:* All five companies used spot heavily in all six markets. However, General Mills substantially outspent Kellogg's, which had nearly double the market share, and outspent Ralston at a rate of eight to one.[6] The stable pattern of sales and brand shares makes it hard to find a direct demonstration of how spot TV advertising affects them (see Table 3.2).
- *Instant coffee:* All the major brands were supported by spot TV, but in some markets, some brands ran only one or two spots a month. Sanka was a consistent advertiser in all three markets. As Figure 3.9a shows, in New York its share went up by 50% when its schedule went from 3 to 47 spots a week, but this accompanied a price cut. Its share fell when it more than doubled its commercial pressure to 102 spots.
- *Paper towels:* Scott advertised consistently with spot television flights in New York and Chicago but not in Los Angeles. Isolated commercials for various other

TABLE 3.2 Dry Cereals—Spot Television

	Six-Market Share (%)	Comparative Spot TV Spending
General Mills	21	100
Kellogg's	38	63
Ralston	5	12

brands crop up without any pattern in all three markets. There is no sign of the short-run effects of spot TV on market share for any brand.

- *Margarine:* Imperial made heavy use of spot in Chicago and Los Angeles. Figure 3.9b shows that in Chicago, brand share was only half as great in weeks where there was spot activity; in Los Angeles there was no difference. There was no use of spot television in New York by any major brand.

- *Dishwashing detergent:* Most of the major brands were using spot TV in all three markets. Here, too, in some cases there was only a single commercial per week per brand. Far more spot television dollars were spent in Los Angeles than in New York or in Chicago. Even though brand shares show great volatility from week to week, there is no indication that they are higher in weeks with spot TV activity than in other weeks, as Figure 3.9c illustrates for Sunlight in Los Angeles, Dawn in Chicago, and Ajax in New York.

Altogether, there were 29 instances in which spot television was used by a brand during only part of the total period. In 9 of these cases, the brand share was higher during the weeks the spot schedule ran; in 18 cases it was lower; in 2 cases it was the same.

Television is used to build and reinforce brand image and awareness. Important as this may be, there is no indication in the data that it creates an immediate response in market share. Spot television schedules for individual brands generally seem to reflect intermittent and sporadic pressure market by market from one week to the next. The case of Sanka in New York (Figure 3.9a) provides the only instance for the three markets and the five product classes in which there is a substantial direct market share effect from a heavy-up in spot TV. This accompanied a price reduction and was followed by a loss in share after the weight was doubled.

In sum, by the most generous possible interpretation we find no consistent short-run effects on market share from spot TV.

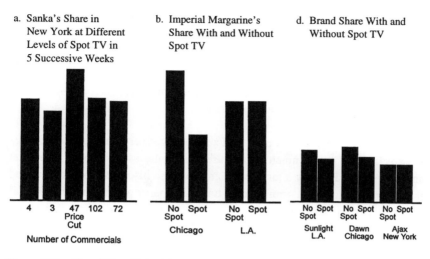

a. Sanka's Share in New York at Different Levels of Spot TV in 5 Successive Weeks

b. Imperial Margarine's Share With and Without Spot TV

d. Brand Share With and Without Spot TV

Figure 3.9. Use of Spot Television

Newspapers

More than $1 billion was invested in newspaper retail food advertising in 1983, most of it in support of packaged goods. This was spread out over many product classes and thousands of individual brands. An overall appraisal of the newspaper support (retail and national) for major brands in our five product classes in these six markets shows far less visibility than might be expected.

- *Instant coffee:* The use of newspaper advertising, particularly retailers' support of individual brands in local store ads, was inconsistent and sporadic. The timing of national ads (both ROP and inserts) varied by market. In no case did ads appear everywhere at the same time on a coordinated schedule.
- *Paper towels:* Newspaper ads generally appeared sporadically. The use of ROP coupons and inserts was timed differently from market to market. One market, Los Angeles, had no newspaper advertising at all in this category, national or retail, during the entire period.
- *Dishwashing detergent:* In some markets some brands had no newspaper support at all during the entire 12 weeks measured.

- *Margarine:* This is one product class in which all brands got some newspaper advertising, generally in retail ads. But this did not apply to all brands in all markets, and the scheduling was not consistent.
- *Dry cereal:* The massive consistent use of newspaper national advertising may help to explain the stability of market volume and brand share in this category. There was a heavy use of national inserts and ROP coupons everywhere, but very little support from retailers in supermarket ads.

What are the measurable effects of newspaper advertising? In this analysis we are looking not so much at increased unit sales as at changes in market share position. By now a large collection of case histories has accumulated that demonstrates from scanner data how newspaper advertising, both retail and national, increases product movement. These analyses show that larger space produces greater sales and that sales increases above a benchmark period continue for weeks after a national ROP ad appears.[7]

Until now, the ads themselves have been the starting point for investigation; each one has been examined to see what additional sales it has generated for the advertised item. But in the present analysis, we have been looking at the market as a whole, recognizing that any given ad occurs in the context of many competing messages in a dynamic situation and that the effects of national advertising, retail advertising, and price changes are interrelated. Unfortunately, we have no data on shelf space and positioning, or on point-of-sale promotion. One purpose of manufacturer co-op allowances (which are reflected in supermarket ads) is to ensure favorable treatment and visibility for a brand within a store's limited space. (Special merchandising and promotion efforts usually accompany dealing—temporary price reduction—which is reflected in the pricing changes analyzed above.)

Newspaper Retail Ads

Each appearance of a brand in an ad can be regarded as a case history. We can examine sales for the advertised brand in stores of the supermarket chain that runs the ad in a particular newspaper, but we would not normally expect this movement to affect the brand's market share on a national scale. Even among the 36 stores in this six-city sample, 12 different chains are represented, each running its own advertising for a different assortment of products and brands every week.

TABLE 3.3 Newspaper Retail Advertising: Paper Towels
(Jewel stores—four paper towel items in 12 weeks)

		Share (%)	
Brand	Type	Pre-Ad	Post-Ad
Scott	feature	8.2	41.8
Bounty	promo	7.1	22.7
Viva	promo	6.4	19.4
	liner	19.4	18.5

However, we are able to look at the effects of retail newspaper ads on market share in Chicago, where all six stores in the Nabscan sample were in the same chain: Jewel. Here we find the familiar pattern of sales responsiveness translated into increases in relative market share. For example, during the 12 weeks of the study, the three major national brands of paper towels appeared only four times in the chain's newspaper ads. Scott was "featured" in one week and, as Table 3.3 shows, its share went up fivefold. Bounty had a "promotional" position in another week and tripled its share. With another retail promotional position (at the same time as a national coupon, freestanding insert ran), Viva also tripled its share, and it held at that level in the following week with the help of a "liner."

The retail chain advertised dishwashing detergent in six ads during the same period, all as promotional items. Market share showed an average increase of 84%. By contrast, margarine repeatedly recurred as an advertised item, six times as a feature. In five of those instances, there was also a price reduction, and market share nearly tripled. (In the remaining case, without a price reduction, the item's share went up even more.) Two ads carried promotion-size units, one with and one without a price reduction; their share nearly tripled (see Table 3.4).

Seven ads carried liners for margarine brands, and their average share actually went down. Does this mean that a one-line mention in an ad is worse than no mention at all? Not in the least. The changes in market share for these brands must be examined in relation to what was happening with their competition at the same time. For example, a liner for Imperial left its position unchanged, from 12.3% to 12.5%. But in the same week, Parkay got promotional ad treatment for a price cut and raised its share from 11.5% to 34.5%. Liners for Parkay and Land O'Lakes were followed by relatively small drops

TABLE 3.4 Newspaper Retail Advertising: Margarine (Jewel stores)

	Average Change in Share (%)
5 features (with price cut)	+186
1 feature (no price change)	+242
2 promos (1 with price cut)	+181
7 liners	−18

in share from 10.9% to 9.6% and 7.2% to 5.9%, respectively. But in this same week, a retail promotion ad and national coupon insert for Imperial pushed its share up from 12% to 31.7%.

These instances merely illustrate the observation that the effects of advertising are always entangled and generally at cross-purposes with the effects of other advertising. The "unsuccessful" liners may have helped their brands resist the competitive onslaught more effectively than they might otherwise have done.

What happens to a brand within a given store as a result of the store's own advertising is offset by what is happening in other stores in the same market. The pattern is complicated further when we look at brand share fluctuations from week to week across the country, which reflect the net sum of all the local product movements. The data in this analysis are consistent with the great body of evidence (much of it assembled by the Newspaper Advertising Bureau) that newspaper retail advertising has immediate effects in the supermarkets that advertise.

Newspaper National: FSIs

By contrast, national newspaper ads apply to sales of the advertised products in all the stores in the markets in which they appear. Let's first consider free-standing inserts. Many inserts appear on Sundays, midway in the measured 7-day period, so the best indication of change is to compare market share in the week before the ad runs with share in the first full week after it has run.[8]

Table 3.5 shows all the cases in New York for dishwashing detergent: Share increases range from 50% to sevenfold. The pattern is similar in other markets. Table 3.6 shows what happened for all 18 insert ads for dishwashing detergent in the six markets and the comparable results for the other products. It will be noted that dry breakfast cereals made tremendous use of inserts—58 cases in

TABLE 3.5 Newspaper FSIs—New York: Dishwashing Detergents

	Share (%)		
	Pre-ad	Ad Week	Next Week
Sunlight	2.2	4.6	14.4
Ajax (+ price cut)	3.1	9.4	12.2
Palmolive	16.2	22.7	33.1
Ivory	16.4	14.4	23.7
Joy	12.1	12.4	20.7

TABLE 3.6 Newspaper FSIs: Various Product Categories

	Total Ads	Share Up	Share Down	Same Share	Average Percentage Increase
Dishwashing detergents	18	14	3	1	61.6
Instant coffee	20	15	5	0	35.5
Dry cereals	58	32	24	2	2.5
Paper towels	4	2	2	0	75.6
Margarine	6	3	3	0	97.9

all. With this consistent competitive use of coupon promotions by all major brands, and with the bewildering array of varieties offered by most brands, it would seem hard for any one brand to win a short-run advantage. Yet in a majority of cases, the post-ad week share was up over the pre-ad week.

Newspaper National: ROP

Freestanding inserts have the obvious advantages of color and convenience, but national ROP advertising shows similar immediate effects on share when the pre-ad week is compared with the week the ad ran. The results are shown in Table 3.7.

Because all of the national newspaper ads in this sample—ROP and inserts—used coupons, the pricing incentive cannot be separated from the purely promotional aspect.[9] National packaged goods advertisers can use newspapers to build brand image and to announce product innovations, but their preponderant use is for couponing promotions, as we have seen.

TABLE 3.7 Newspaper ROP: Various Product Categories

	Total Ads	Share Up	Share Down	Same Share	Average Percentage Increase
Dishwashing detergents	11	9	2	0	53.4
Instant coffee	4	2	2	0	2.8
Dry cereals	65	34	31	0	0.6
Paper towels	10	8	2	0	18.5
Margarine	16	9	6	1	42.7

TABLE 3.8 Short-Run Effects of National Advertising on Brand Share

	Total Number of Cases	Brand Share Higher	No Change	Brand Share Lower
Magazines	8	4	0	4
Network TV	14	6	2	6
Spot TV	29	9	2	18
Newspapers FSI	106	66	3	37
Newspapers ROP	106	62	1	43

To sum up what the data show about the short-run effects of different media: For newspaper ads—retail, national inserts, and national ROP—the changes in market share are overwhelmingly positive. And the use of different media may produce synergistic effects greater than the individual components. For magazines, network TV, and spot TV, there is no consistent change (see Table 3.8).

Conclusions

Several conclusions can be drawn from the analysis presented above:

1. What appears to be a stable national market for packaged goods is actually extremely volatile. The volatility of purchase volume and brand share parallels what is found in studies of consumer behavior—a constant movement in buying plans and intentions, a constant switching of individual purchase preferences among brands.

2. There is great variability from market to market and from store to store. In every link of the distribution chain, the national manufacturer confronts a different

competitive environment, a different mix of consumer attitudes. With more detailed census, marketing, and media data available in every marketer's personal computer, there will be more and more reason to look at markets under a microscope and to plan advertising with an understanding of distinctive local needs.

3. Pricing and promotion are the two key marketing elements that are under the manufacturer's control. This analysis shows that both have an effect on a given brand's market position, but rarely is the effect great enough to change the total volume of consumption in the whole product class.

4. In total category sales, peaks and valleys seem to follow each other. This suggests that added sales at any given moment (at least for widely used grocery items such as the five examined here) are generally made at the expense of future sales in the category. But, naturally, this is not true if a specific brand is on the rise, and it is a strong argument for sustained advertising pressure.

5. There are direct indications of the effects of pricing action on sales and on brand share, but price action does not lead predictably to changes in market share, and it is most effective when it is communicated to the consumer.

6. Newspaper national insert and ROP coupon ads, which are essentially price promotions, have direct market share effects.

7. This analysis reaffirms the substantial body of evidence on the immediate pulling power of supermarket newspaper ads that feature, promote, or even merely list branded merchandise, whether or not the advertising is accompanied by a price reduction. These immediate effects are found on brand shares as well as on unit sales for the advertised items.

8. Except in a few scattered instances, the occurrence or absence of national television advertising (network or spot) or of magazine advertising cannot be connected with shifts in brand share or in category volume. This does not mean that advertising in these media is ineffective, but rather that it works differently and with less immediate and universal impact. Effects of advertising in these media are usually spread through time, absorbed into the dense competitive communications environment, and untraceable, in the short run, at the point of sale.

9. Dramatic and important changes in market share position occur even when no pricing or advertising activity takes place. Shelf frontage, store positioning, in-store display, and point-of-purchase promotion have a great deal to do with product movement. They represent some of the most important residual elements that were not measured in this analysis. To a very large extent, these forces are beyond the control of individual manufacturers, no matter how aggressive or effective their field forces may be.

10. All of the brands covered in this analysis were major, well-known, heavily advertised national brands. Yet in most cases, in individual key markets, there is no significant advertising support for these brands in any given week. A respectable proportion of all ad messages in newspapers, magazines, and spot

TV are disseminated sporadically and on a small scale. In the case of TV, these may be make-goods or barter spots, but whatever the explanation, it is clear that this type of random diffusion of isolated messages can hardly have a measurable effect. Given that there is no reinforcement for these messages, what value do they have? Brands need consistent advertising visibility. The evidence indicates that newspapers can provide it, efficiently and powerfully.

One final point: Scanner data provide a picture of the market that is infinitely richer, more detailed, and more comprehensive than any hitherto available. Although data are now produced for weekly periods and reported at 4-week intervals, it is only a matter of time before they become available overnight and will be usable online by market planners. On the one hand, this opens up incredible opportunities to react with speed and flexibility to competitive conditions. On the other hand, it threatens to drown marketers in vastly more information than they can intelligently handle, unless they can develop systems through which the significant can be sifted automatically from the unimportant. A new era of marketing intelligence has arrived, in which the traditional distinctions between practice and research will no longer apply.

Notes

1. The full set of data analyzed fills nine thick volumes, which were available for consultation at the Newspaper Advertising Bureau (NAB). Nabscan was set up by the NAB, which has since been merged into the Newspaper Association of America.

2. Newspaper Advertising Bureau, *Supermarket Ads Move Merchandise* (New York: Newspaper Advertising Bureau, 1981).

3. Only pricing changes of more than a few cents were coded in the analysis.

4. Five of these magazine campaigns carried coupons, of which two were associated with gains in share and three with losses, for an average gain of 3.4%. Of the three that did not include coupons, two showed gains and one a loss of share, with the average showing a 1% loss.

5. Television advertising is reported by the calendar week (Sunday through Saturday). For alignment with product movement data, the last full week before a shift in television scheduling was taken as the benchmark.

6. In this single instance the three-market spot TV analysis was extended to a projection for all 4 weeks of each month in all six markets.

7. Newspaper Advertising Bureau, *The Sales Effects of National Newspaper Advertising for Two Packaged Goods Products* (New York: Newspaper Advertising Bureau, 1978).

8. Because retail and national ROP ads generally appear on Wednesday, the week ending on Wednesday is used as the benchmark against the week immediately following.

9. The value of the average ROP coupon was 25 cents. For the FSI coupons it was 28 cents. Margarine and detergent coupons in ROP were worth less; paper towel coupons were worth more.

4

Brand Growth

The Past, the Present

Josh McQueen
Alice K. Sylvester
Scott D. Moore

The Past

Modern marketing practices in the United States have been associated with four distinct phases of development. In each phase, category and brand growth has been achieved and measured differently.

Phase I (Circa 1950-1965)

The advent of television in the 1950s enabled marketers to reach huge and widely dispersed audiences efficiently. At the same time, the efficiency of wartime industrial automation efforts was extended to domestic consumer businesses. Booming growth in real income enabled consumers to buy more products than ever before. Category growth was easy and explosive; brand growth seemed unstoppable. During this initial phase of modern marketing, annual shipments and store research were crucial measures of performance.

Phase 2 (Circa 1965-1980)

Years later, the nature of markets and competition had changed. Category growth momentum had disappeared as the national market stabilized or grew at a declining rate. Category structures changed as major manufacturers gobbled up regional competitors. Two, three, four, and sometimes five major companies could all see their market share soar through buyouts, consolidation, and of course, baby boomers coming of buying age. Attention was focused on improving product quality and on the logistics of stocking shelves and development of brand image. Inflation caused marketers to get into the habit of raising prices. Nielsen's concept of "market share" became increasingly important and brand growth was measured on a bimonthly basis in relative, not absolute, terms.

Phase 3 (Circa 1980-1994)

The third phase, the "push/pull era," was characterized by an almost schizophrenic approach to marketing. Consumer loyalty was at the forefront of marketers' awareness, but pressure to shore up the bottom line drove them to price-promote heavily. Retailers joined consumers in marketing's target audience. The balance of power between retailers and manufacturers shifted. Slower inflation made the practice of increasing sales through higher prices more difficult. Deal-sensitive, price-driven consumers sought value and variety. Brands grew, but, in this phase, grew differently. More brands and microvarieties were managed in a portfolio framework. In this context, the decline of big-name "base" brands was acceptable as long as total portfolio shares were up. Information Resources Inc. (IRI) and Nielsen competed to provide data that showed weekly share surges, reinforcing the short-term importance of below-the-line activities.

Phase 4 (1995 and Beyond)

The mid-1990s have been characterized as the "brand customization" phase of brand growth. Manufacturers are focused on one-on-one relationship marketing, and terms like *share of customer* articulate brand strength. Aggregate measures of growth and performance have been replaced by measures that focus at finer levels, on households and individuals. Brand growth and leveraging efficiencies come from customizing marketing programs to unique segments of the brand's customer base. We have come to understand that marketing activities at different points of time are relevant to different types of buying patterns.

The Present

IRI's "Advertising Works" study has raised many interesting challenges to current thinking on the sales effectiveness of advertising.[1] Of significant note is the finding that when advertising has a demonstrable short-term effect on volume, it also produces a long-term effect. In this study, advertising's effect on volume in Years 2 and 3 was to increase buying rate (the number of purchases), not penetration (the number of purchasers). The finding that buying rate plays a major role in long-term volume suggests that a better understanding of purchase frequency, or buying rate, is in order.

We recently undertook a broad-scale study of brand growth in our capacity as researchers for Leo Burnett Company. U.S. scanner panels make it possible to evaluate dimensions of growth, routes to growth, and buyer segment contribution to growth at a disaggregated level. Our study differed conceptually from the "Advertising Works" study in that we looked at brand growth as a result of the total marketing effort; we did not break out advertising's contribution specifically.

Our data set included 2 years of household panel data from Nielsen and Information Resources Inc. We analyzed 1,251 brands in 14 different packaged goods categories and 82,000 households. The purpose of the study was to examine growth and the manner in which growth occurred between Year 1 and Year 2. In addition, we set out to assess the relative contributions of particular buyer groups to brand growth.

TABLE 4.1 Amount of Brand Growth

Percentage of Brand Growth	Percentage of Brands
10 or less	27
11-20	34
21-50	19
50+	21

How Many Brands Grew?

Of the 1,251 brands analyzed, 38% grew and 60% experienced a decline in volume from Year 1 to Year 2; 2% of brands remained the same. (New brands—those with no sales in Year 1—were removed from analysis.) This finding is quite startling: 60% of marketing efforts fail to maintain or grow their businesses.

Many brands that grew were very small. Minimal absolute increases appeared as big percentage increases, so as we proceeded, we included in the analysis only brands with a 1% share. Another set of brands grew, but at a slower rate than the category. These brands, whose shares declined despite absolute sales increases, were also eliminated from the data set. A total of 95 brands remained.

How Much Growth?

Most brands grew moderately—60% grew less than 20% year to year (see Table 4.1).

Assessing Brand Growth Mechanics

Integrating household purchase data was essential for understanding the manner in which brands grew. Each "brand household" (each household that purchased a given brand during the 2 years) was assigned a "purchase status value." Households were characterized as follows:

- *Lapsed:* Bought brand in Year 1, not in Year 2.
- *New:* Bought brand in Year 2, not in Year 1.

TABLE 4.2 Route to Brand Growth

Ratio of Penetration to Buying Rate	Percentage of Brands
100/0	24
75/25	28
60/40	15
50/50	9
40/60	8
25/75	8
0/100	8

- *Decreased:* Bought brand less in Year 2 than in Year 1.
- *Same:* Bought brand same amount in both years.
- *Increased:* Bought brand more in Year 2 than in Year 1.

Changes in a brand's penetration and buying rate were calculated from the household's purchase status value:

- *Penetration:* Lapsed and new households.
- *Buying rate:* Decreased and increased households.

Assigning penetration and buying rate values to individual households also enabled us to assess brand growth in the context of previous Burnett work on buyer segmentation.[2]

Growth Mechanics: Penetration or Buying Rate?

At least some penetration gains were responsible for almost all brand growth. Some 92% of brands grew volume, at least partly, through penetration increases. In more than half the brands, penetration was the major contributor to volume, accounting for 75% or more of all growth.

Buying rate (i.e., purchase frequency) increases, however, were important too, in a large number of brands. Buying rate played an important role in brand growth for 76% of brands. In fact, it was the predominant source of growth for 25% of brands. It appears that few brands grow exclusively through penetration or buying rate (see Table 4.2).

TABLE 4.3 The Effect of Brand Size on Growth Mechanics

| Brand Year 1 Penetration (%) | Percentage Contribution to Growth | | Percentage of Brands |
	Penetration	Buying Rate	
0-5	92	8	23
6-10	77	23	34
11-30	68	33	32
30+	54	46	11

Growth Mechanics and Brand Size

Brands with room to grow will grow more through penetration. Brands with high penetration also tend to grow through penetration, but are more likely to grow through increased buying rates.

Low-penetration brands grow almost exclusively through penetration. These small brands make up a fairly large proportion of many packaged goods categories. In the ground coffee category, for instance, 60% of brands have less than 10% penetration. Similarly, 70% of brands in the analgesic/headache remedy category have less than 10% penetration.

The larger the brand, the more likely it is to grow through buying rate, although penetration still contributes the most. For the top two or three brands in many categories, buying rate is extremely important.

The predominance of growth through penetration is understandable. By definition, most brands are small, have low penetration, and, if they manage to grow, do so by first attracting new users (see Table 4.3).

Brand Growth: Buyer Segment Contribution

In order to assess which buyer groups contribute most to brand growth, we overlaid the Buyer Strategy Segmentation system developed by Leo Burnett on household purchase data. We characterized each brand initially by buyer segment and assigned the characteristic of its most dominant group. We assigned only one buying segment per brand (although brands typically are purchased by buyers from all segments) because we were concerned with primary routes to growth, not secondary or idiosyncratic patterns. We then evaluated brand growth mechanisms (penetration or buying rate increases).

TABLE 4.4 Buyer Segment Contribution to Brand Growth
(brands designated by dominant buyer group)

Brand Buyer Segments	Percentage of Brands	Contribution to Growth	
		Percentage Penetration	Percentage Buying Rate
Price-driven consumers	29	75	25
Rotators	20	68	32
Light users	19	100	0
Deal selectives	17	50	50
Loyals	15	43	57

Buyer segments contribute to brand growth differentially. Brands dominated by "price-driven" consumers outnumber brands dominated by "loyal" consumers two to one. Only 15% of brands are dominated by loyal buyers. This finding undoubtedly reflects U.S. marketing practices, where heavy price promotion has been the focus for years (see Table 4.4).

Interestingly, buyer segments grow volume in different ways. Brands dominated by "light users" generate volume exclusively through penetration gains. "Rotators" and "price-driven" brands grow volume primarily through penetration, but gains in buying rates are also seen.

"Light users," who buy only one or two products a year in a category, are extremely likely to buy a different brand each time they enter the category. A brand dominated by light users is extremely vulnerable—current light users are very likely to defect. This phenomenon helps explain why growing brands and large brands seem to do well—they attract a disproportionate share of these uninvolved shoppers. Continued emphasis on price will likely draw new users, but this aggregate picture seems to demonstrate that they are likely to be gone tomorrow. In-market experimentation seems justified to see what level and type of price activity can more efficiently draw at least a fair share of more habitual shoppers to a brand.

Brands dominated by "rotators"—people who shift on performance, not price—enjoy an attractive position. The 68/32 split between penetration and buying rate indicates that it is possible not only to draw new users but to gain additional buying rate volume.

Brands characterized by deal-selective consumers are also interesting. Like price buyers, "deal selectives" buy only on price, but only from a very select list of brands. Volume gains come from both penetration and buying rate. Marketers scaling back retail spending and price promotions face the challenge of converting these buyers to a more loyal, habitual segment. These data suggest that enough volume is generated through buying rate gains to make this a reasonable objective.

"Loyals" demonstrate vividly what more and more customer relationship programs are proving—that there is more volume to be gained from those already committed to a brand.

Conclusion

This detailed look at panel data highlights the results of three distinct phases of historic marketing practices. We see loyalty, built in the early phase; brand rotation, a response to the era of brand proliferation; and price sensitivity, the legacy of the 1980s.

As we go forward in the next phase, marketing practitioners must recognize the existence of all these buyer segments and develop customer strategies that will most profitably and efficiently attract volume from each segment.

Notes

1. Michael J. Naples, Randall S. Smith, Leonard M. Lodish, Beth Lubetkin, Josh McQueen, Larry Bisno, Horst Stipp, and Andrew Tarshis, *Breakthrough Marketplace Advertising Research for Bottom Line Results* (New York: Advertising Research Foundation Conference, November 1991).

2. Carol Foley, Josh McQueen, and John Deighton, *Decomposing a Brand's Consumer Franchise Into Buyer Types,* in David A. Aaker and Alexander L. Biel (eds.), *Brand Equity and Advertising* (Chicago: Leo Burnett, 1993).

Penetration, Brand Loyalty, and the Penetration Supercharge

John Philip Jones

The normal way of monitoring the effect of advertising is by measuring the sales of the advertised brand, for example, ex-factory or through retail stores. Yet there is no direct link between advertising and sales measured in this way, because advertising is addressed to consumers, and a number of factors can impede advertising's ability to induce consumers to act. It can be countered by the efforts of competitive brands; there may be large stocks of the brand in the trade or in the home to absorb any increased demand; and the brand may not achieve full retail distribution, so that the consumer's efforts to buy it are frustrated. To get a more reliable picture of what advertising is accomplishing, we should therefore look not only at sales, but also at measures of how advertising impinges on consumer behavior.

Relating Sales to Consumer Behavior

The relationship between sales and the key measures of consumer behavior is expressed in the following simple formula:

Sales of a Brand in a Defined Period = Household Population (A)
$$\times \text{ Penetration (B)}$$
$$\times \text{ Purchase Frequency (C)}$$
$$\times \text{ Packs Bought per Purchase Occasion (D)}$$
$$\times \text{ Average Size of Pack (E)}$$

This formula is based on methods first developed by the British mathematician Andrew Ehrenberg, who has worked with large accumulations of data from the United States and a number of other countries.[1]

When we compare different brands in any product category using the above formula, we find no important differences as far as measures A, D, and E are concerned. The household population—which imposes a theoretical upper limit to the extent of any brand's sales—is precisely the same for every brand. People tend to purchase the same number of packs on every occasion, no matter what brand in the category they may be buying. And the packs of different brands are generally sold in more or less uniform sizes.

We can therefore conclude that the sales of any brand are determined by the brand's penetration, which is a measure of the number of people who buy it at least once, and its purchase frequency, or how often they buy it in the period we are looking at.

Penetration

When we measure penetration, there is an important technical reason why we must specify the time period. A brand's penetration tends to be the same when measured in any individual periods of roughly equal length, such as January, February, or March; or 1995, 1996, or 1997. But as the time period itself is extended, penetration goes up; for instance, it is higher in the whole of 1997 than in January 1997, because as the period is extended infrequent users are drawn to the brand, thus boosting its net penetration. This rule does not apply to market share, which does not change greatly as the period is lengthened. When we extend the period, total category sales and sales of any particular brand increase approximately in step, so that the ratio between the two—which is the brand's market share—remains relatively constant. Market share in the whole of 1997 is approximately the same as market share in January 1997.

Purchase Frequency/Brand Loyalty

Purchase frequency—which is essentially a technical expression of consumers' loyalty to a brand—is a measure of how often a brand is bought in a defined period. It expresses volume sales per buyer via purchasing occasions. Because volume sales differ by category (not to speak of the differences among categories in the units used to measure sales), the calculation should be based on the category itself, by indexing each brand's volume sales per buyer on the average sales of all brands in its category.

Penetration and purchase frequency are significant measures for two separate reasons. First, their relative importance varies according to the size of the brand, which means that their relevance to advertising strategy is determined to a large degree by market share. The most common example of this is that small brands are normally driven by a penetration-based advertising strategy, whereas large brands are much more directed toward increasing purchase frequency. Small brands attempt to drive penetration by addressing nonusers and pointing out the advantages of the small brand over the competition. Large brands attempt to drive purchase frequency by addressing existing users and suggesting reasons for additional uses (e.g., recipe advertising for food products). (See also McQueen, Sylvester, & Moore, Chapter 4, this volume.)

The second reason penetration and purchase frequency are important is that they hold the keys to three further measures of consumer behavior: the frequency distribution of purchases, the patterns of repeat purchase, and multibrand buying (see Ehrenberg, Chapter 6, and Jones, Chapter 7, this volume). Regular and uniform relationships exist for each of these measures, whose very consistency has enabled them to be modeled mathematically. This was part of Ehrenberg's groundbreaking work. His models, which he developed before 1970, were derived from a broad range of empirical data and were rooted in penetration and purchase frequency.

Table 5.1 displays the penetration and purchase frequency of 142 brands of repeat-purchase packaged goods. These brands are ranked by market share,

TABLE 5.1 All Brands—Penetration and Purchase Frequency

Quintile	Average Market Share (% points)	Average Penetration (% points)	Purchase Frequency (index)
First	1.8	6.3	84
Second	2.8	7.7	94
Third	3.9	11.0	92
Fourth	6.8	18.6	97
Fifth	18.7	26.9	125

based on their sales over the full year 1991. This makes for a proper comparison with the penetration figures for the same period. The brands are analyzed in quintiles, ranging from the smallest to the largest. (In a quintile analysis, all the brands are ranked and then divided into five equal-sized groups.)[2]

The penetration growth is plotted in Figure 5.1, which shows that penetration and market share progress upward together, demonstrating that sales growth is essentially a function of growth in the numbers of buyers of a brand. However, Figure 5.1 also shows that the growth of penetration takes place at a declining rate as brands get bigger.

The decline in the rate of increase of penetration is shown in Table 5.2, which displays the ratios of market share/penetration. In this table, we can see a sharp decline for the biggest brands.

Given that penetration grows less quickly than market share when a brand reaches and grows above 10 percent, the largest brands must obviously be driven by something else. This factor is increased purchase frequency. This is clear from Table 5.1, which shows that the major increase in purchase frequency takes place in the fifth quintile, covering the largest brands.

The growth of small brands is driven by increasing penetration. Purchase frequency does not change much as a brand grows to an approximate 10 percent share of market. But when it gets to this level, its increased penetration is accompanied by a measurable step-up in its purchase frequency. People begin to buy the brand more often, primarily as a result of satisfaction with the brand's functional properties, operating in conjunction with the added values nurtured by advertising. This phenomenon has been described as the *penetration supercharge.*

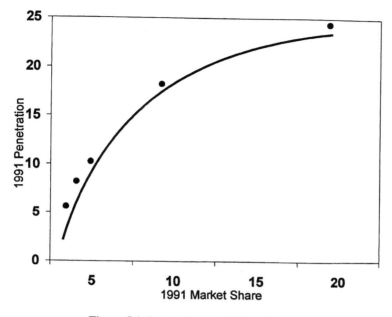

Figure 5.1. Penetration and Market Share

TABLE 5.2 All Brands—Market Share/Penetration Ratios

Quintile	Penetration (market share = 100)
First	350
Second	275
Third	282
Fourth	273
Fifth	144

The Penetration Supercharge

The penetration supercharge represents a scale economy of large brands as this relates to their advertising budgets. The penetration supercharge is derived from two connected phenomena:

1. As a brand's market share grows beyond about 10 percent, its purchase frequency will go up progressively. (As already explained, purchase frequency does not vary much among brands with shares below this level.)
2. As a brand increases in market share, its advertising investment will not need to increase at quite the same rate. Its "share of voice" (i.e., share of total media advertising in the category) will move upward at a *declining* rate as its market share rises. In other words, an extra dollar spent on advertising will work more productively as a brand increases in market share. Small brands have a share of voice higher than their share of market. This difference narrows as a brand grows. Above a share of market of approximately 20 percent, share of voice will be progressively below share of market.

The way in which these two phenomena can be related is that, as a brand grows in size, habit plays an increasingly important role in boosting repeat buying; the advertising does not need to work quite so hard to stimulate sales. Advertising budgets therefore need not go up as fast as a brand's sales.

The value of this scale economy can be quantified according to the following hypothetical but realistic example. If the total media investment in a category totals $100 million:

- A brand with a 5 percent market share will probably have to spend up to a 9 percent share of voice. This brand therefore spends $9 million, or $4 million more than the "parity level" (at which share of market equals share of voice).
- A brand with a 25 percent market share will probably spend approximately 20 percent share of voice. This brand therefore spends $20 million, or $5 million below the parity level. This $5 million is a quantitative expression of the penetration supercharge—the advertising-related scale economy accruing to the large brand. Comparing the two brands, the advertising-related scale economy becomes as much as $9 million ($4 million plus $5 million) for the 25 percent brand in comparison with what the small brand needs to invest.

Notes

1. John Philip Jones, *What's in a Name? Advertising and the Concept of Brands* (New York: Simon & Schuster-Lexington, 1986), chap. 5.

2. John Philip Jones, *When Ads Work: New Proof That Advertising Triggers Sales* (New York: Simon & Schuster-Lexington, 1995), 136.

Repetitive Advertising and the Consumer

Andrew S. C. Ehrenberg

Advertising is in an odd position. Its extreme protagonists claim it has extraordinary powers and its severest critics believe them. But both are wrong. Advertising is often effective. But it is not as powerful as is sometimes thought, nor is there any evidence that it actually works by any strong form of persuasion or manipulation.

Instead, the sequence Awareness–Trial–Reinforcement seems to account for the known facts. Under this theory, consumers first gain awareness or interest in a product. Next, they may make a trial purchase. Finally, a repeat buying habit may be developed and reinforced if there is satisfaction after previous usage.

NOTE: This chapter is based on a report prepared for the J. Walter Thompson Company in New York and published in the *Journal of Advertising Research,* April 1974. Used by permission.

Advertising has a role to play in all three stages. But for frequently bought products, repeat buying is the main determinant of sales volume, and here advertising must be reinforcing rather than persuasive.

These conclusions are based largely on studies of consumer behavior and attitudinal response. They are important both to our understanding of advertising's social role and to the execution and evaluation of advertising as a tool of marketing management.

In this chapter, I first examine advertising and the consumption of goods in general. I then discuss competition among brands and the factors affecting consumers' brand choices, particularly for established brands of frequently bought goods.

The Demand for Goods

Advertising is widely credited with creating consumer demand. Sol Golden was quoted in 1972 in the *Journal of Advertising Research* as saying, "Advertising is the lynch-pin by which everything in the system hangs together—the consumer benefits, the economic growth, the corporate profits, the technological advancement."[1]

Some years earlier, John T. Connor, then U.S. secretary of commerce, said:

> Without advertising, we most certainly could not have had the unprecedented prosperity of the last 67 months, because advertising is an absolutely indispensable element in the economic mix of the free enterprise system that produced that prosperity.
>
> We would not have had, without advertising, a drop in unemployment from over 7 percent to less than 4 percent.[2]

And we would not have had, without advertising, a rise in unemployment since. Many of advertising's critics, from Professor Galbraith downward, also believe it has such powers to create demand, to manipulate the consumer, to build our acquisitive society. But let us look at these supposed powers.

Product class advertising as a whole—"Buy more cars," "Drink more tea," and so on—certainly cannot be held responsible for consumer demand. For one thing, there is relatively little of this form of advertising. For another, it generally has only minor effects, increasing a market by a few percentage points or slightly slowing a rate of decline. These effects are worthwhile to the producer, but neither can be credited with creating demand or manipulating the consumer on any substantial scale.

The primary target of criticism is repetitive advertising for individual brands—"Buy Ford," "Drink Lipton's Tea," and so on. This is where the bulk of mass advertising is concentrated. Such competitive advertising for different brands can lead to a higher level of consumption of the product class as a whole than would exist without it, but there is no evidence that such secondary or even unintended effects are either big or particularly common. There are not even any dramatic claims in the literature. In many product classes with heavy competitive advertising, total consumption is rising little if at all; in some it is falling. On the other hand, there are many product classes with little if any mass media advertising—such as sailboats or marijuana—where consumption is increasing quickly.

Advertising for new products cannot bear the blame for consumer demand either. Undoubtedly, advertising can help to speed up the initial adoption of a new product by creating awareness and, indirectly, by gaining retail distribution and display. But advertising works as a lubricant in such cases—to ease and speed things—and not as the prime mover. Getting an initial purchase for a new product is not the point at issue in understanding society's continuing demand for goods.

The key question is whether people continue to buy something after they or their friends and neighbors have used it. This applies equally to frequently bought goods like frozen foods and cigarettes and to once-only or once-in-a-while purchases like atomic power stations or lawn mowers, where the satisfied users' influence makes itself felt through word-of-mouth recommendation over the garden fence (or the industrial equivalent), through retailer and press comments, and so on.

By and large, one cannot go on selling something that people do not like after they have had it. Sometimes people are sold a new kind of product, by advertising or other means, that they find afterward they did not really want. Some initial sales volume may be created in this way, but generally that is all.

The usual reason why people buy things is that they want them. Anyone who has washed dishes knows that the demand for nonstick frying pans and dishwashers did not have to be created. Rather, suitable products had to be developed, and then advertising undoubtedly helped to speed their adoption.

There is no need to suppose that the role of advertising here is fundamental. It is a peculiar form of snobbism to suppose that if other people want to smoke cigarettes, to smell nice, to have bathrooms, or to drive in motor cars, it is only because they have been manipulated by advertising. Sometimes this view can go as far as the advertising industry itself. The well-known British advertising practitioner John Hobson made this statement in his Cantor Lectures: "Almost certainly the increase in motoring has been the result of competitive petrol [gasoline] advertising."[3] The alternative is to suppose that people want to go from A to B, or like driving, or want to get away for weekends; that, rightly or wrongly, they often find cars more convenient or pleasing than walking or other forms of transport.

An often-cited example of the alleged effects of advertising in "creating" demand is the growth of men's toiletries. But this has been part of the great nonadvertised change in men's fashions: clothing, hairstyles, and so on. Advertising by itself could not have created such a toiletries market 20 or 40 years ago. Instead of leading it, advertisers generally follow fashion or product innovation. Anything else would be bad marketing—spending millions to convince people to buy something just because someone can produce it.

The effects of paid advertising on consumer demand must not be confused with the effects of the mass media as such or with people's developing education and greater mobility. People increasingly see how other people live, and this has led to vastly increased expectations.

People "want" many things once they have become aware of their existence—food, warmth, good looks, money, power, to drive a car, to be a concert pianist, to avoid washing dishes, and so on. Some of these things are very difficult to achieve, others are easier. To acquire goods, one only needs some money, someone to produce them, and a precedent of other people owning them in order to overcome cultural habits or inhibitions.

People go on wanting things because they like them. Increased if highly uneven affluence, increased availability of products, and vastly increased awareness through mass communication and education are three factors that account for the growing acquisitive nature of Western society. The glossy images of affluence shown in advertisements and in the media generally reflect a real demand. Eliminating advertising would not eliminate the demanding consumer.

The products the consumer demands are mostly genuinely wanted or even needed. Manufacturers seldom create the needs, but they do attempt to fulfill them. As a result, we have competition and competitive advertising among different brands or makes of the same product. This we now examine in more detail.

Competition and Persuasive Advertising

Most advertising aims to promote a particular brand or make of product in a competitive situation. Because it often takes an emotional instead of an informative tone, such advertising is generally thought to work by persuasion. Boulding, a typical critic, has written:

> Most advertising, unfortunately, is devoted to an attempt to build up in the mind of the consumer *irrational preferences for certain brands or goods.* All the arts of psychology—particularly the art of association—are used to persuade consumers that they should buy Bingo rather than Bango.[4]

It is generally recognized that advertising's effects on sales are not necessarily immediate or direct. Instead, advertising is thought to work through people's attitudes as an intermediary stage to changing their behavior.

Advertising therefore is often thought of as aiming to attach an image or some special consumer benefits to a brand, in an effort to distinguish it from its competitors in the mind of the consumer. This is attempted especially in situations where there are no physical or quality characteristics to differentiate the brand. Gasoline advertising that stresses "extra mileage," or "enjoyment," or "power" is a case in point, and Rosser Reeves's Unique Selling Proposition (USP) was an extreme version of the view that advertising can only work by offering buyers of Brand X something that no other similar brand has.

In the past 50 years, various theories have been put forward to try to explain how advertising works, taking attitudes into account.[5] One simple version is the well-known AIDA model, which stands for the chain

$$\text{Awareness} \rightarrow \text{Interest} \rightarrow \text{Desire} \rightarrow \text{Action.}$$

This sequential pattern—or something like it put in different words—is treated as common sense: It only says that people need to be aware of a brand before they can be interested in it, and that they can take action and buy it. This imputes two roles to advertising: an informational role, making them aware of the product; and a persuasive role, making people desire it before they have bought it.

In its informational role, it might seem that when there are no deeper benefits to guide brand choice, the consumer will be influenced by the last advertisement seen or by the general weight of past advertising. This assumption has led to the use of awareness and recall measures in pretesting and monitoring advertisements. But there is little direct evidence that advertising for established brands works like this. The evidence that does exist is either negative or at best shows effects that are not dramatically large and that still require confirmation.[6]

In its persuasive role, advertising is thought to create a desire or conviction to buy, or at least to "add value to the brand as far as the consumer is concerned."[7] For this reason, advertisements take on such persuasive methods as creating a brand image, selling a USP, and informing consumers that they need a special product to meet a special need (e.g., a special shampoo for oily hair). But again, there is no empirical evidence that advertising generally succeeds in this aim, when there are no real differences to sell.

In fact, these models of hierarchical or sequential effects have generally been criticized on the grounds of lack of evidence.[8] They also fail to explain many of the known facts. For example, they do not explain stable markets where shares of advertising and shares of sales are roughly in line for each brand. The small and medium-sized brands survive year in and year out, even though their consumers are exposed to vast amounts of advertising for the brand leaders.

Nor do the models account for the situation where, following a drop in sales revenue, advertising expenditure is cut and yet no catastrophe results. If consumers must be continually persuaded to buy a brand, then surely a cut in advertising should turn a minor setback into a major disaster. But it generally is not so.

Again, the models fail to account for the fact that at least four out of five new brands fail. There is no suggestion that failure occurs less often for highly advertised new brands.

More generally, the models do not explain why advertising usually has only a marginal effect on total demand for a product group, or why it is only rarely capable of shifting people's attitudes and behavior on social issues such as smoking, racial discrimination, voting, and so on.

It is not enough to claim that persuasive advertising depends on the quality of the campaign, or that advertising in general is inefficient. What is needed is a new explanation of the ways in which advertising actually works.

In recent years a good deal of attention has been paid to alternative explanations of the advertising process, based on such mechanisms as satisfaction after previous usage, reinforcement, reduction of dissonance, and selective perception. The argument presented later in this chapter is grounded on these processes. But the most direct advances have been in our understanding of consumers' buying behavior and attitudinal responses in a competitive brand situation.

Buyer Behavior

Making brand choices and repeat buying are regular and predictable aspects of buyer behavior. The economic viability of any frequently bought product depends on repeat buying. It follows simple patterns: If 10% of consumers buy Brand X an average of 1.5 times each in a given time period, then in the next time period 45% of that group can be expected to buy the brand again an average of 1.8 times each (as modeled, for example, by the "NBD" theory).[9] This is what is normally found under a wide range of conditions, for both food and nonfood products, in the United States and the United Kingdom, for leading brands and smaller ones.

The 55% who do not buy the brand in the second period are, however, not lost for good. Instead, they are merely relatively infrequent buyers of the brand who buy it regularly but not often. No special efforts therefore have to be made either to bring them back or to replace them (the "leaky bucket" theory). Few things about the consumer in competitive markets can be more important than knowing this, and a successful theory of repeat buying was needed to establish it.

The existence of regular and predictable patterns of repeat buying for a brand, however, does not mean that people mostly buy one brand only. Instead, the majority of buyers of a brand regularly purchase other brands as well. In general there are relatively few 100% loyal or sole buyers of a brand over any extended period of time. A typical and predictable finding for frequently bought grocery products is that in a week, 80% or 90% of buyers of a brand buy only that brand, that in half a year the proportion is down to 30%, and that in a year, only 10% of buyers are 100% loyal.[10] To expect any substantial group or segment of consumers to be uniquely attracted to one particular selling proposition or advertising platform would therefore generally seem entirely beside the point.

Although many consumers tend to buy more than one brand, this does not signify any dynamic brand switching. Instead, the evidence shows that individual people have a repertoire of brands, each of which they buy fairly regularly. Consistent clustering or segmentation of the brands over the whole population is, however, relatively rare. When it occurs, it is usually an above-normal tendency for buyers of Brand A also to purchase Brand B, compared with the patterns for all the other brands, rather than any special tendency for buyers of one brand not to buy the other.[11] But consumers generally buy brands that are similar as if they were directly substitutable.

In general, then, repeat buying and brand switching patterns do not vary materially from one brand or product to another. A particularly simple result is that in a relatively short time period, the frequency with which consumers buy a brand varies only marginally within the same product or group. The main difference between a leading and a small brand is that the leader has more buyers. With ready-to-eat breakfast cereals, for example, consumers make on average 3 purchases of a brand over a 3-month period. This varies between only $2\frac{1}{2}$ and $3\frac{1}{2}$ for different brands.[12] This small variation is itself highly predictable from buyer behavior theory, with the larger-selling brands generally being bought slightly more frequently by their buyers (see Jones, Chapter 5, this volume).

This is what occurs in relatively short time periods. In periods that are very long compared with the product's average purchase cycle (e.g., well over a year), the opposite sort of effect may operate, because most consumers will have had some experience of most brands (even if only a single purchase). This leads to the view that a brand's sales can increase only if people buy it more often.[13] But in a shorter period, higher sales show themselves in terms of having to have more people buy in that period.

These various results are no longer isolated empirical regularities, but are becoming increasingly well explained and integrated into coherent theory.[14] The theory applies primarily when a brand's sales are more or less steady. This holds true most of the time—it is a basic characteristic of the market structure of branded, frequently bought products that sales levels are not in a constant state of flux.

Occasional trends and fluctuations caused by promotions and the like may be important from a marketing management point of view, but they do not amount to big, dynamic changes in consumer behavior as such. The individ-

TABLE 6.1 Typical Evaluative and Descriptive Attitudinal Responses to Different Brands

	Evaluative (e.g., "right taste")		Descriptive (for Brand C) (e.g., "convenient")	
	Users of the Stated Brand (%)	Nonusers of the Brand (%)	Users of the Stated Brand (%)	Nonusers of the Brand (%)
Brand A	67	6	19	3
Brand B	69	5	17	2
Brand C	62	4	55	48
Brand D	60	3	17	2

ual's buying behavior remains broadly characterized as steady and habitual rather than as dynamic and erratic.

Attitudes and Attitude Change

Because on the whole there are no large behavior-related differences among brands except that more people buy one than another, there are not many things that need to be explained by differing motivations and attitudes. In fact, attitudinal responses to branded products tend to be fairly simple.

The evidence shows that most attitudinal variables are largely of an "evaluative" kind, plus some highly specific "descriptive" differences for certain brands.[15] An evaluative response to a brand is equivalent to saying, "I like it" or perhaps even only "I have heard of it." Evaluative attitudes therefore differ between users and nonusers of a brand, but they do not differ among brands. For example, 67% of users of Brand A say it has the "right taste," with only 6% of nonusers of A saying so about it, and 69% of users of Brand B say that B has the "right taste," with only 5% of nonusers of B saying so, and so on, as illustrated in Table 6.1. Brand A may therefore have more people in all saying it has the "right taste" than Brand B, but only because more people use Brand A, not because its users look at it differently: Giving an evaluative response about a brand largely depends on whether or not one is using it.

Certain large exceptions to this pattern occur. These usually reflect some physical descriptive characteristics of one particular brand. For example, if a brand is fairly new, consumers tend to be aware of this and dub that brand exceptionally "modern" compared with older brands. If one brand of indigestion remedies can be taken without water and the others not, people notice this and far more regard it as "convenient," as illustrated for Brand C in Table 6.1. Promotional policies can also make a brand appear descriptively different: A slim cigarette advertised in women's magazines as being smoked by feminine women may be rated more "female" than a standard full-flavored cigarette packaged predominantly in red, with advertisements placed in sporting magazines and featuring cowboys.

A descriptive characteristic is usually perceived also by people who do not use the brand. For instance, a "female" cigarette will be seen so by people who smoke it and by those who do not. Nonusers of an indigestion remedy that does not require water will also regard it as exceptionally "convenient" (as for Brand C in Table 6.1), but they nonetheless do not use it. Descriptive differences between one brand and another therefore seldom relate to whether anyone actually uses the brand. Evaluative responses, on the other hand, while distinguishing between users and nonusers, generally do not differentiate one brand from another. Such results are therefore simple but not very helpful in explaining brand choice.

Attitude Change

The conventional results of research into consumers' attitudes show how they feel about products, but not how they *change* their feelings. Very little work has been reported about changes in attitude, and the work that has been conducted is difficult to interpret.[16]

It seems to be generally assumed that improving the attitudes of a nonuser toward a brand should make him or her use the brand, or at least become more predisposed to doing so. But this amounts to assuming that people's attitudes toward or images of a brand can in fact be readily changed, and that such attitude changes must precede the desired change in behavior. There is little or no evidence to support these assumptions.

The most commonly cited example of a successful change in image is that of Marlboro cigarettes. Few people volunteer another. Marlboro as a brand dates back to the beginning of the 20th century. It was considered a "ladies' " brand, at one stage holding a major share of the "older society women's market." But in the 1950s, Philip Morris, the maker, started advertising it very differently, in a male, outdoor manner—Marlboro Country, the Marlboro

Man, and the famous tattoo on the cowboy's arm in the first advertisements. Sales rose dramatically and Marlboro became a market leader. There is little doubt that a change in consumers' attitudes caused the vast increase in sales.

The real explanation, however, is much simpler. The change in Marlboro was a change in *product.* The new Marlboro of the 1950s was a standard-tipped cigarette, full-flavored, packed in a new flip-top box, with a strong design, and introduced at the start of the growth of the tipped market (the tipped sector of the U.S. market grew from 1% in 1950 to more than 60% by the mid-1960s). For the first half of the century, Marlboro had been expensive, high quality, and with a pink paper wrapper (so as not to show up lipstick). No wonder people thought of it as different.

Subsequent attitude surveys in fact showed that smokers thought of Marlboro not as a ladies' cigarette but as male, outdoor, for young people, for people with average jobs, and so on. But it did not have a special image—it differed little in these respects from other brands of similar product formulation. It scored extra on points where its advertising was played back (male, outdoor), but these differences—some 11 or 12 percentage points in a recent survey—were "not as great as might have been anticipated," to quote Stephen Fountaine, Philip Morris's director of marketing research. The change in Marlboro was real—it became a standard-tipped cigarette—and not a change merely in the mind of the consumer.

Other Factors

Conventional thinking about how advertising works rests on the sequence Awareness $\rightarrow$ Attitudes $\rightarrow$ Behavior. Although this appears to be common sense, various studies in social psychology have cast doubt on it. There are well-established psychological mechanisms that can act in the opposite direction, with behavior actually affecting attitudes. For instance, behavior (the act of buying or using a brand) can lead to greater awareness of information to which one is normally exposed (selective perception). Behavior can even lead to the deliberate seeking out of information, and to changes in attitude (notions of congruence and reduction of dissonance). Consumers have been shown to be more attentive to advertising for the brands they have chosen, particularly if the ticket prices are high.[17]

Usually, a consumer is not convinced that a brand he has not bought before has all the advantages over the alternatives. To reduce the "dissonance" between what he has done and what he knows or feels, he changes his attitudes after the purchase to make his chosen brand appear adequate. He needs to do this even more if the chosen brand in fact differs little from the others, because there is then no tangible reason or "reward" to justify his choice—for example, "Maybe it is not very good, but at least it cost less."

These processes are consistent with the known facts of consumer attitudes, such as those illustrated in Table 6.1. We will now see how they also fit into the broader picture.

Brand Choice and the Consumer

The consumer's choice among different brands or products is widely thought of as irrational and based on ignorance. This is how advertising is supposed to get its effect: "The scope of advertising depends on the ignorance of the people to whom it is addressed. The more ignorant the buyer, the more he relies on advertising." [18]

No one doubts or criticizes advertising's role when it is a question of supplying basic information or creating awareness, such as a house for sale, a job vacancy, a play at the local theater, or even a new consumer product. But where advertising is regarded as persuasive rather than informational, there is criticism because of the view that the ignorant consumer's choice is influenced by the last advertisement she saw or by the brand image she is being told to believe.

But this is all wrong. Buyers of frequently bought goods are not ignorant of them. They have extensive usage experience of the products—after all, they buy them frequently. As we have seen, they usually have direct experience of more than one brand, plus indirect word-of-mouth knowledge of others. The average housewife is far more experienced in buying her normal products than the industrial purchaser buying an atomic power station. She is also far less likely to make a mistake.

In regarding the private consumer's brand choice as irrational, the view seems to be that if there is little real difference among the brands, then it is not possible to choose rationally among them. This ignores the fact that the consumer knows there is little difference and she wants to buy the product. In choosing among similar brands, it is equally rational to choose the same brand as last time or to deliberately vary it, or even to toss a coin. Any brand will do, because the differences do not matter. Just because Brand X is advertised as having some specific "consumer benefit," it does not follow that anyone buying that brand must have believed or been influenced by that aspect of the advertising.

In practice, people seem to find it simplest to develop repeat-buying habits covering a limited repertoire of brands. Our task is to discover and understand consumers' reasons for choosing brands, instead of imposing our own preconceptions of how they ought to think and behave and dubbing anything else irrational. The questions are, How do these habits develop? and What is advertising's role in this?

ATR: Awareness–Trial–Reinforcement

Three main steps can account for the known facts of brand choice behavior: (a) gaining awareness of a brand, (b) making a first or trial purchase, and (c) being reinforced into developing and keeping a repeat-buying habit.

Some initial awareness of a brand usually has to come first, although occasionally one may find out a brand's name only after buying it. Awareness operates at different levels of attention and interest and can be created in many different ways, of which advertising is clearly one. Awareness may build up into the idea of looking for more information about the brand, asking someone about it, and so on.

A trial purchase, if it comes, will be the next step. This does not require any major degree of conviction that the brand is particularly good or special. Buyers of Brand A do not usually feel very differently about A from how buyers of Brand B feel about B, as is illustrated in Table 6.1. If that is how one feels afterward, there is therefore no reason a consumer should feel strongly about a different brand before she has tried it. All that is needed is the idea that one might try it. A trial purchase can arise for a variety of reasons: an out-of-stock situation of the usual brand, seeing an advertisement or display, knowing others who use it, an occasional urge for variety, and so on.

After trying a different brand, people usually return to their habitual brands as if nothing had happened. This is so even when new purchasers have been attracted on a large scale, with free samples or an attractive short-term promotion.[19] But sometimes a repeat-buying habit develops. This is the crucial determinant of long-term sales. The way this habit develops for a particular brand is primarily a matter of reinforcement after use. Any feeling of satisfaction that the brand is liked at least no less than the previously bought ones has to be nurtured. Evaluative attitudes have to be brought into line with the product class norms. But no exceptional "liking" need arise, because similar brands are known to be similar and the consumer does not inherently care whether she buys Bingo or Bango (which matters only to the manufacturer).

According to this viewpoint, development of a repeat-buying habit remains a fragile process, probably influenced by a variety of almost haphazard factors. The consumer knows there is little difference among brands, but she must choose. The critical factor is experience of the brand, and no other influences seem to be needed. Thus it has been found that something close to normal repeat-buying habits can develop without any explicit external stimuli, such as product differentiation or advertising, and preferences for particular price levels can also develop without any external support or manipulation, just by trial and the development of habits.[20]

But this process does not in itself determine how many people become aware, make a trial purchase, and are reinforced into a repeat-buying habit. This and hence the sales level of a brand can therefore be influenced by other marketing factors, including advertising.

The Place of Repetitive Advertising

Advertising can act in the various stages of the ATR process. First, it can create, reawaken, or strengthen awareness. Second, it is one of the factors that can facilitate a trial purchase. For an established brand, the consumer may already have been aware of it and even have tried it, but this would have been in the past. The problem is that now she is ignoring the brand and may even be unconscious of the general run of its advertising. Typically, a special effort such as a new product feature, a new package, a new price or special offer, or a new campaign—anything "new"—is needed to give the advertising an edge for this purpose and be noticed.

Obtaining awareness and trial for a brand is nonetheless relatively easy. The difficulty is at the third stage, of turning new triers into satisfied and lasting customers. This generally has to be achieved in the context of consumers already having a repertoire of one or more other brands that they are buying more or less regularly.

What happens in detail is not yet known—do heavy buyers of X switch to being heavy buyers of Y, or is this a gradual process, or is it the *light* buyers who are the most easily affected? What is it in fact that advertising has to try to support or accelerate? The knowledge of buyer behavior outlined earlier puts some constraints on the possibilities, but this is one of the purely descriptive features of consumer behavior that is not yet understood.

The process can, however, seldom amount to manipulating the consumer. Real conversion from virgin ignorance to full-blooded, long-term commitment does not happen often. A substantial leap forward in sales occurs only once in a while, and sales levels of most brands tend to be fairly steady. Trends and even short-term fluctuations tend to be smaller and more exceptional than is often thought.

The role of repetitive advertising of well-established brands is therefore predominantly defensive—to reinforce already developed repeat-buying habits. The consumer tends to perceive advertising for the brands she is already buying, and repetitive advertising enables the habit to continue to operate in the face of competition. The consumer does not have to be persuaded to think of her habitual brands as better than others, but has to be reinforced in thinking of them as at least no worse.

This view of repetitive advertising—as serving mainly a defensive role, reinforcing existing customers and only occasionally helping to create new customers or extra sales—seems in accord with many of the known facts. It deals also with some of economists' fears about the social costs of advertising and its possibly oligopolistic tendencies.[21]

It is consistent with the fact that advertising by itself generally is not very effective in creating sales or in changing attitudes. It also explains why most people feel they are not personally affected by advertising. They are right. Advertising for Brand X does not usually work by persuading people to rush out and buy it.

The primarily reinforcement function of repetitive advertising is in line with the fairly steady sales levels of most brands in most markets. Advertising is not produced by evil people who are trying to manipulate consumers (or if it is, these people must be very ineffective). No one is more eager to cut advertising expenditures than advertisers themselves, who actually have to pay for the ads. Advertisers see advertising of established brands mainly as a price that has to be paid for staying in business; they dare not cut advertising for such brands—and they are right (unless all manufacturers act together; e.g., aided by government edict, as in the case of TV advertising for cigarettes). For the consumer, large fluctuations in a firm's market share would also not be helpful, in terms of availability, quality control, or lower prices.

According to the ATR model, increasing the amount of advertising would not by itself have much effect on sales, but cutting it is likely to lose sales. This is because some reinforcing action would be withdrawn, allowing competitive brands to gain customers more easily. For an established brand the loss of sales would by definition be quite slow, and no special theory of lagged effects of advertising is needed. Furthermore, reducing an advertising budget after a drop in sales to bring the two in line would not necessarily lead to any further substantial drop in sales.

The model also explains the survival of a small brand with a small advertising budget. For users of the small brand, the large amount of advertising for a larger brand that they do not use performs no function and generally is not even noticed. When a consumer buys two or more brands, some more heavily advertised than the others, each brand's advertising primarily reinforces that brand, and the status quo can continue.

High levels of advertising mostly occur in product fields where consumer demand is strong and the product is easy to supply (because of low capital costs or excess capacity). This leads to active competition and hence the need to defend one's share of the market, either by price-cutting or by heavy advertising.

Economists are frequently concerned that high advertising levels act as a barrier to entry for new brands and hence deter competition. This is wrong on two accounts. First, it is the high risk of *failure* with a new brand that acts as the barrier. *At least four out of five new products fail.* The barrier is spending millions and probably having nothing to show for it. Second, heavily advertised product fields are in fact characterized by heavy competition and a high incidence of new brands—but generally launched by firms with experience and the other factors in the marketing mix (e.g., a suitable sales force) that are also needed.

Remaining Problems

The ATR approach outlined here is no more than a broad verbal statement of how advertising works that seems consistent with the known facts. Detailed quantitative flesh needs to be put on the model, but its differences from the theory of persuasive advertising already raise many questions, such as about the content of advertising, about the setting of advertising appropriations and the evaluation of advertising, and about product policy.

Regarding content, for example, use of attitudinal research results to try to improve one's image or to produce persuasive messages of how Brand X is "best" seems mostly to mislead the advertiser and critic rather than the consumer. Advertising research has failed to show that consumers of a particular brand regard their brand as any more superior than consumers of other brands regard those other brands as superior. Consumers need to be told merely that the brand has all the good properties they expect of the product, and there can be renewed emphasis on creative advertising, telling a good advertising story well.

More generally, because consumers rightly see competitive brands in most product fields as very similar, it seems unnecessary to strive compulsively to differentiate brands artificially from each other. The clutter of marginally different brands, types, and sizes and the corresponding costs of product development and distribution may be unnecessary. This is not a plea for uniformity, but for real research into consumers' attitudes and motives to gain a better understanding of their—rather than advertisers'—needs for product differentiation.

Conclusion

Most mass-media advertising is for competitive brands. It is a defensive tool and a price the producer pays to stay in business.

Consumers' attitudes toward similar brands are very similar. Purchasers of frequently bought goods usually have experience of more than one brand, and they mostly ignore advertising for brands they are not already using.

It follows that there can be little scope for persuasive advertising. Instead, advertising's main role is to reinforce feelings of satisfaction for brands already being used. At times it can also create new sales by reawakening consumers' awareness and interest in other brands, stimulating them to trial purchases, and then sometimes, through subsequent reinforcement, helping to facilitate the development of repeat-buying habits. This is the main determinant of sales volume.

The Awareness–Trial–Reinforcement model of advertising seems to account for the known facts, but many quantitative details still need elucidation. Such developments could markedly influence the planning, execution, and evaluation of advertising.

With persuasive advertising, the task might be seen as persuading the pliable customer that Brand X is better than other brands. Under the ATR model, advertising's task is to inform the rather experienced consumer that Brand X is as good as others. The language of the advertising copy might sometimes look similar (still "better" or "best"), but the advertiser's aim and expectations would differ.

Notes

1. Quoted in A. A. Achenbaum, "Advertising Doesn't Manipulate Consumers," *Journal of Advertising Research,* vol. 12, no. 2, 1972, 3-13.

2. John T. Connor, *Advertising: Absolutely Indispensable* (address before the Cleveland Advertising Club, Cleveland, OH) (New York: American Association of Advertising Agencies, 1966).

3. John Hobson, "The Influence and Techniques of Modern Advertising," *Journal of the Royal Society of Arts,* vol. 112, 1964, 565-606.

4. Kenneth Boulding, *Economic Analysis* (New York: Harper & Row, 1966), 513; as quoted in Achenbaum, "Advertising Doesn't Manipulate Consumers."

5. Timothy Joyce, *What Do We Know About How Advertising Works?* (London: J. Walter Thompson, 1967).

6. Achenbaum, "Advertising Doesn't Manipulate Consumers"; Colin McDonald, "What Is the Short-Term Effect of Advertising?" in *Proceedings of the ESOMAR Congress, Barcelona* (Amsterdam: ESOMAR, 1970); M. Barnes, *The Relationship Between Purchasing Patterns and Advertising Exposure* (London: J. Walter Thompson, 1971).

7. J. A. P. Treasure, "The Volatile Consumer," *Admap,* vol. 9, 1973, 172-182.

8. K. S. Palda, "The Hypothesis of a Hierarchy of Effects: A Partial Evaluation," *Journal of Marketing Research,* vol. 3, 1966, 13-24.

9. Andrew S. C. Ehrenberg, *Repeat-Buying: Theory and Applications* (New York: American Elsevier, 1972), Table B4.

10. Ibid.

11. M. A. Collins, "Market Segmentation: The Realities of Buyer Behavior," *Journal of the Market Research Society,* vol. 13, 1971, 146-157.

12. P. Charlton, Andrew S. C. Ehrenberg, and B. Pymont, "Buyer Behavior Under Mini-Test Conditions," *Journal of the Market Research Society,* vol. 14, 1972, 171-183.

13. Treasure, "The Volatile Consumer."

14. Ehrenberg, *Repeat-Buying*; G. J. Goodhardt and C. Chatfield, "The Gamma-Distribution in Consumer Purchasing," *Nature,* vol. 244, no. 5414, 1973, 316.

15. Michael Bird, C. Channon, and Andrew S. C. Ehrenberg, "Brand Image and Brand Usage," *Journal of Marketing Research,* vol. 7, 1969, 307-314; Michael Bird and Andrew S. C. Ehrenberg,

"Consumer Attitudes and Brand Usage," *Journal of the Market Research Society,* vol. 12, 1970, 233-247 (see also the ensuing exchange of commentary on this article in the same journal, vol. 13, 1971, 100-101, 242-243; and vol. 14, 1972, 57-58); M. A. Collins, "The Analysis and Interpretation of Attitude Data," lecture delivered at the Course on Consumer Attitudes, Market Research Society, Cambridge, England, March 1973; T. K. Chakrapani and Andrew S. C. Ehrenberg, "The Pattern of Consumer Attitudes," paper presented at the American Association of Public Opinion Research Conference, Lake George, May 1974.

16. Jack E. Fothergill, "Do Attitudes Change Before Behavior?" in *Proceedings of the ESOMAR Congress, Opitija* (Amsterdam: ESOMAR, 1968).

17. James F. Engel, "The Psychological Consequences of a Major Purchase Decision," in William S. Decker (ed.), *Marketing in Transition* (Chicago: American Marketing Association, 1963), 462-475.

18. T. Scitovsky, *Welfare and Competition* (Chicago: Richard Irwin, 1951).

19. G. J. Goodhardt and Andrew S. C. Ehrenberg, "Evaluating a Consumer Deal," *Admap,* vol. 5, 1969, 388-393; Ehrenberg, *Repeat-Buying.*

20. J. D. McConnell, "The Development of Brand Loyalty: An Experimental Study," *Journal of Marketing Research,* vol. 5, 1968, 13-19; J. D. McConnell, "The Price-Quality Relationship in an Experimental Setting," *Journal of Marketing Research,* vol. 5, 1968, 300-303; P. Charlton and Andrew S. C. Ehrenberg, "McConnell's Experimental Brand-Choice Data," *Journal of Marketing Research,* vol. 11, 1973, 302-307.

21. P. Doyle, "Economic Aspects of Advertising: A Survey," *Economic Journal,* vol. 78, 1966, 570-602.

Is Advertising Still Salesmanship?

John Philip Jones

The question posed in the title of this chapter is not a joke, although many American advertising people will find it curious if not incomprehensible. The notion of advertising as a branch of salesmanship is so obvious and has such a long history that few American advertisers have ever been able to imagine advertising as being anything else. The question will, however, cause less surprise to European, especially British, practitioners, whose styles of advertising are only too often difficult for Americans to comprehend. In European advertising, understated softness, quirkiness, indirectness, unusual visual effects, and bizarre humor are taken to extremes. If such advertising works at all, it must obviously work in unexpected ways.

NOTE: This chapter is an adaptation of an article that appeared in the *Journal of Advertising Research,* May/June 1997. Used by permission.

In contrast, American advertising has traditionally been written with straightforward and aggressive intentions—to boost sales, to attack the competition and increase market share, to build a consumer franchise and drive loyalty, to launch and develop strong new brands. Its methods have mostly been equally direct: "constructing advertisements which grab a woman's attention and don't let go of it until the message has been fully planted." [1]

It is obvious from this rather typical statement by an American advertiser that his advertising is expected to work by conversion: by addressing apathetic or even hostile prospects and persuading them with powerful arguments to buy his brand. This happens. But I believe that it happens far less often than many advertisers believe—a point to which I shall return.

In 1990, I examined the different attitudes of American and European practitioners in an article titled "Advertising: Strong Force or Weak Force? Two Views an Ocean Apart." The article generated a good deal of interest, and it has been reprinted in at least six different publications, most recently in 1996.[2] The phrase *strong force* was meant to describe the normal American attitude toward advertising, as discussed above; *weak force* was meant to describe a typical European view. I did not mean the adjective *weak* to imply ineffective, but rather to illustrate the modus operandi of advertising that might work in a different and more subtle way from how it is most commonly planned to work in the United States. I sometimes think that the process involved is the opposite of browbeating—namely, seduction.

To the surprise of American readers, I developed the argument that effective advertising can far more often be explained by the weak theory than by the strong one—a generalization that I believe holds true equally for advertising on both sides of the Atlantic, as well as for other countries (such as Japan and Australia) that have reached economic maturity and where there is no longer much increase in primary demand for consumer goods and services. I believe that in an environment in which brands can gain share only at other brands' expense, head-on advertising appeals are too unsubtle to be productive. Consumers switch off their attention. Effective advertising must be derived from the competitive environment, which means that it must be based on an understanding of the subtleties of consumers and of the brands they use, with appeals that may be meaningful only to the users of the competitive brands being targeted.

In my article I also asked myself whether the argument about strong/weak forces was very important. I concluded that it, in fact, matters a great deal. Salesmanship is by definition an activity directed at increasing sales. This generally means increasing an advertiser's profit. The question of whether advertising is a strong or weak force—and what salesmanship really means—therefore has a direct bearing on this prime business objective. As a result, it governs the styles of campaigns developed and exposed, and the types of research used to evaluate them. It also influences—or should influence—my own main field of activity, advertising education.

The Weak Theory

The weak theory is derived from the work of the British academic Andrew Ehrenberg. He is a mathematician rather than an advertising specialist, and is best known for his analyses of consumer purchasing patterns derived from very extensive longitudinal consumer panel data.[3] He has published his work widely, and, with a single important exception (the main topic I shall be discussing in this chapter), his conclusions are well supported empirically.

The main points of Ehrenberg's doctrine can be summarized briefly as follows, although this list can only barely do justice to the breadth and integrity of his work:

1. A brand's penetration—the proportion of households that buy the brand at least once in a defined period—is the main determinant of its market share. In general terms, the more buyers, the higher the share, in direct proportion.

2. Purchase frequency—the average number of times a household buys the brand during the defined period—influences the brand's market share, but to a lesser extent than its penetration does. For small and medium-size brands, purchase frequency does not differ much from brand to brand. However, for the approximately 20% of largest brands, purchase frequency increases to an above-average level, and this gives an additional boost to market share.[4]

3. Three other purchasing dynamics—repeat purchase, the frequency distribution of purchases, and multibrand purchases (i.e., the other brands in the category that are bought by the brand's users)—are all closely related to its penetration and purchase frequency. These additional dynamics can be

modeled mathematically, and in general the predictions of such models will match observed data.

4. For established brands, the five factors discussed in the preceding three paragraphs show regularity and uniformity over time, and certain of them are uniform from brand to brand. The numbers expressing these dynamics describe in reasonably precise terms what are in essence habitual buying patterns: patterns determined by forces driven by existing and deeply entrenched behavior uninfluenced in the main by external stimuli.

5. This now leads to an important but difficult question: If existing buying behavior has a greater influence on buying than do external stimuli, what do these stimuli accomplish? In particular, what does the consumer advertising for a brand actually do?

6. Ehrenberg's line of argument hypothesizes that advertising has three functions: (a) It stimulates brand awareness, acting as a reminder, and this prompts purchase and use of the brand; this leads to the growth of favorable attitudes in the minds of the brand's buyers. (b) Further advertising reinforces these favorable attitudes. This interaction of awareness and reinforcement gives the doctrine its name: Awareness–Trial–Reinforcement (ATR). Additionally, (c) advertising has a defensive role in protecting the status quo—maintaining the brand's penetration and purchase frequency against the assaults of competitive brands.

7. Ehrenberg's doctrine assumes that consumer goods markets are essentially stationary—that there is little change over time in either the size of categories or individual brand shares. As I shall explain, this is not a totally realistic assumption.

I must state immediately that the Ehrenberg doctrine explains a great deal about how purchasing takes place and what advertising actually accomplishes, at least in the medium and long term. Ehrenberg's arguments are plausible in terms of consumer psychology. His doctrine is generally more often right than wrong. However, I believe that it is incomplete in one important respect: how advertising works in the short term (as opposed to the medium and long term). Remember that in Ehrenberg's eyes, advertising's only short-term role is to prompt brand awareness. I believe that there is more to it than this.

Advertising and Consumer Behavior

In 1995, I published the results of a substantial piece of pure single-source research.[5] I coined the phrase *pure single-source* to describe a technique aimed at examining in a tightly controlled way the influence of advertising on consumer purchasing. I covered the leading brands in 12 major categories of repeat-purchase packaged goods, using data on brand buying supplied by the A. C. Nielsen household panel. Each of 2,000 homes in this panel was supplied with meters attached to all the television sets in the household; the meters logged when the sets were switched on and to what programs they were tuned. A third data source, with the proprietary name of Monitor Plus, identified the names of all the brands advertised when each set was switched on. The research provided a total of more than 110,000 statistical readings.

This cumbersome but thorough research procedure made it possible for me to relate the purchasing of identified brands by each individual household to the advertising for those same brands received by that household just before the purchase. (I defined "just before" as within a period of 7 days before the brand was bought.) This carefully controlled collection of multiple data from each individual household enabled me to examine in a scientific way the relationship between advertising and buying. I isolated the effect of advertising by comparing purchases in the households that had bought after having received advertising for the brand with purchases in the households that had bought but had not received advertising for it. In other words, I was able to answer the rather important question, What contribution does advertising make on its own?

The research generated some striking conclusions, the most important of which was that advertising had an immediate effect on sales in 70% of cases. The size of this effect varied widely among brands, but with some brands, market share more than doubled. When tough standards were applied to judge effectiveness, the 70% estimate came down to 35%. An important supplementary point was that a single advertising exposure was shown to be all that was necessary to achieve an immediate sales increase. There was not much buildup of additional sales from extra advertising.

I also measured a long-term effect, gauged in the first instance by the influence of advertising on sales over the course of a year (I subsequently called this a *first order of long-term effect*). In every case, the high level of short-term effect was not sustained, so that as an invariable rule the year-end effect was less than the immediate one. I found that of the 70% of brands whose advertising produced short-term sales results, two-thirds (46% of all brands) showed a positive result—but one that was always reduced by the end of the year. With tough standards for judging effectiveness, the 46% figure came down to 25%.

I therefore drew a clear and robust conclusion that advertising is capable of a *sharp immediate effect* on sales—in direct contradiction to Ehrenberg's doctrine that advertising's short-term effect is solely to increase brand awareness. With such a contradiction, how is it possible to reconcile Ehrenberg's well-supported view that advertising has no short-term effect on buying behavior with my own empirical proof that such an effect not only exists, but can be very large indeed?

The gulf between Ehrenberg and me is not as wide as it appears at first glance, but to appreciate this point, we must understand the different ways in which Ehrenberg's and my data were actually collected.

Ehrenberg Versus Jones

The empirical basis of Ehrenberg's work is consumer panel information: reports from consumers giving details of their brand purchasing. Data were collected at intervals of varying lengths—1 week, 4 weeks, 13 weeks, 1 year—but the vast majority of Ehrenberg's figures are presented for periods of 4 weeks or more. (These might have been aggregations of short-term figures collected separately, but this point is not discussed and the separate figures are not given.) It will be remembered that my data relate to a period of a single length—1 week. Herein lies the key to understanding the difference between Ehrenberg and me.

An additional point is that Ehrenberg covers only brand purchasing and makes no attempt also to measure consumers' actual exposure to advertising. His conclusions about the influence of advertising on purchasing must therefore be inferred. Mine are observed.

Two analysts who have carried out work similar to mine, Walter Reichel in the United States and Colin McDonald in Britain, have demonstrated that the short-term effect of advertising on sales is evanescent.[6] The maximum effect comes from advertising received 1 day before buying the brand; it is weaker from advertising received 2 days before, weaker still from 3 days before, and weaker again from 4 days before.

Because advertising's effect decays so rapidly, Ehrenberg's measures of consumer purchasing over periods of 4 weeks, 13 weeks, and a year cannot be expected to show much immediate effect from advertising stimuli. The advertising effect will seem to be much weaker than it really is. Moreover, different brands in a category will advertise competitively in order to take share from one another; therefore, the effective campaign for one brand will tend to cancel out the effective campaign of another, especially if they advertise at different times. As a result, the two brands will constantly exchange market shares.

Ehrenberg's purchasing data show stable patterns because the immediate effects of advertising are smoothed. The effects are undoubtedly there, but his research is not able to show them. The tranquil Ehrenbergian surface of markets conceals the disturbances that are going on below. I am not the only analyst to detect this. Leo Bogart described it in 1984 as the "turbulent depths of marketing." [7] And in a book published in 1986, I discussed it in the following terms:

> An individual's purchasing behavior may at first glance appear erratic and haphazard. But the more we study such behavior over time, and the more we look at the aggregate behavior of large numbers of consumers, the more regular and predictable it all appears to be.[8]

Ehrenberg has always been aware of the short-term ups and downs of brand purchasing, but he has persistently described this phenomenon as a stochastic effect. The word *stochastic* is not easy to grasp, but my best effort at defining it is that it describes random variations in small effects that, when added up, lead to the same total effect each time.

The real difference between Ehrenberg and me is that he sees the short-term variability in consumer purchasing as haphazard, but with the haphazard changes adding up in some mysterious way to a total effect that is always the same. I see the short-term variability in consumer purchasing as the result of measurable and controllable marketing inputs; it is the mutual cancellation of the effects of such inputs from competitive brands that leads to stability.

Ehrenberg says that the short-term variations in consumer purchasing cannot be managed. I am convinced that they can.

How Does Advertising Really Work?

It is important to start with a clear distinction between the short term and the long term. It is also useful to divide the long term into two parts: a first order and second order of effect.

In the short term, advertising is demonstrably capable of generating a powerful effect on consumer purchasing. Advertising does more than make consumers aware of a brand (as Ehrenberg believes). Effective advertising sells. Advertising is indeed salesmanship.

However, the real meaning of salesmanship is not as obvious as many people might believe. The advertising campaigns shown by my pure single-source research to have the greatest effect in the marketplace are certainly not hard-selling in the conventional sense: "no 'Slices of Life'; no men in white coats making product demonstrations . . . none of the most widely used—and tiresome—advertising clichés. The campaigns are not didactic and verbal." [9] Rather, the successful campaigns have three general characteristics: (a) They are likeable and offer a reward for watching because they are entertaining and amusing, (b) they are visual rather than verbal, and (c) they say something important and meaningful about the brand being advertised.

All the research into the creative process that I have ever examined demonstrates that successful advertising does its job—or at least can do its job—in subtle and rather unexpected ways. The European styles of advertising described at the beginning of this chapter are often surprisingly effective when evaluated by hard measures. [10]

As already mentioned, Ehrenberg talks about advertising reminding the consumer; in his own words, advertising gives a nudge. In the more precise words of Herbert Krugman, advertising rearranges in consumers' minds "the relative salience of attributes." [11] To both analysts, the effect is cognitive.

Despite my respect for these two views, I am convinced that the short-term effect of advertising goes beyond simple awareness. By saying something important about the brand, advertising reinforces brand preferences. However, such reinforcement falls far short of what most people would describe as persuasion—overcoming apathy or resistant attitudes on the part of consumers. If at the one extreme there is an Ehrenbergian nudge, and at the other there is full-blown persuasion, I think that the actual process falls somewhere in between.

One proof that successful advertising works in a more positive way than as a simple low-key reminder is that, to be effective, the content of the advertising must be substantial enough to stand up to the competition. On the basis of a simulated consumer choice between competing brands in a research setting, the sales success of an advertisement can be predicted. The test scores (representing choice of the advertised brands) vary widely from advertisement to advertisement, and what determines effectiveness is usually the strength of the underlying proposition. There must therefore be something more at work than a simple reminder, which would be expected to produce relatively uniform scores.

I have drawn this conclusion from data that compared the pretest scores of a range of television commercials with facts about their effectiveness in the marketplace.[12] The data, which I examined with great care before publishing them, came from the leading American research company in the field of television advertising pretesting, research systems corporation (rsc). The proprietary name for rsc's system is the ARS Persuasion® technique. As suggested in the preceding paragraphs, I suspect that the word *persuasion* may not be a precise description of what is going on, and I am working with rsc to clarify this matter. However, irrespective of the actual effects of the tested advertisements on the consumer's psyche, the test scores for the commercials that go through the ARS Persuasion system can be shown to predict sales fairly accurately in the majority of cases. The test scores not only forecast the direction of sales movements, they also predict reasonably well the extent of the sales effects.

The main conclusion that I believe can be drawn about short-term effectiveness is that to achieve results, the campaign must have a creative edge in comparison with its competition. Since my research demonstrates unambiguously that an advertisement does not have to be exposed repeatedly to work, the creative content is clearly all-important—on the assumption that the initial media exposure achieves a large enough coverage of the market with at least one advertisement. On the other hand, if the advertisement is creatively ineffective, repeated exposures will not bring it to life.

The first order of long-term effect is the result of a repetition of short-term effects. This naturally presupposes that the campaign has produced a short-term effect in the first place. It also demands a sufficiently large advertising budget, and enough continuity in the media plan, to support the brand without too much loss of sales to the advertising and sales promotions of competitive brands.

TABLE 7.1 Total Category Volume Sales Trend and Volume Shares of Leading Brands

	Year 1	*Year 2*	*Year 3*	*Year 4*	*Year 5*
Total category volume sales index	100	106	108	108	108
Brand shares (%)					
Brand A	18.3	17.2	16.2	16.3	17.2
Brand B	17.7	17.4	16.6	15.8	14.7
Brand C	11.2	11.1	10.8	10.3	10.0
Brand D	—	2.0	7.0	8.5	8.2
Brand E	6.4	6.4	6.0	6.2	6.9
Brand F	6.1	5.6	5.9	5.8	5.7
Brand G	5.1	5.8	5.5	5.0	4.8
Brand H	5.9	5.4	4.8	4.7	4.4

Remember that it is the countervailing pressures from competitors that shorten the duration of the effect from often powerful short-term advertising stimuli. There is a tendency for short-term effects to cancel out. This is essentially what leads to inertia in markets: Ehrenbergian stability. In order to shake a brand free of this, not only must the advertiser expose advertising that produces immediate sales, but the advertising must be run with enough media weight to outperform the competition for longer periods than the periods during which the competition outperforms the brand. The race will be won by the competitor with the greatest and most carefully husbanded reserve of media energy.

How often do brands succeed in doing this? I believe more often than Ehrenberg admits, as he is constantly being hemmed in by his underlying assumption of stationary conditions. Consider the product category described in Table 7.1. The category itself is large, mature, and advertising-intensive. The brands, most of which are manufactured by four large oligopolists, are used—one or another—in virtually all American households on a daily basis. The table examines a run of 5 years, none of which is to any degree atypical.

Total sales volume and individual brand shares are reasonably stable, but hardly stationary. Brand D was newly introduced, and from a standing start grew to an 8.2% share of market. Brands B and H lost 10% and 20% of their volume, respectively, and four of the remaining five brands also declined marginally.

I must emphasize that the category is more typical than untypical of repeat-purchase packaged goods in the United States and other developed countries. Brands rise and brands fall, although this happens over a period of years, not months. And the brands that grow are those that not only have functional superiority in at least some respect vis-à-vis their competitors, but also manage to develop and deploy their advertising with competitive efficiency. They have campaigns that have a creative edge. And they invest large enough budgets to ensure that there is a reasonably continuous advertising presence, which brings about more sales "ups" than sales "downs" over the course of a year, leaving a net gain at the end.

But are there cases in which advertising works in a more overtly persuasive, forceful, and dramatic way, along the lines hypothesized by the advertiser quoted at the beginning of this chapter, who sees advertising working by conversion? In the field of repeat-purchase packaged goods, I am convinced that this is rare. But this model explains how advertising works in fields where highly rational arguments are used at great length and the advertisements work with little repetition. I am referring to direct-response advertising, an activity that represents a substantial and growing minority of total advertising. It will, however, remain a minority. With advertising in repeat-purchase fields, long-term effectiveness is gradual. It also embraces an important new factor, which can be described as advertising's *second order of long-term effect.*

Consider the following words of an American consumer (who was being interviewed for a market research study, the researcher employing a projective technique). The lady is describing her feelings about Campbell's soup:

> She is a very warm, genial lady who sits in her kitchen and brews delicious soups and cares about your nourishment and cares about your children and has a flock of grandkids, and has her ration of liver spots on the backs of her hands.[13]

To the lady who spoke these words—and to millions like her—Campbell's is an old friend, and in a small way a part of the life of her family. In blind product tests of canned soup, consumers will rate Campbell's higher than other brands; and in named tests, Campbell's will be rated higher still—a research device that measures neatly and ingeniously the added values of a brand's name and reputation.[14]

To the manufacturer, this powerful attachment between brand and consumer is the end product of years of that consumer's satisfaction with the brand's product quality, augmented and reinforced by advertising planned to be harmonious with this functional excellence. The result is something of specific measurable benefit to the manufacturer. In fact, there are three such benefits: (a) Successful brands can generally command a premium price and are less driven by the need for money-off promotions. (b) Because they often sell a large volume, successful brands benefit from above-average purchase frequency—a direct expression of above-average brand loyalty. (c) Successful brands are relatively less advertising-intensive than smaller, less secure brands, and can therefore use their advertising budgets more economically and productively. These points, which are all clearly demonstrable, provide important scale economies for successful brands.[15] They make a significant contribution to the manufacturer's bottom line.

It is this second order of long-term effect that transforms a successful brand into a great one: Campbell's, Coca-Cola, Hershey's, Ivory, Kleenex, Kodak, Kraft, Tide—also American Express and Ford. Advertising does not create a great brand on its own, but it makes an important contribution. This is what Ehrenberg means by reinforcement. And I think he is totally right.

Notes

1. David Ogilvy, *Ogilvy on Advertising* (New York: Crown, 1983), 70.

2. John Philip Jones, "Advertising: Strong Force or Weak Force? Two Views an Ocean Apart," in J. C. Luik and M. J. Waterson (eds.), *Advertising and Markets: A Collection of Seminal Papers* (Henley-on-Thames, UK: NTC, 1996), 79-93.

3. See, for instance, Andrew S. C. Ehrenberg, *Repeat-Buying: Facts, Theory and Applications,* 2nd ed. (New York: Oxford University Press, 1988); Andrew S. C. Ehrenberg, "Repetitive Advertising and the Consumer," *Journal of Advertising Research,* April 1974, 25-34.

4. John Philip Jones, *When Ads Work: New Proof That Advertising Triggers Sales* (New York: Simon & Schuster-Lexington, 1995), 133-139.

5. Ibid. See also John Philip Jones, "Single-Source Research Begins to Fulfill Its Promise," *Journal of Advertising Research,* May/June 1995, 9-16.

6. Walter Reichel, "Beyond 'Effective Frequency': How to Maximize Marketplace Impact Using New Data-Base Approaches to Media Scheduling," in *Proceedings of the Effective Frequency Research Day Conference* (New York: Advertising Research Foundation, 1994), 91-105; Colin McDonald, "How Frequently Should You Advertise?" *Admap,* July/August 1996, 22-25.

7. Leo Bogart, *The Turbulent Depths of Marketing: An Analysis of Supermarket Scanner Data* (New York: Newspaper Advertising Bureau, 1984).

8. John Philip Jones, *What's in a Name? Advertising and the Concept of Brands* (New York: Simon & Schuster-Lexington, 1986), 105.

9. Jones, *When Ads Work,* 66.

10. See, for instance, the more than 200 individual cases analyzed in the eight volumes titled *Advertising Works* (London: Institute of Practitioners in Advertising, 1981-1995).

11. Herbert E. Krugman, "The Impact of Television Advertising: Learning Without Involvement," *Public Opinion Quarterly,* vol. 29, 1965, 350-356.

12.   John Philip Jones, *Getting It Right the First Time: Can We Eliminate Ineffective Advertising Before It Is Run?* (Henley-on-Thames, UK: Admap Publications, 1996); John Philip Jones, "Look Before You Leap," *Admap,* November 1996, 18-22.

13.   Quoted in John Philip Jones, *How Much Is Enough? Getting the Most From Your Advertising Dollar* (New York: Simon & Schuster-Lexington, 1992), 164.

14.   Jones, *What's in a Name?* 32.

15.   Jones, *When Ads Work,* 61-64.

Expansion Advertising

Brian Wansink

Instead of using advertising to generate preference or choice, many high-share, low-growth brands are now using advertising to suggest new ways to use the brands, or new situations in which they can be consumed. That is, instead of simply encouraging consumers to choose a brand, they are encouraging consumers to use it more frequently. For mature brands, such as Arm & Hammer Baking Soda, A-1 Steak Sauce, and Campbell's soups, this type of advertising campaign may be a cost-effective way in which to build sales. For such brands, encouraging current users to eat an additional can of soup each month or to use steak sauce twice as often may be more effective at boosting sales than trying to convince nonusers to switch from competing brands. There is a point where further penetration of a saturated market becomes very costly. This is the point at which category expansion takes precedence over market penetration.[1]

TABLE 8.1 Expansion Advertising Opportunities for Mature, High-Share Products and Services

Product or Service	Possible Expansion Advertisements
Campbell's soup	Eat with a nice family dinner Eat for breakfast
Clorox bleach	Clean counters and sinks
Heinz vinegar	Clean windows
Jell-O Brand Gelatin	Use in recipes Eat after exercising Consume (in liquid form) as a cold drink
Pepsi-Cola	Drink in the morning
Burger King	Celebrate "small" events (e.g., good report cards) Carry-out for picnics "Take-home" food
Kodak film	Take photos of dinner parties and guests Take photos of "minor" holidays (e.g., Father's Day) Take photos of pets
AT&T	Use business calls as "personal" calls Use calls to "relive" good memories
American Express	Use for small purchases Consider as short-term (30-day) loans

Expansion Advertising Defined

Advertising that attempts to expand the ways in which a brand is typically used is referred to as *expansion advertising*. It includes any advertising campaign that attempts to expand category usage by encouraging a particular segment of customers to use the brand in a situation in which they do not regularly use it. Table 8.1 suggests some expansion advertising opportunities that may exist for various brands.

Attitudes toward using brands are very situation-specific. A person who is generally favorable toward a particular soft drink may be less favorable about drinking it in the morning. An individual's general attitude toward a brand is conventionally denoted as A_{brand}. In contrast, a person's attitude toward using a particular brand in a new target situation in which the brand is not generally used is referred to as his or her "attitude toward the new use" ($A_{new-use}$), and it is specific to the particular usage situation under examination. The objective of expansion ads is to increase brands' usage by improving consumer attitudes toward these new uses.

Although expansion advertising takes many forms, three kinds are most common: noncomparison ads, product comparison ads, and situation comparison ads. In its most basic form, a *noncomparison ad* simply states that a target brand is a reasonable choice for the target situation ("Use Arm & Hammer Baking Soda as a refrigerator deodorant"). In contrast, a *product comparison ad* associates the target brand with the target situation by positioning or comparing the target brand with another product that is already more closely associated with that situation ("Eat Orville Redenbacher's popcorn as an afternoon snack instead of potato chips"). A *situation comparison ad* associates the use of the target brand in a new situation with the brand's use in a more familiar situation ("Special K breakfast cereal is as good at snack time as it is at breakfast").

It is important to determine which kind of expansion ad will be most effective for a particular brand in a particular situation. As Patricia Winters has noted in an article in *Advertising Age,* "Soft-drink marketers have already dubbed the morning an opportunity to offer 'cold caffeine' in a nation where hot beverages have lost favor." [2] The question is, What advertising strategy would be most useful for encouraging soft-drink consumers to drink their favorite colas in the morning? Laboratory research on expansion advertising provides some insight into how to answer this question, as well as related ones.

How Expansion Advertising Affects Usage

What form of expansion ad—noncomparison, product comparison, or situation comparison—is most effective? It depends on the objective of the campaign. Product comparison ads tend to stimulate higher brand recall, whereas situation comparison ads tend to be more persuasive and tend to encourage more usage of the brand.

Situation comparison ads lead consumers to think about the positive aspects of using the target brand in a more familiar and conventional situation.

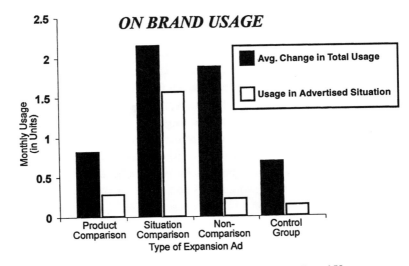

Figure 8.1. The Impact of Expansion Advertising on Brand Usage

These positive thoughts, in turn, have a favorable impact on attribute ratings and on attitude ($A_{new-use}$). Conversely, product comparison ads often stimulate negative thoughts about the target brand because they generally position it with a favored product that is already used in that situation. Although these negative thoughts about using the target brand have an unfavorable impact on attribute ratings and on $A_{new-use}$, they make the brand memorable because they associate it with the more typically used product. As a result, product comparison ads can make the target brand more memorable, even though not all of these memorable thoughts will be positive.[3]

How do these ads affect the total amount of the product that is used? This question was examined in a laboratory study that exposed homemakers to one of three different executions for each of three different brands (Campbell's soup, Jell-O Brand Gelatin, and Ocean Spray Cranberry Sauce).[4] The results of viewing these ads were to be compared with the responses of a control group who had seen no ads. Three months after exposure, telephone callbacks indicated that the expansion ads stimulated use of the brand in the target situation and also increased total usage of the brand. The aggregated results, shown in Figure 8.1, suggest that all executional forms can be effective in stimulating use. These results also emphasize that situation comparisons appear to be most effective, whereas product comparisons are less effective.

Let us return to the question asked earlier: What advertising strategy should be used to encourage soft-drink consumers to drink colas in the morning? The answer depends first on the forms of comparison ads that are feasible and second, the intermediate advertising objectives desired. Not all forms of expansion advertising are equally feasible in a particular situation. A product comparison campaign is appropriate only if there is a similar, substitutable brand that is strongly associated with the target situation (such as coffee in this case). Likewise, a situation comparison campaign is appropriate only if the target usage situation and the brand's more typical usage situation have something in common that is being used as the point of comparison (Pepsi stimulates alertness in the morning just as it does in the midafternoon).

Second, selecting the most successful advertising strategy also depends on whether the intermediate objectives of the advertising campaign are to improve attitudes or to improve recall. If all three forms of expansion advertising are feasible, situation comparison ads may have the greatest impact on attitude, whereas product comparison ads may have the greatest impact on recall. Although Figure 8.1 indicates that situation comparison ads more effectively increase usage, the differences may be less clear if a consumer is exposed to the ads a number of times, as would be the case in a campaign.

Future research might suggest, for instance, that both of these situations have an important place within the life cycle of a particular brand's expansion campaign. That is, situation comparison ads might be used during the first months of a campaign to develop favorable attitudes toward the new use ($A_{new-use}$). After these attitudes are well developed, product comparison ads might then prove valuable in strengthening the association between the target brand and the target situation. Perhaps the reverse scheduling or a staggered scheduling would be more effective with other brands.

How Expansion Ads Change Brand Attitudes

Expansion ads can have a favorable impact on attitudes toward a brand (A_{brand}) for three different reasons: (a) They can enhance perceptions of $A_{new-use}$, (b) they can enhance perceptions of the product's versatility, and (c) they can evoke favorable product attributes.

Expansion ads can have an unfavorable impact on A_{brand} when they elicit negative attributes about product attributes that are not offset by correspond-

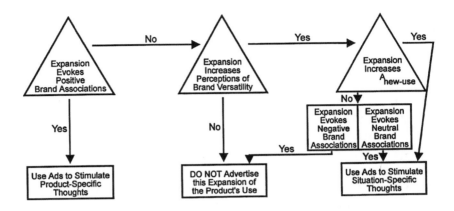

Figure 8.2. Suggested Advertising Strategies for Various Expansion Advertising Situations

ing increases in $A_{\text{new-use}}$ or increases in the perceived versatility of the brand. Copy-testing research can suggest what specific attributes are likely to be evoked by a particular expansion ad. Given this information, the flowchart in Figure 8.2 provides a framework that can help a manager decide which form of expansion ad would be most appropriate for a specific situation.[5]

In general, if a manager fears that an expansion ad will evoke too many negative thoughts about a brand's attributes, using a situation comparison ad would lessen this problem by minimizing the number of negative attributes that are evoked. On the other hand, if there is no doubt that the expansion ad will be well received, a product comparison ad will be most effective at increasing A_{brand}, whereas a situation comparison ad will be most effective at increasing $A_{\text{new-use}}$. If the advertising objectives for the campaign are to strengthen A_{brand} and $A_{\text{new-use}}$ jointly, then a product comparison campaign may be better than a situation comparison campaign. Whereas the former campaign has a combined impact on both A_{brand} and $A_{\text{new-use}}$, the latter is instead likely to have an impact that is primarily focused on $A_{\text{new-use}}$.

Encouraging Substitution With a Competing Product

Up to this point the discussion has centered on the general options a brand manager has in attempting to introduce a target brand into a target situation.

Sometimes, however, a brand manager wants to encourage consumers directly to substitute the target brand for a competing product. For instance, consumers have recently been encouraged to drink Pepsi in the morning *instead* of coffee, to eat Special K breakfast cereal as a midnight snack *instead* of crackers, and to eat Orville Redenbacher's popcorn as an afternoon snack *instead* of potato chips. These particular campaigns have had varied success, but for other campaigns the outcome is still unclear. What is clear, however, is that a substitution-oriented campaign will be successful only if a specific usage situation is targeted and two critical questions are answered: (a) What comparison product should be targeted for replacement? and (b) What brand attributes should be advertised?

To substitute the target brand into a new situation successfully, in place of a product from a different category, there is evidence that the target brand must be perceived as being "different, but not too different" from the use of that replacement product in that situation. In this way the target brand will not be rejected for being too noncomparable to the replacement product, nor will it be dismissed as being too similar. In short, expansion ads are most likely to change usage attitudes if they either (a) advertise common attributes when the replacement product is dissimilar or (b) advertise distinct attributes when the replacement product is similar. Regardless of the specific situation and the specific products being considered, it is critical that an expansion ad make a consumer consider both common and distinct attributes when it offers comparisons with a potential replacement product.[6]

How to Copy Test Expansion Advertising Campaigns

Both industry professionals and academics have criticized traditional copy-testing methods for their inability to capture accurately the usage-related responses generated by expansion ads. Traditional measures that are used in copy testing—purchase intention and brand attitude—are ineffective for capturing the response toward a brand that a person already has in inventory. Measures of purchase intention are insensitive and too distantly removed from the actual use of a brand already in the home. Measures of brand attitude suffer from the "ceiling" problems that exist when a high percentage of consumers are already loyal and regular users of the brand.

By measuring *usage intentions,* copy testing can more directly and sensitively assess the impact of advertising on usage than it can with measures of purchase intention or brand attitude. Measures of usage intentions can be obtained through either likelihood measures or estimates of usage volume. Likelihood measures can be obtained by asking individuals how likely (e.g., on a scale from 1 to 9, in which "highly unlikely" = 1 and "highly likely" = 9) it is that they will consume the brand within a certain time period, such as "within the next 2 weeks." Usage intentions can also be measured by asking individuals to estimate the amount of a brand they will consume within an upcoming time period, such as "within the next 3 months." Comparison of these two measures with actual usage has shown that the measures are effective under different circumstances. Heavy users of a given brand tend to be more accurate when estimating their usage volume of a brand than when estimating their likelihood of using the brand. Conversely, light users tend to be most accurate when estimating their likelihood of using the brand.[7]

This finding also has important implications for how different types of products are copy tested. For infrequently consumed brands (such as Ocean Spray Cranberry Sauce), likelihood measures will be more valid than volume estimates. For more frequently consumed brands (such as Campbell's soups), volume estimates will be more accurate.[8]

When copy testing expansion advertising campaigns, it is critical to realize that a comparison between two or more executions will not be valid unless two conditions are met. First, usage intentions must be the primary focus of the copy test, not purchase intentions or brand attitudes. Second, measures of usage likelihood and estimates of usage volume must both be obtained. These data will enable a researcher to distinguish between the impacts different executions have on heavy users and the impacts they have on light users.

Summary

Many consumer packaged goods companies are beginning to pursue aggressive expansion advertising campaigns. The increased competition brought on by store brands and the desire to leverage brand equity guarantees that the strategic importance of expansion advertising will continue to grow. This growth, however, will not be confined to branded consumables. The importance of expansion advertising will increasingly find its way into the advertising campaigns of industry associations (such as the Florida Citrus Commission and the American Beef Council) and service organizations (such as AT&T and VISA).

Notes

1. Brian Wansink, "Advertising's Impact on Category Substitution," *Journal of Marketing Research,* vol. 21, no. 4, November 1994, 95-105.

2. Patricia Winters, "Cola Companies Are All Abuzz Over 'Cold Caffeine' Products," *Advertising Age,* September 4, 1989, 38.

3. Brian Wansink and Michael L. Ray, "Advertising Strategies to Increase Usage Frequency," *Journal of Marketing,* vol. 60, no. 1, January 1996, 31-46.

4. Wansink, "Advertising's Impact."

5. Brian Wansink and Michael L. Ray, "Expansion Advertising's Impact on Brand Equity," in David Aaker and Alexander L. Biel (eds.), *Advertising and Building Strong Brands* (Lexington, MA: Lexington, 1993), 177-194.

6. Wansink, "Advertising's Impact."

7. Brian Wansink and Michael L. Ray, "Estimating an Advertisement's Impact on One's Consumption of a Brand," *Journal of Advertising Research,* vol. 32, no. 3, May/June 1992, 9-16.

8. Brian Wansink and Michael L. Ray, "Developing Copy Tests That Estimate Brand Usage," in William Wells (ed.), *Measuring Advertising's Effectiveness* (Lexington, MA: Lexington, 1997), 359-369.

Part II

Research Before
the Advertising Runs

Market Research

Why We Need to Be Careful

John Philip Jones

Market research was originally made possible by the discovery of techniques of sample selection, and it is virtually the only scientific tool available to marketing and advertising practitioners. Over the years there have been continuous improvements in the way market research is carried out, particularly in the recent past in methods of analyzing data. But while we cannot deny the increasingly important contribution of research to marketing and advertising, we must also be aware of four endemic concerns with all research. In ascending order of importance, these are the sample, the sample frame, causality, and the questions.

Users of research should always remember that research should be employed as an aid to judgment, not as a substitute for it. Researchers, like most people, find it easier to apply a formula than to puzzle over difficult uncertainties. One of the troubles with market research is that it provides an alluring range of seemingly magical techniques—attitude scales, continuous tracking indexes, simple and multivariate regressions—whose very elegance seems to provide scientific respectability. Such techniques are invariably useful, but useful solely to the thinking researcher who is continuously and energetically aware of their limitations.

The Sample

The reliability of research results depends on the size and representative nature of the sample. A great deal is known about both sample selection and margins of error. It is nevertheless common practice to use small samples of about 100 for quantitative surveys and even smaller ones of about 20 for qualitative investigations. Although such samples can be employed to produce meaningful or at least directional results, researchers do not always make it explicitly clear in reporting their findings that the range of possible error is extremely wide—sometimes as high as 10 percentage points on either side of a figure estimated by the research. In the case of qualitative investigations, the data from samples with as few as 20 subjects are not valid for any type of quantitative extrapolation at all.

The Sample Frame

Another issue of concern for researchers is whether they are questioning the right type of people: Are they selecting the sample from the correct population group (also known as the *universe*)? This decision is often heavily judgmental. For instance, in researching advertising, should we talk to users or nonusers of a brand? This is, in turn, most often decided by the target group described in the brand's advertising strategy. But users of the research should review whether that is, in fact, the specific group whose behavior or views it is most appropriate to examine to answer the problems specifically addressed by the research.

There is also the obvious problem of finding a reliable list of names describing the universe. Up to 10% of the population of the United States change their addresses in any one year. The list of names in a telephone directory reflects this deficiency, besides of course excluding the households that do not have telephones and those who choose not to have their numbers listed.

Causality

It is not always safe to assume a causal relationship between two variables that are moving in the same direction. There is a fundamental question, particularly important for continuous tracking studies, of which of two variables is the cause and which the effect. Does A cause B, or does B cause A? Or are they both perhaps caused by C? This difficulty normally calls for both quantitative and qualitative research, to provide complementary information. For example, an examination of the sales and advertising of breakfast cereals shows that there is generally a correlation between the amount of household viewing of television and the amount of breakfast cereal purchases. It cannot, however, be inferred that the heavy viewing causes the heavy buying. In fact, they are both a result of a common cause—the presence of children in the household. More children mean more television viewing *and* more cereal consumption.

The Questions

This is the worst problem of all, because people are only rarely capable of responding to possibilities outside their range of direct experience. (It is sometimes said that if the development of household lighting systems had depended on market research, houses would be lit today with highly sophisticated kerosene lamps.) The problem is exacerbated by researchers' almost universal habit of framing questions in ways that may be easy to ask and tabulate, but often create a blocked conduit when it comes to providing insights into consumers' beliefs and attitudes. All too often, instead of asking people a range of direct and oblique questions for them to answer in their own way, researchers make startlingly bald statements, many concerned with matters of trivial importance and questionable relevance, and expect people to respond, according to varying degrees of agreement or disagreement, on rigid 5- or 7-point scales. The users of such research should beware.

In addition to the central problems discussed above, there are common solecisms in the description of research findings; the mathematically skilled user of research will immediately notice these. One of the most common and most irritating mistakes is the habit of percentaging data on the basis of totals much smaller than 100. The person who does this needs to be reminded that this procedure involves making projections. Before we can accept such projections, we need evidence that when the smaller total is projected upward, the internal composition of the figures is not going to be changed in important ways.

David Ogilvy has also often remarked on the opaque and inelegant language in which most research reports are written. The eminent physicist Lord Rutherford once remarked that if a theory in physics cannot be explained to a barmaid, it is not very good physics. In their ability to communicate research findings, universities are generally no more lucid than commercial research organizations. Many observers believe that universities are in fact far worse—mainly because university faculty nurture their academic language as an almost sacerdotal rite. (I teach in a university.)

10

Likeability

Why Advertising That Is Well Liked Sells Well

Alexander L. Biel

A s Timothy Joyce has shown Chapter 2 of this volume, one of the more unexpected results of the Advertising Research Foundation (ARF) Copy Research Validity Project was that scaled response about the likeability of a commercial was the single best predictor of sales effectiveness. The ARF's study compared the copy-testing techniques most frequently used in the United States to measures of sales from a split-cable source. In each case, two commercials for the same established brand of repeat-purchase packaged goods that had produced significant sales differences in the marketplace were

NOTE: This chapter is an adaptation of an article that appeared in *Admap*, September 1990. Used by permission.

run through a formidable gamut of copy-testing measures. Perhaps the most striking result of this study was that a simple advertising likeability scale predicted sales winners 87% of the time. This made it a better predictor than any of the many other measures tested, including day-after recall, persuasion, and recall of key copy ideas.

Specific Likeability Studies

The Ogilvy Center for Research & Development in San Francisco was active in probing the relationship of likeability to effectiveness. The objective: to better understand *why* advertising likeability seems to relate so well to sales. The center's first study on likeability was conducted in 1985. The study was undertaken in an effort to help resolve the long-standing issue concerning the relationship of advertising's likeability to its potential to motivate customers. One school of thought was that likeability enhances persuasion. But an alternative view held that advertising that was likeable was probably not very effective. Supporters of this idea would point to very entertaining commercials that had failed in sales terms. And, indeed, an extreme viewpoint held that advertising that was actively *disliked* could conceivably be very effective. Those who endorsed this view pointed to disliked advertising that had done well in the marketplace.

To resolve some of these issues and to separate fact from folklore, a study was designed to obtain a brand persuasion measure as well as a measure of commercial liking. Both measures would be taken among the same consumers for a large sample of commercials. To this end, the first study included 73 prime-time commercials aired in the United States between January and April 1985. In this study, advertising for high-ticket consumer durables was excluded, because single-exposure measures of persuasion are generally thought to be insensitive in this category. For the same reason, corporate advertising and advertising for services were also excluded. The mechanics of data collection precluded the inclusion of local retail advertising. The advertising included in the study spanned 57 products in 11 categories.

As a stand-in for sales effectiveness, the proprietary persuasion procedure developed by Mapes & Ross was selected. Several factors led to this choice. The weight of the evidence *at the time* strongly favored the general category of persuasion measures as having a demonstrable relationship to purchase

TABLE 10.1 Percentages Liking Specified Commercials

Like a lot	28
Like somewhat	30
Neutral	34
Dislike somewhat	3
Dislike a lot	1
No answer/don't know	5

behavior. It was also felt that there was an advantage in using a measurement that already had reasonable acceptance in advertising research circles, at least in the United States.

The Mapes & Ross procedure can be summarized as a pre- and postexposure measure administered over the phone to a sample of consumers recruited for this purpose. In addition to the standard Mapes & Ross questions, a 5-point scaled question (running from "liked it a lot" to "disliked it a lot") was inserted to measure how well the respondent liked the commercial. A total of 895 consumers living in major cities across the United States were interviewed. On average, each respondent provided persuasion and liking data on 1.7 commercials, which resulted in a total of 1,555 observations on which the study was based.

Although the plan had initially been to divide the sample into a group of enthusiasts, a neutral group, and a negative group, the data did not allow this. Indeed, only 4% of the sample described commercials as those that they disliked somewhat or disliked a lot. Although it was disappointing that the data did not support probing reactions to commercials that were actively disliked, the fact that there were so few commercials in these categories was a finding in itself. At least by 1985, few commercials of national advertisers were actively disliked (see Table 10.1).

The remainder of the responses indicated that reactions fell into three groups of roughly the same size. Some 28% of consumers were enthusiastic about the commercial that they had seen, describing it as one that they "liked a lot." A second group—30% of those interviewed—was positive, but only mildly so. These people described the commercial they had seen as one that they "liked somewhat." A third group—34%—described the commercial they had seen as neutral; they neither liked nor disliked it.

With the sample divided into three groups, it was possible to examine the relationship of liking of commercials to changes in brand preference. These changes were measured by the Mapes & Ross procedure that elicits brand

TABLE 10.2 Persuasion by Liking—Percentage Changes in Brand Preference

Neutral	8.2
Like somewhat	9.5
Like a lot	16.2

preference among an individual's considered set prior to and then again after exposure to the commercial (see Table 10.2).

Among consumers who described a commercial as neutral, there was a net change of 8.2% in favor of the advertised brand. Those people who were mildly positive toward the commercial exhibited a slightly higher net positive change of 9.5%. However, when people were enthusiastic in their descriptions—that is, when they described commercials as those that they liked a lot—the net change in preference was dramatically higher: 16.2%. On the basis of these data, one reasonable conclusion that could be drawn is that it pays to produce advertising that people like, and the more they like it, the more they are persuaded by it.

It would be easy enough for creative directors to argue that the kinds of commercials that are best liked are those that win awards. In fact, however, the data said nothing of the sort. The only conclusion that could be drawn at this point was that likeable commercials were more persuasive. That led to the next obvious question: What makes a commercial likeable? Is it humor? Believability? Or is it how clever the commercial is? Does a commercial need to devote itself entirely to entertainment to evoke this response, or are there other paths to likeability?

And that led to another study. Again, a large sample of commercials was required, as well as a large sample of people. The Ogilvy Center's second study achieved this by examining a new representative sample of 80 prime-time commercials. The second study was based on a new nationwide sample of target market consumers. The commercials were an accurate representation of national prime-time advertising, excluding any local spots that may have appeared during prime-time hours. The Mapes & Ross persuasion measure was used as the dependent variable. The independent variables consisted of 26 descriptive adjectives in the form of a checklist. This adjective checklist was based on an extensive review of the copy research literature and was an arguably robust, well-grounded instrument. Through the use of a statistical procedure (factor analysis), five important independent variables were isolated, and a cluster of adjectives was associated with each of these. The five factors that emerged were dubbed *Ingenuity, Meaningful, Energy, Rubs the Wrong Way,* and *Warmth.*

The terms "clever," "imaginative," "amusing," "original," "silly," and "not dull" have their highest loadings on the Ingenuity factor. These are the descriptions that conventional wisdom associates with likeability because they relate to entertainment.

The Meaningful factor consisted of the descriptors "worth remembering," "effective," "not pointless," "not easy to forget," "true to life," "believable," "convincing," and "informative."

The Energy factor was defined by the adjectives "lively," "fast-moving," "appealing," and "well-done."

Rubs the Wrong Way consisted of "seen a lot," "worn-out," "irritating," "familiar," and "phony."

Finally, the Warmth factor consisted of the adjectives "gentle," "warm," and "sensitive."

A score was constructed for each factor for each commercial.

Analysis of the data clearly revealed that product category had an important bearing on commercial liking. Consumers were more inclined to applaud the food and beverage commercials, which, on average, had a 25% "liked a lot" response, compared with only 16% for the other commercials studied. In contrast, the latter group, which consisted primarily of medicine, personal care, and household products, received more "ho-hum" responses in the form of neutral ratings: 32%, compared with 25% for the food and beverage group. It would appear that this product categorization is to some extent reflecting "the approach/avoidance" dichotomy associated with the name of researcher William Wells.

These differences led to separate treatment of the two groups in subsequent analyses. To discover the relationship of the five descriptive factors to liking, a multiple regression analysis was run for the 38 food and beverage commercials and for the non-food and beverage commercials (see Table 10.3). In the food and beverage category, the regression equation accounted for 73% of the variance in liking, so it could be concluded that the checklist did a good job of capturing the essence of liking.

The factor most related to liking was not, as might have been expected, Ingenuity. Instead, the most important factor driving likeability was Meaningful, which was defined as "worth remembering," "effective," "true-to-life,"

TABLE 10.3   Relative Contributions of Factors to Liking of Food and Beverage
Commercials

Meaningful	.71
Energy	.50
Ingenuity	.28
(Doesn't) Rub Wrong Way	.24
Warmth	.18

TABLE 10.4   Relative Contributions of Factors to Liking of Non-Food and
Beverage Commercials

Meaningful	.54
(Doesn't) Rub Wrong Way	.52
Energy	.36
Ingenuity	.23
Warmth	.22

"believable," "convincing," and "informative." It was also defined as "not being easy to forget" and "having a point to it."

The second most important factor contributing to likeability of food and beverage commercials was Energy, primarily defined by a "lively, fast-moving pace." Ingenuity, (Not) Rubbing the Wrong Way, and Warmth are far less important contributors to likeability.

Turning to the non-food and beverage category, quite a different set of guidelines emerged for the 42 commercials in this group. In thinking about this category, it is important to remember that 9 out of 10 commercials in the group were for medicine, household, and personal care products. In this case, the regression/equation accounted for 81% of the variance in likeability. Three factors in particular seemed to have the most influence on how well a commercial was liked (see Table 10.4).

Again, most important was how "meaningful" the commercial seemed to people. However, for these products it was just as important to avoid irritating people with a tired, worn-out approach that seemed to rub the consumer the wrong way. The third most important contributor to likeability for these commercials was Energy. Ingenuity and Warmth did not add much to how well consumers liked these commercials.

Possibly the best way to summarize the impact of this research is to think about how creative people were briefed on the function of likeability before the research was reported. At that point, it was standard practice to advise creative people that there was no evidence that liking had anything to do with effectiveness. Furthermore, the available folklore suggested that commercials people hated could indeed be very effective.

After the two studies discussed previously, this advice was clearly not valid. Based on the research, the best advice for creative people now is that making commercials that people like *enhances* the probability that those commercials can be persuasive. However, it is important to caution them about exactly what likeability means. In particular, it is important that they understand that the commercials people like best are those that have something to say, that are worth remembering, that people view as effective, true-to-life, and convincing. In other words, people most like commercials they find personally *meaningful.*

Contrary to conventional wisdom, a commercial that sacrifices meaningfulness for sheer ingenuity is *not* likely to be persuasive. If a commercial is merely clever, imaginative, and amusing without being relevant, consumers are not likely to be impressed. It is also important to point out that a high level of energy makes an important contribution to likeability. And so does not rubbing the consumer the wrong way—especially if the advertiser is in a sector other than food and beverages.

A logical question that follows from this research is, Why should liking be so closely related to sales? Five possible reasons are explored below.

Five Hypotheses

1. Commercials that are liked get better exposure.

This hypothesis is elegantly simple. If I like a commercial the first time I see it, I am less likely to avoid it the next time I have an opportunity to see it. Avoidance can of course mean zapping in the physical, mechanical sense. However, many commercials that are not physically zapped are nevertheless perceptually screened out as having been seen previously. A consumer may be willing to see a well-liked commercial repeatedly.

Interestingly, this hypothesis suggests that likeability can convert a creative characteristic into a media attribute. Another way of looking at likeability is to see it as a "gatekeeper" to further processing. One model of advertising might suggest that a primary affective response to the commercial per se governs the decision to process further. This model suggests that consumers form an overall first impression of an advertisement on a visceral or gut level. To the extent that impression is positive, they are likely to maintain attention and process the advertising more fully.

2. Commercials serve as brand personality attributes.

In product categories where the functional characteristics of different brands are perceived to be very similar, consumers may consider advertising itself to be a brand attribute. For example, if we accept that consumers make few distinctions among brands of cigarettes on the basis of functional attributes, it could be argued that advertising images like the Marlboro Man become attributes of the personality of the brand and thus form part of the basis of selection. Likewise, the Pepsi advertising that gives the brand connotations of being the "actively rebellious" cola is clearly part of the brand's personality. Because the ARF validity study dealt with established brands and existing categories, this hypothesis might be particularly attractive as an explanation for the correspondence that was found.

However, the phenomenon may not be limited to packaged goods. As an extreme example, it is not unreasonable to suggest that an important personality attribute of the Volkswagen Beetle was the sophisticated advertising for the car created by Doyle Dane Bernbach. By buying the car, the consumer could "participate" in that advertising. We are all familiar with advertising that symbolizes the brand—here is a case where the brand may well have symbolized the advertising!

3. Liking is a surrogate for cognitive processing.

There is a good deal of evidence in the cognitive response literature that suggests that when consumers actively process messages, rather than passively receive them, they are more likely to act on those messages. Jeremy Bullmore, former chairman of J. Walter Thompson, London, developed this argument and was strongly associated with its conclusions. He argued that good advertising entices the consumer into mental collaboration. He suggested that if an advertisement goes beyond mere message registration to elicit a contribution from the consumer, it is likely to be more effective. The consumer has moved from being an observer or maybe even an adversary to being an accomplice or, as Bullmore put it, a "part author."

Having been drawn in in this manner, the consumer would likely be positively disposed toward the ad that he or she had "coauthored." This particular hypothesis would appear to be supported by the finding that consumers are most likely to be favorably disposed toward advertising that they describe as meaningful or personally relevant.

One of the aspects of cognitive processing in which psychologists have been particularly interested is the extent to which a persuasive message evokes counterarguing on the part of the receiver. For example, the commercial trumpets the mildness of a brand of detergent, while you, in comparing it to your own experience, find that you disagree. If this happens, preference for the brand will be reduced.

It is possible that likeability and lack of counterargument might work both ways. A commercial that does not evoke counterarguing may be better liked than one that does. And commercials that are liked reduce the probability of counterargument. Put another way, one is less likely to argue with a friend than with an adversary.

4. Positive affect is transferred from commercial to brand.

The concept of affect transfer suggests that simple proximity of the brand to a well-liked commercial may operate so that the positive affect of the commercial rubs off on the brand, unbeknown to the viewer. In the social psychology literature, perhaps the best demonstration of this effect is Gorn's experiment in which well-liked music paired with a gift enhanced the choice of that gift, compared with music that was not liked.

5. Liking evokes a gratitude response.

This hypothesis, which has been advanced often in the past, specifies that consumer behavior is in part due to gratitude for the pleasure of the advertising itself.

Summary

Hypotheses 4 and 5 are included here for the sake of completeness. However, note that the research reported above found meaningfulness to be the factor that drives liking. If the gratitude hypothesis (Hypothesis 5) were correct, it could be the case that meaningfulness might have been less important than the more entertainment-oriented factor that we identified as Ingenuity. The same reasoning applies to the transfer of affect hypothesis (Hypothesis 4).

Obviously, more research is needed to understand which of the mechanisms discussed above is actually at work. Equally obviously, the mechanisms are not mutually exclusive, so several could well be operating simultaneously for the same consumer. Or different mechanisms may be at play among different segments of consumers.

However, even in the absence of further research, the mere fact that these hypotheses can be constructed is helpful. It demonstrates that the results are not necessarily mysterious, on the one hand, or simplistic, on the other. And in that sense, they lead to an opportunity for useful progress in our understanding of how advertising works.

Finally, although it might be tempting to adopt liking as the single standard of commercial effectiveness based on the ARF work, that would be extremely dangerous. The ARF study, well designed as it was, used a tiny sample of commercials. Moreover, those commercials were all for established brands of repeat-purchase packaged goods. Liking might very well be a more important measure for these kinds of brands than for services, durables, or new products. In addition, the specific job that advertising is expected to do clearly will have an impact on which measures serve best. Although likeability is surely worthy of inclusion in the advertising research repertoire, overdependence on it would probably be both unproductive and misleading.

11

Qualitative Research in Advertising

Jan S. Slater

A n avid proponent of research, advertising legend David Ogilvy, has said, "Advertising people who ignore research are as dangerous as generals who ignore decodes of enemy signals." [1] Indeed, advertising people cannot afford to ignore research. Advertising is big business, with more than $100 billion spent annually in main media.[2] It is just too big an investment for advertisers to speculate or rely on gut instincts. Research is needed to reduce uncertainty and to provide data for developing strategies and advertisements. But research is not an insurance policy; it is only a tool that advertisers can use to gain information on and better understanding of consumers and how advertisements might communicate with them. In fact, no amount of research will answer all questions about consumers or guarantee that an advertisement will work in the marketplace. What it will do is provide advertisers with consumer information, offer insight into consumer unknowns, and help narrow the range of alternative creative decisions.

Advertisers rely primarily on two types of research: quantitative and qualitative. *Quantitative research* is used to determine the identities of consumers—who they are and where they are. Such research is generally described as marketing research and is completed prior to the planning of an advertising campaign. This research is designed to gather basic information about markets, target groups, and competitors. Additionally, quantitative research is used after a campaign has been implemented, to track its effectiveness and memorability. *Qualitative research* seeks to understand how consumers behave and why they behave as they do. Qualitative research can be very useful for providing information for concept development as well as for testing alternative creative ideas and executions for the consumer.

The use of quantitative research in advertising has been well documented in textbooks and journals. In this chapter I will attempt to explore the use of qualitative research in the development and creation of advertisements.

What Is Qualitative Research?

More than 50 years ago, the Advertising Research Foundation (ARF) was established by the Association of National Advertisers and the American Association of Advertising Agencies. ARF's role is to assist the industry in increasing the effectiveness of advertising through objective and impartial research. ARF defines qualitative research as follows:

> The intent of qualitative research is to gain insights concerning consumer attitudes, beliefs, motivations and behaviors. When creatively and perceptively analyzed and reported, qualitative research offers insights which go beyond the surface. The qualitative research approach provides "feel," "texture," a sense of intensity, and a degree of nuance. Qualitative research is usually reported discursively, often in respondents' own words.[3]

Qualitative research is usually exploratory and involves relatively small numbers of people who are not sampled with the aim of projecting the findings. Although small in size, qualitative samples are representative of the consumers or target groups being studied. However, in qualitative research no attempt is made to generalize findings to an entire population or to draw concrete conclusions that the results will be the same in every instance. In fact, qualitative research is considered impressionistic rather than definitive.[4] The methodology of the research is not ensconced in theory or hypotheses; rather, it is based on subjectivity and insight. The aim of qualitative research is to provide a greater understanding of what needs to be studied; the findings are not intended to represent entire populations.

There are six basic characteristics of qualitative methodology that distinguish it from quantitative research:[5]

1. Qualitative researchers are concerned primarily with process, rather than with outcomes or products.
2. Qualitative researchers are interested in meaning—how people make sense of their lives, their experiences, and their structures of the world.
3. The qualitative researcher is the primary instrument for data collection and analysis. Data are mediated through this human instrument, rather than through inventories, questionnaires, or machines.
4. Qualitative research involves fieldwork. The researcher physically goes to the people, setting, site, or institution to observe or record behavior in its natural setting.
5. Qualitative research is descriptive in that the researcher is interested in process, meaning, and understanding gained through words or pictures.
6. The process of qualitative research is inductive in that the researcher builds abstractions, concepts, hypotheses, and theories from details.

There are several uses of qualitative research in advertising: (a) to obtain background information where nothing or very little is known about a situation or target group; (b) to identify relevant behavior patterns, beliefs, opinion, attitudes, or motivations of consumers (which may allow greater insight into consumers' perceptions of a brand and often how they use it); and (c) to assist in concept identification and development, as well as the testing of creative alternatives. Qualitative research tends to be more flexible than quantitative research and is often less expensive to conduct (because of the smaller samples). It is used to give advertisers a general impression of consumers and their relationships with products or particular advertising. According to Bozell CEO Charles Peebler, "What is now important is discovering what 'bonds' a consumer to a product."[6] But qualitative research in advertising has been trying to discover that for years.

Historical Perspective

Qualitative research is not new to the advertising industry. Perhaps some methodologies are relatively new or the emphasis has changed, but qualitative research has played a role in advertising for more than 50 years.

In the late 1940s, an Austrian psychologist named Ernest Dichter began applying psychoanalytic principles to consumption and advertising. Dichter established a new form of research, which he called *motivational research.* Instead of using the statistical techniques of polling and counting derived from social science methods, Dichter's motivational research delved into the subconscious, the nonrational level of the mind, to examine why people behave in certain ways. Believing that consumers do not know what they want or why, Dichter used motivational research to determine how advertisements should be directed or focused.[7] He borrowed some techniques from the field of social science and described motivational research as a brand of market research that concentrates on the "why" of buying. His techniques included depth interviews, projective techniques, word association, and sentence completion tests. He believed that research cannot be successful without being creative, and he strove to make scientific research and creativity compatible.

Dichter believed that advertising has psychological requirements that go beyond an advertisement's commercial purpose. His work provides an interesting example concerning ice cream. Dichter noted that ice cream advertising generally strove to impress the public with the superior quality and flavor of a particular ice cream. These claims were augmented and illustrated by beautiful dishes of ice cream. Dichter showed in a psychological study that the "voluptuous" nature of ice cream is one of its main appeals. However, most ads were not designed to satisfy people's desires for voluptuousness. Instead, they created a feeling of neatness, an expectancy of sober enjoyment—all far removed from the emotionally loaded feelings most people have for ice cream. For example, Dichter noted, when interviewees said that they considered the flavor the most important thing about ice cream, they were expressing only a symptom. The function played by ice cream in their lives actually stemmed from the whole emotional aura of voluptuousness, childhood experiences, and uninhibited overindulgence. It is such functions that form the basis on which an advertiser can build an effective campaign.[8]

Pierre Martineau, research director of the *Chicago Tribune,* was an advocate of Dichter's motivational philosophy. He has written:

> Any advertising will be more effective if it can tap the underlying emotional and attitudinal concepts which are important in specific areas as well as utilize the practical advantages of the product. This is an objective of motivation research— to prove and to evaluate these underlying forces and thereby to supply directions helpful to the creative people.[9]

Martineau, an advertising outsider, understood the concept perfectly: Advertisers must view the product through the eyes of the consumer.

By 1957, motivational research had its proponents and opponents. There were 80 research companies that claimed to specialize in motivational research, among them Dichter's own Institute for Motivational Research. Advertising agencies such as Leo Burnett, Foote, Cone & Belding, Young & Rubicam, and Grey all embraced the concept. Individuals such as Charles Brower of BBDO cautioned their peers to avoid "outside witch doctors and head shrinkers." [10]

Research in advertising agencies has carried over to the 1990s, although it has gone through many changes and still has its critics. The recession and budget cuts of the 1980s forced many agencies to reduce or eliminate their research departments. When the industry was faced with cost pressures, research departments, not thought of as profit centers, were among the first casualties. Today, Leo Burnett and BBDO, despite Brower's concerns in the 1950s, are at the forefront of agencies maintaining strong research departments. Other agencies have opted to use outside research firms, and still others are moving research into an account planning concept that incorporates qualitative research.

Account Planning

Introduced in Britain in 1968 by Stanley Pollitt, account planning was imported to the United States by Chiat/Day in 1981. A 1987 study showed that almost 90% of British ad agencies used account planning.[11] Although it has been embraced by several American agencies—including Hal Riney; Goodby, Silverstein & Partners; Kirshenbaum and Bond; Fallon McElligott; and Wieden and Kennedy—it has not swept the country.

Account planning does not employ exclusively the conventional research techniques used in advertising agencies and brought in from outside organizations. The planner becomes part of the account group and works closely with the creative team in building the creative strategy and seeing it through to development. The planner is positioned as the voice of the consumer and functions as a qualitative researcher, conducting one-on-one interviews and focus groups, providing greater insight about the consumer than general demographic statistics can provide.[12]

Those who use account planning endorse its benefits wholeheartedly. Its critics claim that account planners have simply repackaged what research agencies have been doing all along, while alienating creative people in the process. It is generally agreed by those who use account planning that there are two key elements to making it work: First, the creative people must believe in the concept to allow the process to operate; second, the planning must be done before the creative work begins.[13]

Uses of Qualitative Research

Making advertisements work is the key issue, and whether an agency uses account planning or not, there are several uses of qualitative research in advertising:

1. It can be used to obtain background information where nothing is known about the problem or target group. BBDO's research for the Plymouth Neon campaign included 30 focus groups to understand the target group, Generation X.[14]

2. It can be used in concept identification and development, as well as for testing the concept among actual consumers. Once BBDO had a grasp on what Generation X-ers wanted from an automobile, they employed a target group consumer panel to judge the proposed campaign.[15]

3. It can be used to identify relevant behavior patterns, beliefs, opinions, attitudes, and motivations of consumers.[16] By providing a better understanding of consumers' perceptions of the brand, such research often sheds light on consumers' uses of the brand. Campbell Mithun Esty used an anthropologist to conduct one-on-one interviews with Jeep owners to gather just this type of information.[17]

It is very difficult to uncover why people behave as they do through direct questioning. Dichter compared asking consumers why they buy or why they behave in making certain decisions to a physician's asking a patient to define the disease he thinks he has. Dichter's underlying conviction was that Americans decide to buy things for reasons not necessarily related to the products, and often they are not even fully aware of their motivations.[18]

When confronted with a survey in a supermarket or shopping mall, most consumers do not disclose the truth about their buying behavior, but instead provide answers they believe conform to some standard of correct behavior.

Therefore, it is common for consumers to underreport bad habits and overreport good ones. For example, many people underreport how often they watch television, or what types of high-fat foods they consume. Qualitative research tends to be more flexible than such survey research, in that it can probe into feelings and beliefs of a consumer more thoroughly than can be done using a questionnaire or in a laboratory experiment. However, as the discussion below makes clear, the quality of the data gathered using qualitative research is dependent on the skills of the researcher as interviewer or moderator.

Methods of Qualitative Research

The most common methods used in qualitative advertising research are projective techniques, one-on-one interviews, and focus groups. The method used is dependent on the type of information desired and the time and money available to conduct the research.

Projective Techniques

Projective techniques are used predominantly by psychologists as a means of clinical diagnosis. Ernest Dichter introduced the technique to the advertising industry as a means of exploring the thoughts, associations, and mental images consumers have about a brand. The underlying theory of projective questioning is that in certain situations it is impossible to obtain accurate information about what a person thinks and feels by asking him or her to explain those thoughts and feelings. This information can be obtained, however, by allowing a respondent to project thoughts and feelings onto some other person or object.[19] Sentence completion, word association, picture interpretation, and personality tests are all projective techniques. They can be used within the context of individual interviews or group discussions.

During sentence completion tests, respondents are often asked to describe what others might think in certain product usage or brand choice situations. For example: "If I purchased a Lexus, my friends would say . . . " or "Women who use Ivory Soap are . . . ." In this situation, the belief is that it is easier for people to express feelings if they can attribute them to someone else.[20]

In a word association task, a participant is asked to list words that come to mind when a particular brand name, category, product, or person is mentioned.

An example of a word association question would be "When I say Coca-Cola, what words come to mind?" The respondent then identifies the words he or she associates with that brand, such as "cool," "refreshing," "traditional," "American," "quenching," "polar bears." It is imperative in these types of exercises that the interviewer or moderator allow respondents to associate freely and not lead or influence responses.

Picture interpretation is based on the Rorschach inkblot test used in clinical psychology. A photograph or illustration is shown to a respondent, who then is asked to explain or describe what is occurring in the picture. Respondents are often given a set of photos and asked to select an image for a particular brand. The photos may depict different people, drawings, celebrities, or environmental settings. This method has been beneficial for the selection of suitable spokespersons for various advertisements as well as for the evaluation of effective package designs.

In personality tests—or "psychodramas," as Dichter called them—consumers are asked to imagine that they are the product and to describe their feelings, or to describe the product as a person, giving it human attributes such as personality, lifestyle, gender, and age. This type of research provides a clearer understanding of customers' image of the brand and can suggest key words for describing the product that can be used in advertisements.

One-on-One Interviews

Often, one-on-one interviewing is referred to as an intensive technique. A one-on-one can be semistructured, lasting 20-30 minutes, or in-depth, lasting upwards of an hour. The interview is carefully planned, with a written guide for questioning, but is much less restricted than a standardized questionnaire. The questions asked are predominantly open-ended, allowing the respondent to answer in his or her own words and allowing the interviewer the opportunity to probe the consumer's deeper feelings and individual motivations based on his or her answers. Dichter has described this as a "procedure in which the respondent achieves insight into his own motivations." [21]

One-on-one interviewing requires an extremely skilled interviewer, one who does not ask too many questions but rather leads the interviewee into talking about a general area or topic. It is important for the interviewer to engage the respondent in a full and spontaneous expression of attitudes and feelings. Dichter compared it to the work of a detective, attempting to uncover the motivation for a crime. [22]

The discussion of general ideas often yields the most interesting associations during an interview. The interviewer may use several techniques to draw out the respondent without directly asking for his or her views. For example:

1. The interviewer might ask the respondent about his or her experiences with the product, encouraging a discussion of memories and the feelings related to those memories. For example, the topic may be the first car a respondent owned, or the first time the respondent wore makeup or used a computer. Understanding the emotions that are tied to certain purchases can provide insights into the decision process, and those insights can be transformed into emotional cues within advertisements.

2. In order to look at a respondent's range of emotions or feelings, the interviewer might test for extremes. The interviewer might ask the respondent to describe the best and/or worst experience he or she ever had with the product. This might uncover barriers to purchasing or provide a means either to recapture a good experience with the product or to redirect a bad experience in advertisements.

3. Instead of asking specific questions—When do you eat lunch? How much time do you spend in your car? How much time do you spend watching television?— the interviewer might ask the respondent to describe or relive days at a time. From listening to a respondent explain his or her routine, an interviewer can often uncover information regarding the individual's lifestyle as well as knowledge about how the product fits into that lifestyle.

4. The interviewer might ask the respondent to describe how he or she feels in connection with the brand. This is especially important for exploring areas of social approval and confidence in the brand.[23]

One-on-one interviews can be used for both concept development and concept testing. In the development stage, consumers are interviewed to determine attitudes and feelings about the product, to provide creative people with direction. This helps in identifying not only what to say, but how to say it and show it. By matching the consumer perspective to the visual and copy, advertisers can create more effective advertising. Concept testing uses a number of simple stimuli (e.g., rough layouts, animatics, scripts of ads) to discern if the message is appropriately communicated and understood by the consumer. According to Dichter, "The psychological test of the ad and its graphic presentation demonstrates what happens to the message in the mind of the consumer." [24] There have been many cases in which one-on-one interviews have helped in the creation, development, and improvement of advertisements.

Snapple advertising agency Kirshenbaum and Bond conducted extensive interviews with Snapple consumers to devise its campaign. The account planner for the brand advised the creative department of the strategy in one line: "100% natural advertising." The interviews revealed consumers' attitudes that Snapple is not slickly advertised or packaged. Respondents considered the drink an undiscovered secret, one they would share with friends. They thought the company to be small and perhaps a little naive. An almost obsessive relationship existed between customers and the brand. This was evident not only in the interviews, but in the "soul-baring" letters customers were writing to Snapple; more than 2,000 letters came in each week. Initially, the creative idea was focused on product attributes. However, following the research, the creative team based the campaign on customer letters to the company, which are read by Wendy, the "Snapple lady," and acted out in the commercials.[25] The offbeat, unpolished look of the advertisements, and the use of real people and real stories, worked for Snapple.

Lord, Dentsu & Partners, which handled the introduction of Mead Imaging's Cycolor copying equipment, had difficulty deciding whether to advertise the technology or the use of color. One-on-one interviews with corporate purchasing directors and local retailers provided the information needed. Color was shown to be the better platform for the campaign. Although the interviewees preferred color, the overall feeling was that color copies are overly expensive. It became obvious that the buyers did not want to know about technology; they were interested in how to use color and use it economically. The interviews led to a campaign titled "The power is in the paper." A color magazine advertisement featured the hood of a fire-engine-red sports car and the headline "Red gets more speeding tickets." The visual led the reader into the copy: "The power of color is well-documented. Red cars do get stopped more often. Just like the red on this page had the power to stop you." [26]

It must be noted that one-on-one interviews can be both expensive and time-consuming. Furthermore, the gathering of quality information and the interpretation or analysis of the data are often solely dependent on the skills and expertise of the interviewer. But in many situations, one-on-one interviews are preferred over group discussion research. One-on-ones have been found to be most appropriate when group dynamics might bias outcomes, such as when the subject is copy communication or extremely sensitive intimate or personal products. One-on-ones tend to offer an atmosphere of confidentiality and sincerity. However, there are other situations in which respondents are reluctant to discuss reactions or ideas without group support.

Focus Groups

Focus groups are fast becoming the predominant method of qualitative research for advertising. A focus group is defined as a depth interview with a group instead of with individuals. The group normally consists of 8 to 12 people who fit the profile of the target group or consumer. A great deal of planning and screening is required to recruit focus group participants.

A skilled moderator conducts the group discussion. Although the moderator uses an interview guide for questioning and discussion, the format is less structured than a survey questionnaire and allows for the moderator to react and probe to follow up respondents' answers. The moderator acts as a guide through the discussion and balances the dynamics of the group to ensure the participation of all interviewees. There is little agreement on the most effective communication style for the moderator. Some play a passive, low-key role, whereas others take the devil's advocate position, which is naturally more active.[27] No matter what style is used, it is vital that the moderator remain objective and not identify with the research sponsor so as to avoid bias. Additionally, the moderator must keep the discussion relevant to the topic, encourage the shy or inhibited members while suppressing the opinionated know-it-all, and see to it that no leadership force emerges and takes control.[28]

The biggest problems associated with focus group research are the failure to have the right people in the room, the lack of a skilled moderator, and the confusion that can arise from group dynamics. Actually, group dynamics can be considered both an advantage and a disadvantage. These dynamics are dependent on the problem being discussed and the group assembled—group interaction may stimulate new ideas and often provides for greater spontaneity and candor.[29] On the other hand, the synergy of the group might allow some participants simply to agree with or support the ideas of others in the group, rather than explain their own thoughts. Some experts advise caution in using focus groups for evaluation of advertising executions because the personal interaction within a group can easily shift attention away from the ad, and because the subtle differences between two or more executions may be overlooked in a group discussion.[30] Before using a focus group, the advertiser should make sure that the research problem is appropriate to and can benefit from a group discussion.

A focus group generally lasts from 1 to 2 hours. It is not uncommon for observers, such as copywriters and clients, to watch the discussion via two-way mirrors. Although focus group participants are told they are being observed, after a few moments of discussion they usually become oblivious to that fact. Additionally, sessions are usually video- and/or audiotaped and then transcribed for analysis.

In advertising, focus groups are used in campaign development and evaluation of ad executions. Rubin Postaer & Associates used extensive focus group research to develop a campaign for American Honda Motor Company. In 4 months, 37 focus groups were conducted throughout the country in preparation for the introduction of Honda's new Accord line in September 1993. Since 1989, the Honda Accord had been the top-selling car in the United States, until the Ford Taurus jumped to the top spot in 1992. The pressure was on. Rubin Postaer & Associates needed some new insight into what motivates consumers. They wanted to understand better the consumer's process of buying a car.

Part of what these focus groups identified was that buying a car is a game. The consumer wins by getting the best deal and a car that lasts 7 or 8 years. The ideas of empowerment, brand heritage, and durability also emerged from the focus groups. The discussion led not only to the development of the campaign, but to the slogan "A car ahead." This was how consumers perceived Honda.[31]

Similarly, Arrow's tag for its sportswear line, "We've loosened our collar," was developed from focus group research conducted in the planning stages of the campaign. Arrow had a reputation as a "solid-white dress shirt company," although the company's sportswear line had been in existence for 10 years. Chiat/Day New York was the agency that received the task of understanding men's feelings about fashion—not any easy job; most men do not think about fashion. Chiat/Day turned to focus groups that comprised Arrow consumers and consumers of competitors' products.

Initially, the client and the art director had agreed on a GQ-type image, but the focus groups' comments expressed the view that "they're my father's dress shirts." In fact, the Arrow shirt was not high fashion, and the users were not all that interested in high fashion. Arrow shirts were affordable and the users were just regular guys who had to wear a "uniform" to work and enjoyed getting home to relax—the basis of the "loosened collar" concept. The commercial "Higher & Higher" depicts a solemn men's chorus in white shirts gradually transformed into a hip gospel group in colorful sportswear. Chiat/Day had creatively and successfully supported Arrow's strength— the white dress shirt—while making Arrow hip and somewhat fashion-conscious.[32]

Conclusions

Although much of this discussion has focused on how qualitative research can benefit advertising, there is still much criticism and resistance to qualitative techniques. The criticism stems from how this research is performed, applied, analyzed, and presented. Some critics believe that because qualitative research findings cannot be projected to a larger population, the research is not valid enough to base campaigns on. The resistance often comes from clients who consider such research expensive and unnecessary, and from creative people who believe the science is destroying the art.

Some of the criticism is valid. The biggest problem is the misuse of qualitative research. Many times research is conducted without clear objectives, without appropriate respondents, using the wrong methods, or by researchers who do not understand advertising. Additionally, although qualitative measures are used to gain understanding of the emotions and attitudes of consumers, and those insights are used in creative development, the industry fails to use the same measures for copy testing. Instead, the quantitative measures used for copy testing fail to determine whether the advertisements are indeed tapping the right emotions in executions.

Perhaps the worst problem is people's expectations of qualitative research. It is not a predictor of success. No amount of research, qualitative or quantitative, can guarantee success in the marketplace. Qualitative research is about information that will provide direction, not proof or validation that an idea is right. It can only indicate that a given idea might be the best one right now. One cannot expect the research to be purely scientific and rational when the subjects—consumers—tend not to be scientific and rational.

Despite the criticisms, qualitative research provides measures that are vital to advertising development. It is an aid to creative people. Those who are afraid of it are perhaps insecure. Qualitative research is diagnostic in nature and can only help to improve the ideas. What a boost to the creative process it is to be able to listen to actual conversations of consumers describing their feelings about a product. How can that be a hindrance? Qualitative research is also effective in locating weaknesses in a concept. It provides advertisers the opportunity to understand the emotional and nonrational aspects of advertisements by personally observing consumers interacting with those advertisements. This is a key benefit that cannot be ignored.

Ernest Dichter believed that advertisers understand what they want advertising to accomplish commercially, but most often do not understand the psychological requirements of the advertising message. What happens to that message in the mind of the prospective buyer is what he believed to be important.[33] And if the purpose of advertising is to provide information or to modify attitudes or simply to reinforce attitudes, then the content of the advertising is key. David Ogilvy has said that the most important task is to decide what is to be said about the product, what benefit to promise: "The selection of the promise is the most valuable contribution that research can make to the advertising process." [34] If the message is so crucial, then so is the qualitative research that can help determine it.

Notes

1. David Ogilvy, *Ogilvy on Advertising* (New York: Crown, 1983), 158.

2. "U.S. Advertising Volume," *Advertising Age,* May 12, 1997.

3. Advertising Research Foundation, "Marketing Insights Through Qualitative Research," in *Proceedings of the ARF Qualitative Research Workshop* (New York: Advertising Research Foundation, 1987).

4. John Philip Jones, *How Much Is Enough? Getting the Most From Your Advertising Dollar* (New York: Simon & Schuster-Lexington, 1992).

5. John W. Creswell, *Research Design: Qualitative and Quantitative Approaches* (Thousand Oaks, CA: Sage, 1994).

6. Quoted in Andrew Olds, "Planned and Delivered," *Advertising Age,* January 1, 1990, 8.

7. Stephen Fox, *The Mirror Makers: A History of American Advertising and Its Creators* (New York: Vintage, 1984).

8. Ernest Dichter, "A Psychological View of Advertising Effectiveness," *Journal of Marketing,* July 1946.

9. Pierre Martineau, *Motivation in Advertising: A Summary* (New York: McGraw-Hill, 1957).

10. Quoted in Fox, *The Mirror Makers,* 184.

11. Randall Rothenberg, "The Media Business: Advertising's Good Fortune for Account Planners," *New York Times,* November 18, 1988, 17.

12. Ibid.

13. Olds, "Planned and Delivered."

14. Raymond Serafin and Leah Rickard, "Lighting Up Neon," *Advertising Age,* February 7, 1994, 16.

15. Ibid.

16. Peter Sampson, "Qualitative and Motivation Research," in Robert M. Worcester and John Downham (eds.), *Consumer Market Research Handbook* (Amsterdam: Elsevier Science Publishers, 1986), 29-56.

17. Joshua Levine, "Desperately Seeking 'Jeepness,' " *Forbes,* May 15, 1989, 134.

18. Rena Bartos and Arthur S. Pearson, "Ernest Dichter: Motive Interpreter," in "The Founding Fathers of Advertising Research" (special issue), *Journal of Advertising Research,* February/March 1986.

19. Sampson, "Qualitative and Motivation Research."

20. Ibid. See also Jack Haskins and Alice Kendrick, *Successful Advertising Research Methods* (Lincolnwood, IL: NTC Business Books, 1993).

21. Ernest Dichter, *Handbook of Consumer Motivation* (New York: McGraw-Hill, 1964), 415.

22. Ibid., 416.

23. Ibid., chap. 12.

24. Ibid.

25. "The British Reinvasion," *Advertising Age,* June 1, 1993, 36.

26. Quoted in Terry Kattleman, "Planning in Action," *Advertising Age,* January 1, 1990, 38.

27. Haskins and Kendrick, *Successful Advertising Research Methods.*

28. Sampson, "Qualitative and Motivation Research."

29. Cheri Berlamino, "Designing the Qualitative Research Project: Addressing the Process Issues," *Journal of Advertising Research,* December/January 1990.

30. Thomas L. Greenbaum, "Focus Groups Can Play a Part in Evaluating Ad Copy," *Marketing News,* September 13, 1993, 24. See also Jones, *How Much Is Enough?*

31. Cleveland Horton, "Moving Honda 'Ahead,' " *Advertising Age,* October 11, 1993, 26.

32. Kattleman, "Planning in Action."

33. Dichter, "A Psychological View."

34. Ogilvy, *Ogilvy on Advertising,* 160.

12

Perceptual Mapping

John Philip Jones

Perceptual mapping is a useful analytic device for presenting brands in juxtaposition to their competitors, according to defined criteria. The measures and the relative positions of the brands on the map are derived from research, and the map is an expository device that is capable of leading to action by pinpointing gaps. The criteria mostly relate to how consumers perceive the brands. This perception helps the advertiser to find the uncommon and salient qualities of a brand that should be embodied in its advertising proposition—the basic message communicated by its advertising campaign.

There is no end to the perceived functional and nonfunctional characteristics that the maps can cover. Each characteristic is set out on a continuum, with the ends representing opposite extremes (for example, harshest-mildest, strongest-weakest, youngest-oldest). Because maps are two-dimensional, perceptual maps measure two specific attributes, or rather two ranges or continuums describing each of these attributes.

Figures 12.1 and 12.2 cover various nonfunctional characteristics of the 10 leading brands of toilet soap. Figure 12.1 describes two aspects of brand

136

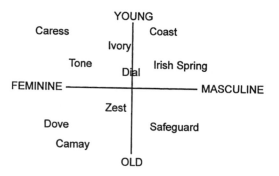

Figure 12.1 Perceptual Map of Toilet Soaps: Perceptions of User Demographics

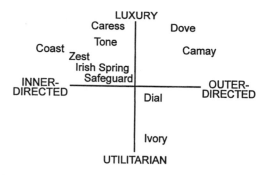

Figure 12.2 Perceptual Map of Toilet Soaps: Perceptions of Selected User Psychographics

imagery: the perceived ages and sexes of users of the brands. This map was drawn based on judgment, through the extrapolation of brand imagery from data from Mediamark Research Inc. (MRI) on the demographics of the actual users.[1] (We do not, of course, know for certain whether user demographics predict user imagery, and we need to carry out qualitative research to confirm the hypotheses embodied in the map before we act on them.)

Figure 12.2 describes two purely psychographic aspects of brand imagery. The first is Inner- and Outer-Directedness, based on Values and Lifestyles (VALS). Inner-Directed groups are made up of highly educated people whose ambitions transcend the economic and social status quo. The Outer-Directed groups represent the majority of people, who like the world more or less as it is.[2] The second aspect is the luxury-utilitarian continuum. Figure 12.2 is also based on judgment and is derived from MRI demographics.

The relative positions of the different brands marketed by each of the main manufacturers are worth a comment. Procter & Gamble markets Camay, Coast, Ivory, Safeguard, Zest, and (more recently) Oil of Olay; Lever Brothers markets Caress and Dove (Lever 2000 has subsequently joined this portfolio, and this brand is settling down and appears to be successful); the Dial Corporation markets Dial and Tone; and Colgate-Palmolive markets Irish Spring.

Procter & Gamble, with the most complex of the brand portfolios, is obviously efficient in keeping its individual brands separate from one another. This efficiency prevents cannibalization. The positions of the two established Lever Brothers brands are particularly interesting. Both Caress and Dove are luxury products; both are oriented to skin care, with a strong feminine emphasis; and in formulation, both, unusually, are nonsoap detergent (NSD; Zest is the only other major NSD bar among those mapped here). On the face of it, Caress and Dove are uncomfortably close to one another in their positioning. Yet, as we can see from Figure 12.1, they have been neatly separated according to the important criterion of the perceived age of their users. MRI data show that Caress is strongly oriented to younger women and Dove to older women. Thus the two brands are complementary and not competitive.

Another thing worth noting about Figure 12.1 is that the brands in the market have a somewhat more feminine than masculine orientation. The reason for this can be supplied by common sense. Most packaged goods, including toilet soaps, are bought by female homemakers, who follow their own brand preferences to a large degree. The brands they buy are used by the men in the house just because the bars happen to be in the bathrooms.

Lever 2000 seems to be settled in Figure 12.1 somewhere between the largest brands in the category, Ivory and Dial. It is directed at users of both these brands, and like them it has a balanced feminine-masculine appeal. Lever 2000's position on Figure 12.2 seems to be similar to what we see in Figure 12.1—at a midway point between Dial and Ivory—although judgment suggests that Lever 2000 might be moving in the direction of the southwest quadrant, embracing a degree of Inner-Directedness. This is apparent from the advertising.

Notes

1. John Philip Jones, *How Much Is Enough? Getting the Most From Your Advertising Dollar* (New York: Simon & Schuster-Lexington, 1992), chap. 8.

2. Arnold Mitchell, *The Nine American Lifestyles: Who We Are and Where We Are Going* (New York: Macmillan, 1983), chaps. 1, 4.

Brain Wave Measures of Media Involvement

Herbert E. Krugman

Television is a medium of low involvement compared with print.[1] Involvement is defined in terms of the number of personal connections between the stimulus and the viewer: the number of thoughts that came spontaneously to mind during exposure and that linked something in the content of the stimulus to something in the content of the viewer's own life.

In 1967, *Time* sponsored a small study in which I reported that the same kinds of advertising in TV and print evoked in the TV form many fewer personal connections between the ad content and something in the life content of the viewer.[2] In a very much larger study, the Newspaper Advertising Bureau confirmed that TV versions of similar print ads evoked fewer personal connections.[3]

NOTE: An earlier version of this chapter was published in the *Journal of Advertising Research,* February 1971. Used by permission.

Television is popular, interesting, and time-consuming, and it is not meant as criticism to say that it is a low-involvement medium. It is, however, very different from print, and perhaps even more so than is generally granted. To learn more about these differences, I became interested in laboratory experiments on the processes of looking and of thinking, and on the processes of attention and of relaxation. In so doing, I sensed that sooner or later I might develop a special viewpoint about the work of Marshall McLuhan. This is a report on that developing viewpoint.

Let us begin with looking. *Looking* was defined in terms of the capabilities and limitations of the Mackworth stand-mounted eye-movement recorder (known as the Mackworth Optiscan), in which the respondent's head is rendered immobile with the aid of a bite-plate and a 6-by-8-inch picture is viewed at a distance of 18 inches.[4] Eye movements are recorded to produce a developed motion picture film of the viewed scene, and a superimposed white spot or marker indicates the path of eye movements. Ten-second exposures are recorded, and from the developed film a plot is made of the locations of eye fixations, duration or dwell time, and shifts to new fixations.[5]

In and of itself, looking was of little concern in the particular research described, because it started with the premise that the respondents were looking at the experimental ads. The concern was with how they were looking when communication was not taking place; that is, what were the response qualities of looking-with-learning?

The respondents in the studies were brought to a laboratory, exposed to different ads for 10 seconds each via the Mackworth Optiscan, and then interviewed for recall of the ads. Recall, therefore, was the criterion of learning. Additional respondents were brought back once a week for 3 weeks, without verbal interviewing, just to note the effects of repeated exposures on looking.

Of various scoring methods, the one of most interest concerned looking in only one place versus looking all over, or "bunched-up" versus "spread-out" looking. These were called *focusing* and *scanning,* and we scored them by dividing the total area of each advertisement into 1-by-1-inch cells and counting the number of different cells that were "looked into."

Initial findings presented an interesting paradox. On a respondent basis, scanning represents looking-with-learning; that is, the respondents who scanned more recalled more. However, on a stimulus basis, focusing represents looking-with-learning; that is, the ads that were scanned less were better recalled. The resolution of the paradox is apparently this: Ads that are easily learned require very little of the respondent and communicate with little work on his or her part. But ads that are not learned easily do require the respondent to be more active, to look around, and to scan.

So a situation occurs here where, at one extreme, the work of communication must be done by the communicator via creation of an easily learnable ad or communiqué, or, on the other hand, where the work of communication may be done by the respondent or communicant via an ability to learn difficult communiqués.

At this point we asked, How is it done? For example, we began to suspect that scanning, as an active learning process, had something to do with the possibility of personal connections taking place between the stimulus and the viewer, but how? It also appeared that focusing permitted much learning without any effort at all, and, again, we asked, How?

Enter William James

It was William James who came to the rescue. This turn-of-the-century Harvard psychologist had been the primary American exponent of the study of conscious experience. As a student of the process of attention, he is still acknowledged as master by contemporary scholars.

James defined two types of attention, voluntary and involuntary, and he noted that voluntary attention cannot be continuous; it is a continual returning of the attention to its object when it wanders away. He said, "*Voluntary attention is always derived;* we never make an effort to attend to an object except for the sake of some remote interest which the effort will serve"; and "*There is no such thing as voluntary attention sustained for more than a few seconds at a time.* What is called sustained voluntary attention is a repetition of successive efforts which bring back the topic to the mind. No one can possibly attend continuously to an object that does not change." [6]

James's distinction between voluntary and involuntary attention means that much of thinking, learning, and reading represents a sequence of successive efforts to attend, whereas much of the viewing of life around us—films, TV, and other changing stimuli—is far less likely to require effort. In other words, the change, the switching, or the rhythmic process goes on inside man when he is working at the job of attention, or it goes on outside man and inside (e.g.) the moving film as it relieves man of that work.

Now in these terms, we may reappreciate scanning as an interrupted series of discrete events. They permit the intrusion of a stimulus inside the head of the viewer in the form of a thought, and particularly in this case in the form of a thought connected to the stimulus.

Thus involvement or thinking, when taking place vis-à-vis a media stimulus, requires that the respondent attend to both internal and external stimuli. It sometimes means that some of the external stimuli may be missed; it sometimes means that pressure to keep up will be felt—that is, to do two jobs of attention, one to the stimulus on the page or screen and one to the reaction inside the head. It is susceptible to motivation and effort, and it fairly may at times be called mental work.

The matter of dual attention seemed to answer the "how" of scanning in a way that one could understand its relation to involvement or to thinking. But what about focusing where attention was easy, and uninterrupted, and somehow still seemed to communicate? What is there about the changing stimulus in film or TV that can relieve man of the work of learning? Is *learning* the right word to use, even qualified as passive learning?

We thought that the entertaining quality of film and TV might have something to do with relaxation. Is relaxation not the opposite of work, and is it not associated with suggestibility? Furthermore, a particular TV commercial continued to pique our curiosity. The commercial was the Clairol Nice 'n Easy advertisement that used a slow-motion technique borrowed from the movie *The Pawnbroker*. That film introduced tricks of flash scenes as well as slow motion, but the Nice 'n Easy commercial used only the slow motion.

The commercial had exceptionally high recall scores but aroused no pupil dilation response. This seemed quite unusual. Was the commercial learned without any excitement whatsoever, or was there another element present, an unmeasured response? Is the opposite of excitement just nothing? Is calm a flat emptiness?

With measures of arousal based upon changes in pupil dilation, skin, heart, or respiration, an absence of excitement brings the measure back to a minimal baseline. No further information is provided. With brain waves, however, a decline in arousal would be evidenced by a lessening of so-called beta waves, or rhythmic frequencies emitted in the 13-40 cycle per second range. As relaxation appeared there would also appear the alpha waves in the 8-12 cycle per second range, the slower theta waves of 4-7 per second, and finally the delta waves at 1-3 per second. In general, brain waves cover the full range of human response activity, from peak arousal to deepest sleep. So we decided to measure brain waves produced in response to television commercials.

Brain Wave Experiment

The Neuropsychological Laboratory of New York Medical College is engaged in basic and applied research, and frequently in practical applications. The paid subject in our experiment was a 22-year-old secretary. She was a high school graduate with a black-and-white television set at home, and she had not served as a subject before. Testing took place in November 1969.

About a half hour after lunch, the subject was seated in a test room, actually a light- and sound-controlled environment that could be viewed remotely via a television monitoring system. The cubicle had drapes, a comfortable couch, magazines on a cocktail table, and a simulated TV set in the corner at a viewing distance of 7 feet.

When the subject entered the cubicle, a single tiny electrode was fixed to the occipital region (the back of the head) with the aid of a tiny quantity of jelly. It was referenced to both ears. A very fine wire lead ran from the electrode to the wall, where it apparently disappeared. It had no discernible weight and was not visible to the seated subject. The lead then went outside to a Grass Model 7 Polygraph, which was connected in turn to a Honeywell 7600 tape system and a CAT 400B computer.

The subject was told:

We have fixed up this room a little bit like a living room at home. This is supposed to be a TV set. Just relax for a while. Look at one of the magazines here or read for a few minutes until some commercials come on the screen. Then watch the commercials. Don't be surprised if the commercials are repeated a few times. There will be three commercials shown. The commercials will be shown several times. When the commercials go off the screen, go back to the magazine and read or look a little longer.

The simulated TV set was a Fairchild 400 rear projector with an 8-by-11-inch screen. (In a later retest with the same subject, an actual TV set and on-the-air stimuli were used, but with almost identical results.) A tape cartridge held three different color commercials to be run in sequence three times, for a total of nine exposures.

Each of the commercials had some outdoor activity involving play, romance, or sports, so that responses to the commercials might also reflect somewhat the responses that might be made to entertainment content as well as to commercials.

The commercials were (a) a story about a boy who could run and play because his defective heart was artificially paced with a medical device developed by GE (a quiet, gentle commercial with pleasant outdoor scenes); (b) the classic and very gentle Nice 'n Easy commercial; and (c) a very explosive GE commercial showing star baseball pitcher Bob Gibson throwing fastballs at what looks like an unbreakable sheet of glass, actually a new product called Lexan. All the commercials were 60 seconds long.

Procedure

Analysis of the brain wave (EEG) data was first made on the total reaction to each of the nine commercial exposures, or specifically to 56 seconds of each, to eliminate transition responses. The type of analysis summed up the *spectrum,* as we name it, of all identifiable brain wave frequencies emitted during the 56-second epoch, as it is called. In simple terms, one obtains a measure of how many seconds' worth of each wave frequency appears during the 56 seconds.

The computer program reported 11 "bands" or frequency class intervals from 1.5 cycles per second up to 32 cps. The first 5 bands were combined and called *slow waves*. The next 4 bands, from 7.6 to 12.33 cps, are usually called alpha waves and are associated with relaxation. They were combined and called *alpha*. The last 2 bands, from 12.3 to 31.8 cps, are usually called beta waves and are associated with alertness, activity, and arousal. They were combined and called *fast waves*.

The subject arrived, was seated, and received her instructions. For about 15 minutes she browsed through magazines while her EEG responses plus impressions from the TV monitor indicated a comfortable and relaxed adjustment to the surroundings. Just before the commercials came on, a full record was made of the EEG spectrum for the last 56 seconds of magazine reading. This involved a Max Factor advertisement that discussed different techniques

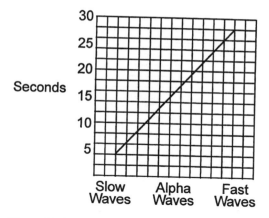

Figure 13.1. EEG Response to One Exposure of a
Max Factor Print Advertisement (56-second epoch)

for applying makeup. The subject reported later that she was very interested
in this advertisement, and was a bit annoyed when the TV commercials came
on. She also reported that she liked the Nice 'n Easy commercial, disliked the
Bob Gibson commercial, and was bored with them all by the third exposure.

Results

First, the print ad, with 5 seconds of slow waves, 16 of alpha, and 28 of
fast waves, all added up to a picture of relaxed attention, interest, and mental
activity, as shown in Figure 13.1.

As the first commercial came on, the subject looked up and an entirely new
pattern or mix appeared, adding up to 21 seconds of slow, 18 of alpha, and 15
of fast. I say *pattern* because closer inspection and analysis showed that the
wave patterns throughout were, at any one moment, mixtures of the overlap-
ping wave actions. It was not some seconds of one frequency followed by
some seconds of another, but an overall state, mode, or style of reception with
elements of different wave types. Thus the 21 slow, 18 alpha, and 15 fast in
response to the first commercial roughly represented constant proportions of
waves active in any one period within the 56 seconds.

We were surprised that the alpha or relaxed element did not change
significantly from print to TV, but we took it as a sign of general relaxation
in the test situation. We had expected that the TV might be more relaxing, but

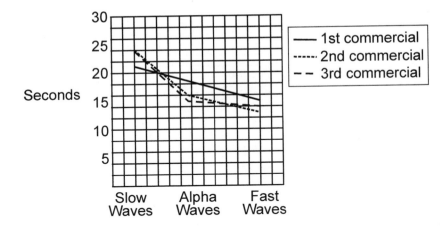

Figure 13.2. EEG Response to Each of Three TV Commercials on First Exposure (56-second epoch)

not that it would instantly produce a preponderance of slow waves and a characteristic mode of response. Rather, we expected that it might develop over time with the three repetitions.

The initial spectrum for the first commercial did not change significantly for the next two commercials. Apparently it was a characteristic mode of response. The 21-18-15 became 24-15-14 for the second commercial, and 24-16-13 for the third. Results are shown in Figure 13.2. There were, however, differences in the proportion of delta and theta, which together constitute the slow waves. These deserve closer attention in future studies.

The question arises as to how immediate this characteristic mode of response was. Did it appear in the first seconds of the first commercial or what? To answer this, we analyzed spectra for three 10-second periods within the first exposure to the first commercial. Within Seconds 2 to 12, there were 2 seconds of slow, 4 of alpha, and 4 of fast waves. Within Seconds 25 to 35, there were 4 seconds of slow, 3 of alpha, and 3 of fast waves; and within Seconds 46 to 56, there were 5 seconds of slow, 3 of alpha, and 3 of fast waves.

In other words, it was about halfway through the first exposure to the first commercial before the slow waves predominated over the fast waves. We can say, then, that the characteristic mode of response took about 30 seconds to develop fully.

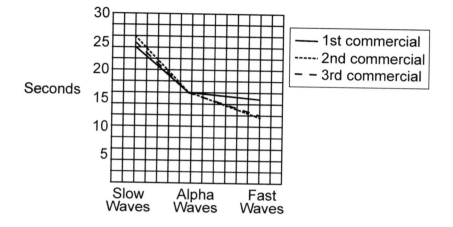

Figure 13.3. EEG Response to Each of Three TV Commercials on Third Exposure (56-second epoch)

Looking at just the first 10-second period, however, we can also say that slow waves were already half as common as the fast waves, compared with the prior print viewing, where the slow waves were only one-fifth to one-sixth of the fast waves. Thus the adaptation, quite reasonably, began immediately upon the subject's viewing the television stimulus.

What about repetition? The second round of viewing went 22-20-13, 24-16-14, and 28-15-12. The third round went 24-16-13, 25-16-12, and 26-16-12. The slow waves gradually increased generally from 23 to 25, and the fast waves decreased from 14 to 12.

More noteworthy was the similarity of response to all three commercials, increasingly so with repetition. The differences between response to the three commercials on third exposure are less than the difference between any one commercial on second exposure. In short, the commercials evoked little difference on first trial and almost none by the third, as shown in Figure 13.3.

The question arises as to the remaining sensitivity to the third exposure of the third commercial, by this time probably boring and well-learned. Again, we analyzed spectra for three 10-second periods within the third exposure to the third commercial. Within Seconds 2 to 12, there were 6 seconds of slow, 2 of alpha, and 2 of fast waves. Within Seconds 25 to 35, there were 4 seconds of slow, 3 of alpha, and 2 of fast waves; and within Seconds 46 to 56, there were 4 seconds of slow, 3 of alpha, and 2 of fast waves. In other words, even on this last dull viewing the subject's initial preponderance of slow waves diminished a little as the commercial proceeded to the halfway point. Thus it appears that there may be a little life left even in what appears to be a satiated condition.

Interpretation

It appears that this subject's mode of response to television is very different from her response to print. That is, *the basic electrical response of the brain is more to the media than to content differences within the TV commercials* or to what, in pre-McLuhan days, would ordinarily have been called the commercial message.

It also appears, as suggested initially by the earlier studies of involvement or of eye movement, that the response to print generally may come to be understood as active and composed primarily of fast brain waves, whereas the response to television might come to be understood as passive and composed primarily of slow brain waves. Further testing is indicated.

In addition to computer analysis of brain wave frequency rates, it is possible to examine visually the actual wave tracing produced. It is a physical record of the wave. Such examination shows the amplitude of the print waves to be consistently about five times that of the TV waves. We may attribute the taller print waves to the fact that the print reader uses effort to converge his or her eyes onto the closer stimulus, and also endures a tension in the muscles of the neck as the head is bent slightly forward and turned. It is possible that reading cannot be maintained without some such tension and that in a completely comfortable chair with perfect head and neck support, the reader would fall asleep.

Old Theory: Learning From Messages

McLuhan might characterize our field of communication theory as horse-and-buggy, or at best a "Pony Express" type of theory. That is, we are wedded to a view of someone preparing a message, the message carried across a distance (hopefully fast), and a receiver reading or decoding the message at the other end. Ours is a transportation type of theory, with a communicator, a communiqué, and a communicant.

Our mass communication theory has much to say about communicators and the influences on them and their media. It is also much concerned with patterns of diffusion of ideas, and it is very concerned with the selectivity and depth of audience responses. Somehow McLuhan seems to say that this has all been made irrelevant by the technological fact of television.

Television is not mass communication in our sense, says McLuhan. Nobody out there is trying to decode or receive any messages. Instead, their eyes and ears have been "extended" into the situation portrayed on the screen. They are participating in an experience even if it is passive participation. And unlike films, a significant portion of television is "live" or, as they say in the computer field, "in real time."

In terms of our old mass communication theory, we would ordinarily say that television is better or richer than radio because an extra dimension, that of video, is added; or richer than newspapers because audio is added. This is a right conclusion from a wrong premise. Radio and newspapers as communication are deficient in that they must omit much information. Similarly, television as experience is deficient in that reality is presented minus the feelings. This is McLuhan's "cool" medium, in consequence said to be breeding a generation yearning for feelings and meanings behind the superficial happenings and encounters in life around them.

Our initial EEG data support McLuhan in the sense that television does not appear to be communication as we have known it. Our subject was working to learn something from a print ad, but the fact that she was passive about television does not appear to be communication as we have known it. *Our subject was working to learn something from a print ad, but was passive about television.* If something happened to communicate, that's fine; if it did not, it went by and was gone and no process of scanning or dual attention would worry over its shortcomings. The subject was no more trying to learn something from television than she would be trying to learn something from a park landscape while resting on a park bench. Yet television is communication.

What *shall* we say of it, a communication medium that may effortlessly transmit into storage huge quantities of information not thought about at the time of exposure, but much of it capable of later activation?

New Theory: Learning From Experiences

The TV viewer is well equipped to recognize many things in life seen beforehand on television. So equipped, he startles into, "Ah ha, I've seen you or this before." This startle is the beginning of an active response, but because this has not been thought out in advance of the time of exposure, it comes out unformed and shapeless.

This suggests the awkward spontaneity of the younger generation, the tendency to act or react in a variety of new but faintly recognized situations where purpose or intent has not yet crystallized. It may look immature or enthusiastic to many observers, but it emanates from the ability to recognize as familiar a wide variety of things in life.

The print viewer, meanwhile, has paused and thought about what he has seen in print, has formed an opinion or mentally rehearsed a plan. When he recognizes something similar in real life, he is ready with a formed or "mature" response. However, print has allowed him to store relatively less information, and so there is much that he does not recognize and to which he reacts not at all. So print man seems very selective, and reacts well or not at all. It looks very mature.

In short, it is suggested that television man, the passive media audience, is a more active but "clumsy," experience-oriented participant in life, whereas print man, the active media audience, is a more selective, less active, and "mature" information- or message-oriented participant in life. Never mind now which is better. McLuhan was aware of some such difference while none of our mass communication theory was relevant.

As to the question, Which is better? we are handicapped by our greater familiarity with active and involved types of learning. Our understanding of how passive learning takes place is still deficient, and we are not yet sure how to measure its effectiveness in a fair manner.

Although further work with brain waves seems indicated, it should be stressed that there is no evidence or speculative inference here to suggest that either print or television is "better" than the other, or that fast or slow brain waves are better than the other. Instead, we have a very great need to understand the differences better, and perhaps especially to understand better the significance of slow brain waves. To do so we must hold in abeyance those historically built-in predispositions in favor of certain behaviors that currently seem more "mature."

Finally, I have pointed out in the analysis of eye-movement patterns involving focusing and scanning that advertising that is easily learned requires very little work on the part of the respondent, but advertising that communicates less easily does require the respondent to be more active. This observation based on eye-movement data seems confirmed or paralleled by the present brain wave data. So the response to television is more passive simply because it is an easier form of communication. The task now is to determine just how easy or hard different communication or even educational materials should be made for optimal learning by various audiences.

Notes

1. Herbert E. Krugman, "The Impact of Television Advertising: Learning Without Involvement," *Public Opinion Quarterly*, Fall 1965, 349-356.
2. Herbert E. Krugman, "The Measurement of Advertising Involvement," *Public Opinion Quarterly*, Winter 1966-1967, 583-596.
3. Leo Bogart, S. B. Tolley, and F. Orenstein, "What One Little Ad Can Do," *Journal of Advertising Research*, vol. 10, no. 4, August 1970, 3-15.
4. N. H. Mackworth, "A Stand Camera for Line-of-Sight Recording," *Perception and Psychophysics*, March 1967.
5. This type of equipment is described and photographed in the cover story of the August 1968 issue of *Scientific American*.
6. William James, *Principles of Psychology* (New York: Dover, 1890).

Consumer Preferences
as Predictions

Alfred Politz
W. Edwards Deming

I f marketing research is to perform a useful function, it must be put finally in the form of predictions for the use of management. The form of the prediction may be, for example, the likely increases or decreases in sales that would result under certain circumstances from this or that change in quality, style, package, color, or price of a particular product, or from some particular method of advertising it. These predictions are to be used by management as aids in coming to a decision concerning the future quality, style, package, color, or price of an article, or the method of advertising it.

NOTE: This chapter is reprinted with permission from *The Politz Papers: Science and Truth in Marketing Research,* published by the American Marketing Association, edited by Hugh S. Hardy, 1990, pp. 100-105.

Decisions Involve Risks

A decision may turn out to be wrong and lead to losses. It can be wrong even when it is made with the aid of good marketing research in the form of predictions, although certainly a decision has a better chance of being the right one if it is made with the aid of good predictions. Otherwise there would be little use for good predictions, and little use for good market research.

Likewise, a prediction may be wrong even when it is made with the aid of good data, although certainly a prediction has a better chance of being correct if it is made with the aid of good data. Otherwise, there would be little use for good data.

Again, predictions involve risks, but the researcher must nevertheless make them. It might seem smart to avoid the risk of prediction by confining research to the mere measurement of a present situation. This viewpoint, however, is illusory; it does not solve the problem. Until the data of a marketing survey have been put into the form of predictions, they cannot contribute to the decisions that management must make.

The principle that knowledge must have temporal spread is well-known in the sciences. The aim here is to translate this principle into the language of marketing research, so that marketing research may be more effective for the use of management.

Every decision entails the expectation of a specific result. Therefore, every decision, if it is rational, depends on a prediction. A decision assumes that a particular action will lead to an anticipated result.

Form and Use of Prediction

What makes marketing research useful are predictions of the causal type, related to circumstances that the management may face. Symbolically, the predictions must be of this character: Under condition C1, action A1 will lead to result R1, and action A2 will lead to result R2. Under condition C2, action A3 will lead to result R3, and action A4 will lead to result R4. For example, a useful prediction may be in this form:

If your competitor retains his red package (condition C1)

  a. Change your package to green, and your sales will increase 20% during the next 2 years.
  b. Retain your package yellow as it is, and your sales will continue to increase at about 5% per year, about as they have increased in the past.
  c. Change your package to red, and your sales will definitely fall below the projected normal by 10% or more.

If you know that your competitor will change to a green package (condition C2)

  d. Change your package to green, and your sales will decrease 20% below the projected normal.
  e. Retain your package yellow as it is and your sales will decrease about 5%.
  f. Change your package to red, and your sales will increase 10% above the projected normal.

If your competitor may change his package to yellow or green, and plays a game of probability for maximum profit (condition C3)

  g. Change your package to green, and your expected sales will increase about 10% above the projected normal.
  h. Retain your package yellow as it is, and your sales will continue to increase at about 5% per year, as in the past.
  i. Change your package to red, and your expected sales will increase about 5% above the projected normal.

With such information at hand, the manufacturer is in a position to make a rational decision—a decision based on reason. It is not the business of marketing research to tell the manufacturer what to do. The manufacturer's decision, in spite of the promised increase to result from a green package, even if he knows that his competitor will retain the red package (condition C1), may be to continue to use the same yellow package. Why? Because the manufacturer is in possession of more information than the predictions that were furnished to him by the marketing researcher. He has the predictions, indeed, but he has also the knowledge that the green color is difficult to purchase, and the supply uncertain; or, perhaps, that the particular green that he wants is controlled by a patent, which is licensed to his competitor.

On the other hand, if the prediction had been a 50% increase as the result of a green package under condition C1, the manufacturer's decision might have been to change to green, as the prospects would perhaps warrant the extra trouble and expense of acquiring enough green color to supply his needs.

Had the marketing researcher merely advised the manufacturer to change the green package, there would have been more than a clash of responsibility; the manufacturer could not have made use of the result of the research or, in an attempt to use it, might well have made a disastrous decision.

The Design of the Survey

The survey, to be useful, must be laid out in advance so that it will provide information on which to base predictions of the kind that management will need. If the design fails to provide answers under the various possible conditions that may face management, and to provide the range of validity of these answers, the research may well turn out to be of no use to management, or even a hazard.

Design must come before, not after. *The first step in the design of a marketing survey is to think of the main relevant causes of sales and drops in sales, and the likely conditions to be faced. The second step is to design the survey to that it will measure the effects of several possible actions, under the conditions already specified.*

The questionnaire must elicit this information, and do so in a form that will indicate which actions (decisions of management) may be important and which actions may not be important.

The sample design must be one that will produce this information with known reliability, sufficient for the needs of management, and it must do so with speed and economy.

The first step, the discovery in advance of the relevant causes and conditions, is the foundation of the survey. The researcher must dig into the problems of management, to be in a position to know the relevant causes and conditions that will face the management next quarter. The survey cannot discover the effects of causes not put into the design, although it may of course show that some causes suspected initially as relevant are really not very important.

The survey on the effect of the color of the package on sales, for example, would not have elicited information on the differential effects of the different colors had not color been built into the design. Neither would it have elicited this information under the several possible moves of the competitor, had not these moves been built into the design. Without proper planning, this particular survey might have measured only, albeit very efficiently and very exactly, the present sales of the yellow package by age groups, area, and income—interesting information and useful as far as it goes, but lacking something far more important, namely, the prediction that under condition C1, a green package would, by itself, increase future sales, and that under conditions C2 and C3, the predictions are different.

Without the initial discovery of the relevant causes and conditions, it matters not how skillfully the questionnaire is drawn up, nor how efficient the sample may be, nor how much care is taken in recruiting field-workers, training them, and supervising them; the survey will still not be maximally useful, as it will fail to make the really important predictions that management needs.

On the other hand, if a survey starts with recognition of the relevant causes and conditions, and thus attempts to solve the right problem, it has some chance of being useful, even with poor and unapproved techniques of questioning and sampling. It is important to use the best techniques, but they cannot overcome the handicap of a bad concept.

This kind of planning for the aid of management may be called merely good marketing research, or merely good statistical research, or it may go by the name of operational research, or some other name. In any case, the aim is to provide the maximum aid to management, with the help of modern statistical tools.

Relevant Causes

Marketing research must study relevant causes, not merely causes. The total number of causes related to why people purchase one thing rather than another is almost always practically unlimited. The function of marketing research is not merely to find causes of people's behavior, or to measure the effects of just any cause, but to discover the relevant causes and to predict what effects on sales will result from various possible actions (decisions) under certain conditions.

If we deal long enough with any particular action, we shall find more and more causes behind it, and we shall find the causes of the causes. The results are interesting; they may even furnish intellectual entertainment, but this does not necessarily mean that we are analyzing, understanding, and predicting in a way that is useful for the management of the particular company that has hired us. There is nothing wrong in the discovery that some of the causes for the growth of plants lie in the chemistry of the soil, which was placed there ages ago, which acts under the influence of the sun's heat, and that the heat of the sun is the result of certain nuclear changes. It looks impressive to trace the yield of a cornfield back to the carbon cycle of the sun, but the immediate problem of the farmer is not to discover the infinite chain of causes. Rather, the problem for the farmer is to discover the differential effects on yield and marketability that arise from varying the very few causes that are relevant to his problem—for example, decisions that he must make now on the variety of wheat, cotton, or fruit that he will put on the market in the future; the choice and method of fertilization, in consideration of the gains, losses, and competition that he may expect from other products and from the more extensive use of farm machinery.

The effects of all these causes will vary with the conditions that he may face, such as over- or underproduction of certain varieties, and shifts in the consumer's preferences. He must try to outguess all these causes under all the possible conditions that he may face. The chemistry of the sun and of fertilizers and of the rare elements of the soil and of the atmosphere are still as important as ever, or more so, but they are important more directly to the manufacturer of fertilizer and of farm machinery; they are not the relevant causes that the farmer must make decisions on.

When we predict that action A will give result R, we can only speak of relevant causes, the causes on which management may take action. If people buy more windows at a certain time because a hurricane has devastated the area, then people have a good reason for buying windows, but the reason is an uncontrollable cause; it is not the result of advertising to "buy more glass."

However, although the cause of the need for more glass is a hurricane, and even though this is an uncontrollable cause, the sales that a particular manufacturer makes may depend largely upon the inventory of glass that he keeps on hand in that area for just such contingencies. They will also depend on his competitor's inventory as well. A good inventory at the crucial moment means sales, and no inventory means loss of sales if his competitor is prepared. Hence if in a particular area hurricanes have an expected frequency that is not negligible, then the inventory is a controllable cause of sales, although the hurricane itself is uncontrollable.

The manufacturer, in coming to a decision on his inventory of glass in the area that is afflicted with hurricanes, must weigh the various risks and balance them. He must weigh the cost of maintaining an inventory when no hurricane arrives against the losses of being caught short if it does. Moreover, he must decide whether to have three blueprints ready—one in case his competitor decides to maintain an inventory, another in case he does not, and a third to maximize his profit in case his competition decides to maximize his profit also by playing a game against the first man on the basis of probability—or one single plan that will be best no matter what his competitor does.

A part of the job of marketing research is therefore to study the frequency of hurricanes in the area and to advise the management on the total amount of glass that would be required to meet the demand so created.

The actual decision on what to do is the responsibility of the management, not of the researcher. The management supposedly possesses not only the results of the research, but certain other information as well, such as the costs of inventories, the cost of machinery, delays in delivery, and some inkling of his competitor's plans.

Standard Error

The standard error of a sample result is not the standard error of a prediction based on this result. We have spoken of predictions, and of the need for data on which to base predictions. Actually, in most problems prediction is unfortunately not a simple matter. A prediction must often be based on several kinds of knowledge, some of which is not so precise as the data from a good survey. Good data are helpful, but they cannot guarantee a good prediction except when the forces are all under control, and they never are.

Through the use of the theory of sampling, we may design a sample that will discover with a standard error of (e.g.) 2% what would have been the result of asking every person in some region, by use of the same procedures and care as were exercised on the sample, how many families in the region own the homes that they are living in, how many homes have mortgages, how many people bought this or that product last week, how much wheat they raised last year on their farms, how many acres were in wheat, and how many families intend to purchase certain items of household equipment next year. However, a small sampling error in the data cannot guarantee a correct prediction of how many families will own their homes 5 years hence, what they will spend for various items of food, clothing, or furnishings for the home, or how much wheat they will raise next year. Unfortunately, there is no way to calculate the standard error of these predictions.

A small sampling error is no guarantee that the figures obtained in a survey will be useful; they may be accurate figures on the wrong questions, and not useful for the predictions that the management will need when they must make certain decisions next month.

The production of figures is really very simple. Anybody can produce figures. To produce figures of known accuracy is another story; and figures useful for good research is something else again.

Research is finished when the interpretive predictions are finished, ready for the use of management. Research is not finished when it is left in the form of mere figures or charts, to show what happened. Research must show what will happen if a decision goes this way, and what will happen if it goes the other way, and what predictions will hold if the underlying conditions turn out to be this or that. Moreover, the research must deal with the relevant causes, because these are what the management can work with.

Quantitative Pretesting for Television Advertising

John Philip Jones

The greatest problem that has always afflicted advertising is the waste that it entails. Almost a hundred years ago, two leading advertisers in two different countries, William Hesketh Lever and John Wanamaker, made the statement—apparently independently of one another—that half their advertising was wasted, but they did not know which half. This aphorism has become folklore, yet no advertising practitioner during the intervening century has made much of an attempt to improve matters at a macro level. The intense conservatism of the advertising industry has ensured that the obvious waste is regarded with complacency and indifference.

This is all perfectly clear from the research I have carried out in both the United States and Germany. This is based on the pure single-source technique, and it demonstrates unambiguously that the situation has indeed *not* improved much over the course of the past century.[1] The main discoveries I have made can easily be described. My top-line findings were that 70% of campaigns in

12 major categories of repeat-purchase packaged goods produced immediate effects on sales, large or small, and that 46% of campaigns generated long-term effects in addition to short-term ones. *Long-term* represents an influence on market share over the course of a year. Long-term can also mean periods much longer than a year, so that a year-end effect is more precisely described as a *first order of long-term effect.*

These figures are based on an optimistic view of effectiveness. If we set tougher standards, the figures drop by about half, to 35% for short-term and 25% for the first order of long-term effect.

If these rather sober estimates represent anything like a general picture—and data published by Colin McDonald in the United Kingdom actually confirm that they do—the advertising industry should regard them as profoundly disturbing.[2] They are much worse even than Lever's and Wanamaker's guesses. My estimates of overall effectiveness indicate a waste of resources that can be measured in scores or even hundreds of billions of dollars spent on campaigns that do not work or work only partially.

How can anyone dispute the need to improve matters? It is not enough to devote attention exclusively to generating stronger campaigns—an endeavor to which agencies have always given their best efforts, though these efforts obviously have not been good enough. More important, we must pay serious attention to finding reliable tools that can help us to identify beforehand what is likely to work, so that media budgets can be spent with some reliable degree of effectiveness. This is an activity about which agencies have been notably less enthusiastic.

One reason why agencies have dragged their feet over pretesting is that they have always had theoretical reservations about the various research techniques—reservations that should be respected, although agencies can be faulted for their unwillingness to try to solve the technical problems they identify. But a second—and more significant and pervasive—reason for agencies' refusal to embrace pretesting systems is a deep-seated fear that these represent a threat to creative autonomy. Pretesting is widely perceived as a weapon available to clients that will allow them to dictate to their agencies, and even to browbeat them.

In this chapter I am concerned exclusively with methods devised to forecast the marketplace performance of campaigns. Such techniques are invariably quantitative. For 30 years in the United States (and for a slightly shorter period in Europe), agencies have made fairly productive use of qualitative research for guiding creative work. But even the most enthusiastic proponents of such research would not claim that it can be used reliably for predictive purposes. Rather, it is employed mostly to detect problems of communication and impact. I will therefore discuss qualitative methods only briefly here.

Pre/Post Preference Testing

The research method to which this chapter is devoted can be described as *pre/post preference testing*. The proprietary name for the method on which I shall be reporting is the ARS Persuasion® technique. In this technique, the commercial to be tested is screened in a "laboratory" setting (actually a theater) as part of an entertainment program, which includes other unrelated commercials. Two "market-basket" lotteries take place, one before the program and another one afterward. The ARS Persuasion measure represents the difference in the preference for the advertised brand in the lottery before the program and the preference after exposure to the advertising. This difference is assumed to be "the net effect of retention and attraction as a result of the advertising stimulus." [3] It purports to measure the immediate short-term effect of an advertisement—something that in the marketplace would generally be manifested in sales.

Advertising practitioners with long memories will immediately call to mind the name Horace Schwerin. Indeed, ARS Persuasion testing is the Schwerin technique in its contemporary form. Schwerin research was developed in the United States and was once widely employed also in Britain. In Britain, it was introduced at the time of the launch of commercial television in the mid-1950s, and was extremely popular in the mid-1960s, a period when one of the major television contractors allowed a rebate from its card rates on the understanding that the savings would be used to fund Schwerin testing of the campaigns that were to be screened. Schwerin became so influential that major clients decided which commercials to run virtually exclusively on the basis of their Schwerin scores. [4]

However, by the end of the 1960s this use of Schwerin research had come to an end. Indeed, Schwerin was effectively discredited, and the Schwerin organization had ceased operations in the United Kingdom. I believe that this was all the delayed result of an extremely unfavorable paper written by Jack Fothergill and Andrew Ehrenberg, which had been published in August 1965. [5]

Fothergill and Ehrenberg's paper was a response to an article by Robert D. Buzzell, who had attempted to show a correlation between Schwerin scores and the marketplace performance of the advertising campaigns that had been tested.[6] Fothergill and Ehrenberg effectively destroyed Buzzell's optimistic conclusions about the Schwerin technique, and with them the British advertising community's belief in this system. Perhaps I should say that it destroyed clients' belief in Schwerin—agencies had been highly skeptical (and, where possible, resistant) from the beginning, and Fothergill and Ehrenberg's work did nothing more than stimulate their *Schadenfreude.*

The remarkable feature of Buzzell's paper was that it was colossally flawed, for reasons other than those given by Fothergill and Ehrenberg. Buzzell attempted to measure the short-term effects of advertising from sales audits conducted at 4-month intervals. From what we know today of the evaluation of short-term effects, it is clear that we ideally need to measure sales at *4-day* (or perhaps 7-day) intervals. There was no way that Buzzell, with the auditing system available to him, could have measured any short-term effects at all. Fothergill and Ehrenberg did not refer even once to this decisive deficiency.

Fothergill and Ehrenberg used their technical virtuosity to destroy Buzzell's attempt to demonstrate Schwerin's predictive powers. But because Buzzell did not employ the right tools for the job, Fothergill and Ehrenberg successfully attacked Buzzell without damaging the Schwerin system itself. Schwerin continued to operate with reasonable success in the United States despite its demise in Britain.

An organization called research systems corporation (recently renamed rsc THE QUALITY MEASUREMENT COMPANY) acquired the equity of the Schwerin organization and registered the name ARS Persuasion for its pre/post preference technique (ARS being an acronym for Advertising Research System). The corporation has become extremely successful and has built a powerful client base—itself evidence that an important collection of sophisticated and influential American advertisers have faith in the predictive value of the ARS Persuasion technique. In the United States, rsc alone carries out 2,000 tests per annum, and there are also three competitive organizations in the business (although their methods are not, in my opinion, quite as good as rsc's).

The company has done more than sell its services and carry out routine pretesting; rsc has invested its own funds in improving its methods and conducting other types of "research into research." The data published in this chapter are practical illustrations of rsc's commitment to validating and improving its system with a view to maximizing its value to the advertising profession.

When my book *When Ads Work: New Proof That Advertising Triggers Sales* appeared in the spring of 1995, rsc approached me and arranged a series of meetings. Two features of my research—my conclusions that advertising is capable of a powerful but selective short-term effect, and that this effect can be achieved by a single advertisement exposure—were harmonious with the findings and underlying theory behind ARS Persuasion testing; rsc immediately seized on these points, and I agreed that we stood on common ground.

Eventually, rsc commissioned me to evaluate the evidence on the ability of the ARS Persuasion measure to predict commercial effectiveness. I accepted the job on the strict understanding that rsc would exercise no sanction over what I would write, except in matters of fact and confidentiality. I was frankly skeptical until I began to scrutinize the evidence—and to appreciate rsc's enthusiasm to demonstrate the validity of its work. The result was a report titled *Getting It Right the First Time: Can We Eliminate Ineffective Advertising Before It Is Run?* which was published in the United Kingdom in 1996.[7]

As an aside, the pure single-source research I have already mentioned in this chapter shows both resemblances and differences among its three countries of origin—the United States, Germany, and Britain. One striking similarity is that in all three countries, the proportion of campaigns that have no short-term effects at all is the same: approximately 30%. Yet at the opposite extreme of the most effective campaigns, the United States scores much better than either of the other two countries. The top 30% of American campaigns are significantly more effective in generating immediate sales than are the top 30% of campaigns in either Germany or Britain. This difference immediately raises the question of whether it is related to the more effective use of advertising pretesting in the United States. Quantitative pretesting of all types is practiced far more widely in the United States than in Europe.

Evaluation of the rsc System

The theoretical objections to pre/post preference testing are relevant only in two circumstances: when the system can be shown not to be predictive, and where there are omissions from what it provides. In my evaluation of rsc's work, I examined briefly two criticisms endemic to the research itself: (a) supposed problems with the sampling and (b) the issue of whether consumers respond to a single advertisement exposure. I also looked, in more detail, into gaps: (c) the special situation of large brands and (d) the uses of open-ended qualitative data. In summary, I found little substance in the two criticisms (a and b), but I found the gaps (c and d) to deserve more extended discussion, which they receive in my monograph *Getting It Right the First Time*. (In this chapter I will also look at another matter—the reliability of the research system to measure emotional as well as rational copy.)

In my work with rsc, I have concentrated mainly on the evidence of the predictive capability of the research technique. If it can be demonstrated that the device is capable of predicting success or failure in a reasonable majority of circumstances, then the objections endemic to the technique itself become substantially irrelevant. This is the main reason I have not become embroiled in the theoretical pros and cons of the two criticisms noted above (a and b).

Assembling a battery of cases to address the all-important question of predictability was a laborious procedure. I set rigorous standards in selecting the examples. First, there had to be accurate measurement of short-term sales effects, which meant that the cases had to be confined in the main to those in which sales were measured by scanner research. The result was that large numbers of cases based on bimonthly audit data had to be omitted. Second, I took great pains to review the remaining cases for statistical contaminations, notably those relating to price or price promotions. Third, when I used groups or collections of cases, I reviewed the complete collections, confirming that all the appropriate cases were included (i.e., that the successes had not simply been skimmed off and the remainder ignored).

Of the enormous number of cases available to rsc, the organization provided more than 800 cases for which in-market sales results were available. In these, the data seemed prima facie to be both pure and "reasonable" (i.e., did not contradict common sense). However, I excluded many of these cases on the grounds of confidentiality, or because of the three conditions mentioned above.

A total of 174 cases remained. These fall into seven groups, which are summarized below. When this corpus of evidence has been built up to 500 cases, I shall publish it in a book.

1. Campbell's Prego spaghetti sauce is a very interesting longitudinal case that gives full consideration to the contribution to sales of a range of marketplace contaminations—factors other than the creative content of the campaign. The power of

the creative content is effectively predicted by the ARS Persuasion scores; this is shown to be strong enough to outweigh the various noncreative contaminations affecting sales.

2. SmithKline Beecham's Citrucel laxative is another longitudinal case. It demonstrates the ability of powerful creative work (also forecast by the ARS Persuasion scores) both to boost volume sales and to support increased unit price.

3. A collection of 37 split-cable tests monitored by Information Resources Inc. (IRI) demonstrates a strong relationship between ARS Persuasion scores and marketplace sales, but a weak relationship between advertising expenditure alone and sales. The best results come from heavy expenditure put behind strong copy—a result that accords well with my pure single-source research findings in the United States and Germany.[8]

4. A clear correlation between the size of the ARS Persuasion score and consumer trial rates is shown for 28 new brands.

5. An important group of 97 miscellaneous cases—a group that is being added to all the time—demonstrates a very good fit between ARS Persuasion scores and immediate market share changes. There is a reasonably good statistical relationship between the size of the score and the size of the resulting sales effect.

6. Seven split-cable copy tests demonstrate a clear relationship between the relative ARS Persuasion scores of the alternative advertisements and their sales performance in the marketplace.

7. Three named longitudinal cases demonstrating the ability of the ARS Persuasion scores to forecast sales effectiveness won David Ogilvy Awards, sponsored by the Advertising Research Foundation. These examine three major American brands: Warner-Lambert's Celestial Seasonings herbal tea, Goodyear Aquatred tires, and Kraft General Foods' Oscar Mayer Lunchables.

Readers will appreciate that items 1, 2, and 7 described selected individual cases, and that items 3, 4, 5, and 6 were total census collections, representing in total 169 of the 174 brands reviewed.

This battery of evidence provides excellent endorsement of the ARS Persuasion scores' ability to predict the direction of sales, and good endorsement of their ability to predict the magnitude of resultant sales change. These conclusions should not be regarded as trivial or unreliable. Nor should they be viewed as an attempt by me to sell the research method. I am a disinterested observer. But there is little doubt in my mind that the system has enormous potential for improving advertising's track record. Even if the technique produces occasionally incorrect predictions, the success rate from using it will be greatly better than the present dismal level of success, as described at the beginning of this chapter. I think that the ARS Persuasion technique is capable of helping the advertising industry toward a far higher rate of effectiveness than it manages to achieve at present.

I am working with rsc to add to these data on a continuous basis. There are, however, three specific aspects of the method that deserve special consideration and discussion with the advertising community and additional "research into research," which rsc is willing to carry out. The first aspect is the special importance of large brands.

Large Brands

In comparison with small brands, large brands tend to show small volume growth but are more profitable because of their higher consumer prices and relatively lower advertising budgets (i.e., measured by share of sales value). There is widespread belief, particularly in Britain, that the ARS Persuasion scores are less predictive in the case of large brands than with small brands, partly because these scores are thought to forecast penetration growth rather than purchase frequency growth (a dynamic of particular importance to large brands).

The extensive experience of rsc with large brands demonstrates that the average ARS Persuasion scores are indeed slightly lower for large than for small brands—a reflection of the way in which large brands make progress without dramatic sales increases. (There is a remarkable fit between the rsc findings and the data from my own pure single-source research on various aspects of the marketing performance of large brands.)

The 97 miscellaneous cases mentioned above include 33 large brands. These show a good agreement between the size of the ARS Persuasion score and the sales outturn. The size of the score is predictive of the size of the sales result. This conclusion suggests strongly that the ARS Persuasion scores predict both purchase frequency and penetration growth. Nevertheless, the ARS Persuasion scores need to be interpreted with special care in the case of large brands. Although rsc has devised systems to help with this, the link between the ARS Persuasion score and operational recommendations—"go" or "no go"—may be more complex for large than for small brands. Careful judgment must be used in the interpretation of the scores.

An important finding for large brands is that the size of the ARS Persuasion score necessary to *maintain constant sales* is slightly higher than the figure for the 97 brands as a group. This "stable sales" level is an implicit demonstration of the fact that the advertising for large brands operates defensively—that is, it must be persuasive *in order to maintain constant sales volume.* The persuasiveness of the advertising contributes to the profitability of large brands, although it does not boost volume dramatically.

Emotional Versus Rational Copy

The second aspect deserving special consideration is whether the ARS Persuasion scores can forecast the sales effects of emotional copy as well as factual copy. A content analysis was carried out of the 97 miscellaneous cases mentioned above. These broke down into 56 examples of predominantly rational copy and 41 cases of partly or substantially emotional copy. The scatterplots for the two groups of cases are virtually identical. The emotional versus rational conflict seems to be a red herring.

Open-Ended Diagnostics

The third aspect deserving fuller consideration is the ability of the rsc system to generate open-ended diagnostics. This is a broader question than it appears, and concerns the advertising industry's beliefs in how advertising works. It is rsc's belief that it can contribute to this debate by opening a dialogue with advertisers and—most important—with agencies, to compare experiences and evidence of how advertising works in terms of consumer psychology.

It is in this context that diagnostic information can be employed as feedback to generate and improve creative ideas. If advertising agencies in the United States and Europe can be persuaded to cooperate, rsc is poised to explore this whole matter further. The heart of the problem that needs to be addressed is the creative process itself. Although rsc has made great headway in understanding the strategy and refreshment stages of the advertising process, there is need for more understanding of this process as a whole. The advertising industry knows too little about the all-important creative aspects of its work, and rsc is eager to push forward this frontier of knowledge. If agencies are willing to cooperate with rsc in this enterprise, the organization is optimistic about the possibilities of real synergy.

To summarize what I have said in this chapter: I have little doubt that quantitative pretesting—and in particular the ARS Persuasion system, which I have examined in much detail—has enormous potential for reducing the uncertainties of advertising decision making. I am certainly far less skeptical of the system than I was when I started to examine the evidence. But it is also fair to say that the advertising industry in the United States has many fewer doubts about the system than is the case in Europe. I personally would like to see European practitioners forget their prejudices. Much would be gained if they could be persuaded to approach the whole debate in a positive and above all experimental fashion. There have been many cases in the past when American experience has led the way to improved efficiency and better performance in European advertising. I believe that pre/post preference testing could be another example of this same traffic in ideas.

Notes

1. John Philip Jones, *When Ads Work: New Proof That Advertising Triggers Sales* (New York: Simon & Schuster-Lexington, 1995). See also John Philip Jones, *When Ads Work: The German Version* (Frankfurt am Main: Gesamtverband Werbeagenturen, 1995).

2. Colin McDonald, "How Frequently Should You Advertise?" *Admap,* July/August 1996, 22-25.

3. Lee M. Byers and Mark D. Gleason, "Using Measurement for More Effective Advertising," *Admap,* May 1993, 31-35.

4. This information is based on my personal experience in the mid-1960s, when I was an account representative with J. Walter Thompson, London. I worked on Unilever business and observed how Schwerin research was used by this client (and also by others) in making decisions about which advertisements to run.

5. Jack E. Fothergill and Andrew S. C. Ehrenberg, "On the Schwerin Analysis of Advertising Effectiveness," *Journal of Marketing Research,* August 1965, 298-306.

6. Robert D. Buzzell, "Predicting Short-Term Changes in Market Share as a Function of Marketing Strategy," *Journal of Marketing Research,* August 1964, 27-31.

7. John Philip Jones, *Getting It Right the First Time: Can We Eliminate Ineffective Advertising Before It Is Run?* (Henley-on-Thames, UK: Admap Publications, 1996).

8. Jones, *When Ads Work: New Proof* and *When Ads Work: The German Version.*

Rough Versus Finished Commercials in Research

Paula Pierce

The practical advantage of testing television commercials as rough prototypes lies in the considerable savings in production costs on ineffective creative ideas, which sometimes amount to hundreds of thousands of dollars. The procedure makes sure that such investments are devoted to ideas that are likely to succeed in the marketplace.

The predictive reliability of rough prototype TV commercials has been amply documented by McCollum Spielman Worldwide (MSW), which has collected a substantial body of empirical evidence. When MSW analyzed 92 pairs of rough prototypes and their finished counterparts, the results demonstrated that the rough prototypes were highly predictive of their finished counterparts on basic evaluative measurements of brand/product awareness and persuasion. It should be noted, however, that this predictability occurs when the finished version closely follows the "blueprint" of its rough prototype. (The copy-testing methodology used by MSW is described in the following section.)

Five types of rough prototypes were found to be highly predictive: animatics, photomatics, rough live action, "stealomatics," and hybrid forms. An advertiser testing a rough prototype commercial can feel confident that the test results on basic evaluative measurements of brand/product awareness and persuasion are reliable, valid indicators (at the 90% confidence level) of how that commercial will perform if it is produced as a finished effort.

AD*VANTAGE/ACT Advertising Testing System

MSW's AD*VANTAGE/ACT advertising testing system is an internationally validated evaluative and diagnostic advertising/communications research system that uses central-location exposure and immediate interviewing to gather information about a commercial's ability to generate recall, communicate its message, and persuade. The system is operational in more than 28 countries on five continents. More than 30,000 commercials have been tested worldwide.

Methodology

Each test is conducted simultaneously in multiple-market central locations. All interviews are videotaped and, therefore, are fully controlled. Respondents view TV commercials in the realistic context of TV programming. All questions are administered on videotape, and respondents record their answers on anonymous numerical questionnaires.

Measures

- *Clutter Awareness (CA):* Unaided recall of the advertised product/brand in a realistic "clutter" format (i.e., in the presence of other commercials)
- *Main Idea Communication (MI):* Unaided recall of factual and emotional communications
- *Persuasion/Attitude Shift (P/AS):* A validated pre/post measure of advertisers' influence on viewers' behavior or disposition toward the advertised brand
- *Diagnostics:* A key feature of the AD*VANTAGE/ACT system—the ability to accommodate standard and customized diagnostics to probe audiovisual brand

bonding, communication, comprehension, believability, advantages, imagery, usage, reactions to executional elements, and affective response

Types of Rough Executions

Storyboard Line Drawings

The most rudimentary pretest production form consists simply of storyboarded line drawings that are filmed or taped with a voice-over or sound track. This form of preproduction was found to be too rudimentary to be predictable in an MSW copy test.

Animatics

The catchall production term *animatic* is often misused to describe all kinds of rough commercials. Technically, however, an animatic is a very specific form of rough production—a series of polished and detailed artwork renderings filmed in rapid succession to give the illusion of motion via rapid, sequential camera framing and movement. The quality of detail of the artwork in an animatic distinguishes it from crude, incomplete, or sketchy line drawings commonly used in storyboards. The quality and detail in an animatic, for example, enable test subjects to recognize instantly a drawing of a brand name or package, or the likeness of a well-known personality.

Photomatics

A photomatic commercial is produced in the same manner as an animatic, except that it uses a series of still photographs. Very often, a photomatic production will appear very close to finished form, owing to carefully crafted "zooms" and "pans" by the camera lens.

Rough Live Action

The rough live action format provides full, filmed action, but costs are kept down by using, for example, nonunion talent, simplified sets, and simulated backgrounds. It is common practice to use videotape for a rough live action effort, and in many cases the final appearance can be surprisingly close to a finished commercial.

Stealomatics

A stealomatic (or "ripomatic") uses existing commercial or stock footage that is reconfigured, adapted, and altered to create a new commercial. The advanced technology of video editing and effects capabilities permits a very professional and near-finished look to the final result.

Hybrids

Many advertisers will create new pretest rough efforts by utilizing two or more of the above techniques. For example, existing stock footage can be combined with new photomatic footage to create a new approach.

Why Pretest Rough Executions?

The pretesting of rough prototypes is especially meaningful in today's economy, where increased advertising productivity is essential amid skyrocketing TV rates. To get last year's mileage, today's advertisers need appreciably larger budgets, or they suffer the consequences of fewer appearances on the air and diminished reach (fewer customers). Thus it is becoming ever more important for advertisers to find ways to obtain greater impact with shrinking ad dollars.

Many advertisers have found that rough prototypes, made with any one of several cost-effective techniques, yield reliable test results and an array of extended benefits. Advertisers who use rough commercials to pretest can accomplish the following:

- Eliminate costly production of alternative finished commercials and "guesstimates" of their potential effectiveness
- Maximize cost-efficiency by producing only cream-of-the-crop commercials that are proven effective in pretest
- Gain valuable diagnostic insight into strategic and executional components that may require alteration or enhancement

- Investigate the viability of new product concepts with clear audiovisual expositions, rather than abstract verbal statements
- Encourage creative experimentation with opportunities to evaluate large numbers of alternative strategies and executions without committing hefty production costs
- Eliminate the tradition of justifying commercials on the basis of costly production investment (research results help determine which efforts meet performance criteria and, therefore, merit production and airing)

Typical Questions About Pretesting

Virtually all types of products, executions, approaches, and strategies are demonstrable and testable using rough techniques. What is important is that the rough version show and say what the advertiser wants to show and say in the finished commercial.

How reliable are rough pretests of celebrity/personality presenters?

Rough pretesting provides advertisers with the freedom to evaluate different celebrities before making their final choices (and financial commitments). MSW has tested hundreds of animatic/photomatic commercials designed to preevaluate personality presenters. The key to a good rough likeness is that the drawing or photo and voice imitation are clearly recognizable as that particular personality. A series of specialized diagnostics are used to gauge the personality's appeal, credibility, appropriateness, and compatibility with the brand, product, and message.

Are rough pretests a valid gauge of mood/image and emotional approaches that are designed for highly visual production?

MSW's experience demonstrates that mood/image and emotional approaches are very testable in rough form. The rough test provides a clear indication of the viability of the executional concept and theme, and whether these elements are consistent with the strategic intent and intended communication. The pretest will also determine whether the advertiser may be on the verge of a costly misunderstanding. Diagnostics pertaining to liking and involvement may show a less intense response to a rough. Even so, the

TABLE 16.1 Product Categories of Rough/Finished Pairs in Study Sample

	Number	% of Total
Total	92	100
Food	31	34
Personal care products	23	25
Beverages	14	15
Household products	10	11
Hard goods	4	4
Automotive	4	4
Miscellaneous	6	7

direction of the diagnostic results will provide a clear indication of positive or negative findings.

Can a rough pretest adequately measure a food product's taste appeal?

If the objective of the advertising is to create high levels of taste appeal, MSW recommends using stock footage of food "beauty shots" for best results. These can be inserted in an animatic or photomatic at critical points.

Detailed Study Findings

A sample of 92 of the most recently tested rough/finished commercial pairs was selected for the purpose of determining rough-to-finished predictability. A rough/finished pair is defined as a rough prototype and its finished counterpart. The finished effort closely follows its rough prototype conceptually, strategically, and executionally.

The sample (described in Table 16.1) was broadly representative of the body of product categories and industries in the MSW AD*VANTAGE/ACT normative data bank. For each case, the data collected were for AD*VANTAGE/ACT basic evaluative measures of Clutter Awareness and Persuasion/Attitude Shift. In each pair, and for each measure, scores for rough and finished versions were indexed to their proper product category norms and then subjected to appropriate statistical tests.

The overall averages for the Clutter Awareness and Persuasion/Attitude Shift measures were highly comparable (statistically equal) for rough and finished commercials in the total sample of 92 (see Table 16.2).

TABLE 16.2 Two Advertising Measures

	Clutter Awareness (%)	Persuasion/Attitude Shift (%)
Rough	51	24
Finished	52	25

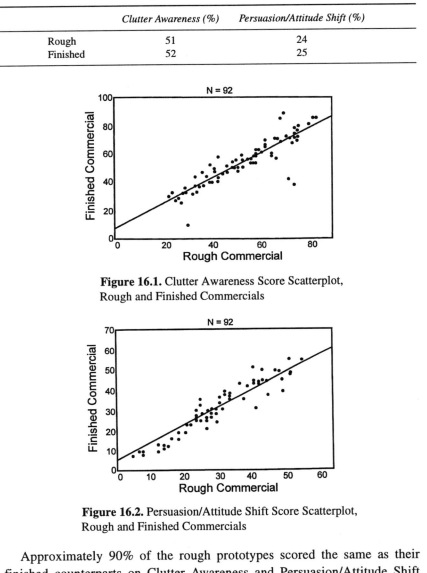

Figure 16.1. Clutter Awareness Score Scatterplot, Rough and Finished Commercials

Figure 16.2. Persuasion/Attitude Shift Score Scatterplot, Rough and Finished Commercials

Approximately 90% of the rough prototypes scored the same as their finished counterparts on Clutter Awareness and Persuasion/Attitude Shift measures at the 90% confidence level. The scatterplots presented in Figures 16.1 and 16.2 illustrate the strong positive relationship between the rough and finished data on Clutter Awareness and Persuasion/Attitude Shift.

TABLE 16.3 Percentages of Rough/Finished Pairs Showing Significant Differences on AD*VANTAGE/ACT Basic Measures

Clutter Awareness	11
Persuasion/Attitude Shift	9

TABLE 16.4 Percentage Scores of Rough/Finished Pairs: Animatics

	Clutter Awareness		Persuasion/Attitude Shift	
	Animatic	*Finished*	*Animatic*	*Finished*
Air conditioner	57	60	36	38
Pet food	65	67	33	36
Beverage	40	50	15	19
Lipstick	70	74	27	29
Fast food	69	67	11	13
RTE cereal	48	51	27	26
OTC drug	51	56	40	32
Jeans	58	53	12	15
Tires	67	66	11	13
Condiment	35	44	20	22

TABLE 16.5 Percentage Scores of Rough/Finished Pairs: Photomatics

	Clutter Awareness		Persuasion/Attitude Shift	
	Photomatic	*Finished*	*Photomatic*	*Finished*
Camera	42	40	61	58
Deodorant	37	41	10	12
Coffee	54	57	26	25
Shampoo	27	30	6	7
Facial moisturizer	54	55	14	16
Hair spray	45	48	11	9
Cologne	32	35	7	6
Gasoline	51	56	4	6

The system is operating at close to the optimal level. The percentage of significant differences between individual rough/finished pairs was about what would be expected at the 90% confidence level (see Table 16.3).

Five types of rough prototypes showed overwhelming majorities of equal scores on both measures. Actual scores of representative pairs of rough and finished commercials for these five types in various product categories are shown in Tables 16.4 through 16.8.

TABLE 16.6   Percentage Scores of Rough/Finished Pairs: Rough Live Action (RLA)

	Clutter Awareness		Persuasion/Attitude Shift	
	RLA	Finished	RLA	Finished
Bar soap	26	30	10	13
Deodorant	50	52	19	19
Pasta	55	57	16	19
Fast food	54	52	33	37
Frozen dinner	61	64	27	29
Household cleaner	33	34	21	14
Mascara	51	56	22	20
OTC drug	39	37	4	5

TABLE 16.7   Percentage Scores of Rough/Finished Pairs: Stealomatics

	Clutter Awareness		Persuasion/Attitude Shift	
	Stealomatic	Finished	Stealomatic	Finished
Candy bar	69	70	47	52
Snack chip	22	28	23	25
Condiment A	55	57	12	19
Condiment B	54	52	33	37
Frozen vegetable	69	67	11	13
Beverage A	45	48	31	35
Beverage B	35	35	21	20
Dinner A	49	54	26	31
Dinner B	57	59	24	24

Why Pretest With AD*VANTAGE/ACT?

The following characteristics of the AD*VANTAGE/ACT copy-testing system make this system suitable for rough pretest studies:

- *Realism:* Respondents are exposed to commercials on TV sets, in the context of programming and other advertising. Rough executions blend in and are perceived as being "on TV."
- *Confidentiality:* Exposure takes place on closed-circuit TV monitors for invited respondents only. The methodology provides complete confidentiality for proprietary new copy and new product development activities.

TABLE 16.8   Percentage Scores of Rough/Finished Pairs: Hybrids

	Clutter Awareness		Persuasion/Attitude Shift	
	Hybrid	*Finished*	*Hybrid*	*Finished*
Detergent A	24	26	22	24
Detergent B	51	54	19	20
Bar soap	69	72	20	21
Fast food	79	81	16	15
Retailer	58	53	24	22
Camera	41	48	47	45
Toy A	25	27	11	11
Toy B	28	33	6	7
Creme rinse	45	45	21	23
Color TV	47	50	18	15

- *Comprehensive measurements and insights:* AD*VANTAGE/ACT's comprehensive series of measures, including tailored diagnostics, provides maximum opportunity to probe all aspects of the pretest commercial, especially when it is desirable to obtain insight into the reasons a commercial did or did not work. The test results provide a blueprint for finished production.

- *Norms and experience:* The AD*VANTAGE/ACT normative data bank contains more than 3,000 brands in more than 500 product categories. Due to MSW's extensive experience with rough executions, separate norms for rough executions are available for most categories.

- *Predictive reliability:* MSW has found high correlations between rough and finished commercial tests.

Electronic Media Audience Measurement

Fiona Chew

The success of a product is generally assessed by the volume of sales it generates: The larger the number of sales, the greater the success. By the same token, the success of a program broadcast on television or radio is measured by the number of households or persons who tune in to that show.

However, the measurement of audiences is not as straightforward as keeping a count of product sales. Several methods are used to assess and estimate the numbers of television viewers, viewing households, and radio listeners. Each has its advantages and problems, and each results in its own particular audience estimates. These estimates are critical from the perspectives of both advertisers and broadcasters, because of the costs associated with the size and characteristics of audiences. In this chapter, I will discuss the specifics of the assessment of audiences for electronic media programs, including some definitions and the data collection procedures used. I will also provide an overview of the organizations that publish broadcast ratings, along with discussion of their sampling approaches, coverage, and timing, as well as the limitations of these methods and procedures.

This type of research is *extremely* important because the research numbers are the main information source determining the rates charged for television and radio time.

Definitions

Rating

When the number of households or persons tuned in to a program is expressed as a percentage of the total market, this is called a *rating*. A rating is strictly a quantitative measure. According to Nielsen audience estimates, as of 1994 the national U.S. television market consisted of 95.4 million households. If ABC's *Home Improvement* is watched by an estimated audience of 17,709,600 households out of that 95.4 million, this translates into a rating of 18.8 ([17,709,600/95,400,000] × 100). With local-market data, ratings are similarly calculated for U.S. TV and radio markets from New York to Honolulu. There are more than 200 TV markets and more than 250 radio markets in the United States. Television ratings include both household and person ratings, whereas radio ratings focus only on individuals. Ratings can be calculated for the average minute by summing and averaging minute-by-minute estimates. Quarter-hour viewing is registered with at least 5 minutes of viewing during a 15-minute block, and average quarter-hour ratings are calculated from the audience estimate during any 15-minute block averaged for a program.

Share

A program's share is simply its audience expressed as a percentage of the market's total households or persons using television at that time. Using the example above, if only 63,248,500 households were using television during the broadcast period when *Home Improvement* was on the air, then the program's share of the household audience is 28 ([17,709,600/63,248,500] × 100). With local-market data, shares can be similarly estimated for various programs.

Cume

Cume is short for *cumulative audience,* which refers to the total number of unduplicated households or persons who tuned in at least once to a program during its broadcast. A cume rating is expressed as a percentage of the market total and assesses the extent of market reach attained by a program. For example, if CBS's *60 Minutes* has a 30% household cume, this means that 30% of the market households tuned in to the program at least briefly.

Data Collection Procedures

Meters, diaries, and telephone interviews are the three basic methods used to collect and report broadcast audience information. Meters are electronic devices that record television viewing automatically. Diaries are instruments in which respondents log their own television or radio exposure. Telephone interviews are conducted by audience measurement organizations with television or radio users to collect information about their media usage.

Meters

The People Meter and the Audimeter are two electronic devices currently used to record the time each TV set in a household is turned on or off, the station to which it is tuned, all the channel changes, and the duration of time the set is on. In addition, the People Meter has a keypad that permits the viewer to register his or her identification with a button whenever he or she enters or leaves the room, starts to watch, or stops watching television. This feature allows individual monitoring of the program viewing of all family members, including visitors.

All viewing data collected by meters are downloaded regularly and automatically to the measurement company's central computer, where they are stored and processed. Because data are collected automatically, audience information is available to users the next day, thus the term *overnights.* The use of meters is very costly, owing to the equipment and technical support required. Currently, People Meters are used primarily to collect national viewing data, whereas Audimeters are used in nearly 30 local markets. A. C. Nielsen has a People Meter service in the Los Angeles market, established in

```
SAN FRANCISCO-OAKLAND DMA
Daily GRID
PROGRAM AVERAGES
QUARTER HOUR RATINGS       THURSDAY   08/25/94   466 REPORTING HOUSEHOLDS
TIME    HUT    7 KGO A     RTG SH    5 KPIX C     RTG SH   4 KRON N    RTG SH   44 KBHK I    RTG SH

3:00P 26.8 DONAHUE           2.4  9 GERALDO        2.1  8 DAYS-OUR LIVES 4.5 17 TALE SPIN      1.7  6
      27.7                   1.9  7                1.7  6                    4.9 18   1.5  6 27.2 1.3  5
3:30P 28.1                   2.8 10               2.1  7                    4.9 17 DARKWING DUCK  0.6  2
      27.3    2.3  8 27.4    2.1  8  2.0  8 27.4  2.4  9  4.9 18 27.4       5.4 20   0.5  2 27.7  0.4  1
4:00P 28.8 OPRAH WINFREY     5.6 19 AMERCN JOURNAL 3.0 10 KICKI LAKE        5.4 19 GOOF TROOP     0.6  2
      30.5                   7.1 23   3.2 11 29.6  3.4 11                    6.0 20   0.6  2 29.6  0.6  2
4:30P 31.3                   7.3 23 INSIDE EDITION 3.2 10                    4.7 15 BONKERS        0.6  2
      33.0    6.9 23 30.9    7.9 24   3.3 10 32.1  3.4 10  5.1 17 30.9      4.3 13   0.6  2 32.1  0.6  2
5:00P 35.4 CHT MVS AT 5      5.1 14 KPIX 5 MVS-5   5.8 16 MVSCNTR 4 AT 5    4.5 13 GROWING PAINS  1.3  4
      36.3 A  5.1 14 35.8    5.1 14   5.6 16 35.8  5.4 15  3.9 11 35.8      3.4  9   1.6  4 35.8  1.9  5
5:30P 38.0 ABC-WORLD MVS     5.1 13 CBS EVENNG MVS 7.1 19 NBC NITELY MVS    3.0  8 FAMILY MATTERS 3.0  8
      41.8    5.4 14 39.9    5.8 14   6.7 17 39.9  6.4 15  3.3  8 39.9      3.6  9   3.3  8 39.9  3.6  9
6:00P 46.3 CHT MVS AT 6      6.0 13 KPIX 5 MVS-6   8.6 19 MVSCNTR 4 AT 6    4.7 10 FULL HOUSE     2.8  6
      47.0 (JOE&SANCHEZ)     5.4 11 B  7.9 17 46.6 7.3 16                    3.6  8   2.8  6 46.6  2.8  6
6:30P 47.2                   5.6 12 CURRENT AFFAIR 6.7 14                    4.7 10 ROSEANNE       3.2  7
      47.2    5.5 12 46.9    5.1 11   6.0 13 47.2  5.4 11  4.4 10 46.9      4.9 10   3.4  7 47.2  3.6  6
7:00P 47.6 JEOPARDY          6.9 14 TW WAIKIKI-CBS 4.9 10 HARD COPY         7.1 15 STAR TK-GENRTN 2.8  6
      49.1    7.5 16 48.3    8.2 17               4.7 10   6.5 14 48.3      6.0 12                2.1  4
7:30P 49.6 WHEEL-FORTNE      6.2 13               4.9 10 ENT TONIGHT 30    5.8 12                3.4  7
      50.9    6.8 14 50.2    7.5 15   5.0 10 49.3 5.6 11   5.9 12 50.2      6.0 12   3.0  6 49.3 3.9  8
8:00P 53.2 MT SO-LIFE-ABC    8.6 16 EYE-CHUNG-CBS  6.7 13 KAD ABT U-THU     7.9 15 STAR TK GEN-AS 2.8  5
      55.1                   8.6 16               3.3 13   8.6 16 54.1      9.4 17                3.0  6
8:30P 54.5                   8.6 16               7.9 14 VINGS-THU         10.7 20                3.0  6
      55.6    8.5 16 54.6    8.2 15   7.2 13 54.6 7.1 13   11.1 20 55.0     11.6 21   2.9  5 54.6 3.0  6
9:00P 55.8 BEHND-DOOR-ABC    6.9 12 HOTEL MLBU-CBS 8.2 15 SEINFELD-NBC     14.2 26 ROBOCOP        1.9  3
      55.8                   5.4 10               6.7 12   14.3 26 55.8     14.2 25                1.9  3
9:30P 56.2                   6.4 11               7.3 13 FRASIER-NBC       13.5 24                3.0  6
      54.7    6.1 11 55.6    5.8 11   7.2 13 55.6 6.9 13   12.9 23 55.4     12.4 23   2.2  4 55.6 2.1  4
10:00P 51.5 PERTN LIVE-ABC   7.1 14 KPIX 5 MVS-10  7.1 14 DATELINE-THU      9.7 19 COPS           1.5  3
      50.4                   6.2 12 (MCEHLTMACHVZ) 6.4 13                    9.7 19   1.5  3 50.9  1.5  3
10:30P 48.9                  7.7 16               5.1 10                    8.2 17 NIGHT COURT    1.3  3
      48.9    6.8 14 49.1    6.4 14   5.8 12 49.1 4.7 10   8.7 18 49.1      7.3 16   1.3  3 47.4  1.3  3
11:00P 41.8 CHT MVS-11       5.4 13 D LETTRMAN-CBS 8.2 20 MVSCNTR4 AT 11    5.1 12 ARSENIO HALL   1.3  3
      39.3 C  5.1 13 40.5    4.9 12               8.8 22   4.8 12 40.5      4.5 11                0.6  2
11:30P 37.1 ABC-NITELINE     4.9 13               7.3 20 TONITE SHW-NBC    4.1 11                0.9  2
      31.1    4.4 13 34.1    3.9 13   7.0 19 37.3 3.9 13                    4.5 14   0.9  2 37.3  0.9  2
12:00M 27.7 HUNTER           2.6  9 INSIDE EDITH R 3.6 13                    3.4 12 MONTEL WILLIAM 0.9  3
      22.3                   2.4 11   3.5 14 25.0 3.4 15   3.6 12 29.5      2.4 11                0.9  3
12:30A 19.3                  2.6 13 BERTICE BERRY  2.6 13 C O'BRIEN-NBC    1.5  8                0.9  3
      17.4    2.5 12 21.6    2.4 14               2.1 13                    0.9  5   0.7  3 21.6  0.6  3
1:00A 16.5 CHT MVS-11 R      2.1 13               2.1 13                    1.7 10 DEAR JOHN      0.9  5
      16.1    2.1 13 16.3    2.1 13   2.3 14 17.3 2.4 15   1.4  8 17.3      1.7 11   0.9  6 16.3  0.9  6
1:30A 14.8 BEST PCTRE SHW    1.7 11 KPIX 5-MV-10 R 2.4 16 PAID PROGRAM     0.6  4 LATE NITE MOV  0.9  6
      14.6                   1.3  9               2.8 19   0.7  5 14.7      0.5  6 (MURPHYS LAW)  0.9  6
2:00A 13.5                   1.1  8               2.8 21 LT-KIMMEAK-NBC    0.9  7                0.9  7
      12.0                   0.9  8   2.5 18 13.7 2.1 18   0.9  7 12.7      0.5  8                1.1  9
2:30A 11.6                   0.9  8 CBS LT-NITE 2  1.9 16 NIGHTSIDE-N-F     0.5  8                1.1  9
      10.9    1.0  8 12.9    0.6  6 B 1.9 17 11.2 1.9 17   0.7  7 11.2      0.6  6   0.9  7 12.2  1.1 10

R = REPEAT              S = SPECIAL         P = PREMIER
A (JNNINGASNCHZ)        B (MCRLHTMAKLLY)    C (JOE)
D (SWEATNG BLLT)
```

```
! - BELOW MINIMUM AUDIENCE LEVEL
( - INCLUDES ONE OR MORE BELOW MINIMUM RATINGS
```

Figure 17.1. Metered Market Overnights for San Francisco, 1994
SOURCE: Nielsen Media Research. Reprinted by permission.

September 1992, that serves as a Hispanic sample. Figure 17.1 shows some of the Audimeter data for the San Francisco market downloaded for an evening in 1994.

One of the problems with the People Meter is that it is an "active" meter; that is, it requires participation by persons in the household to indicate any changes in their own television viewing or that of others who neglect the task, such as children. Viewers are requested to push a response button whenever a red light flashes in order to verify that they are still watching. When they stop watching permanently or temporarily (e.g., to get a snack, go to the bathroom, or talk on the telephone), they are supposed to press the button when they stop and again when they return. Studies have shown that the People Meter tends to underestimate children's television viewing and that "button fatigue" among viewers eventually leads to an overall underreporting of television viewing.[1]

The Audimeter's downside is that it measures television usage (i.e., that the TV set is turned on to a specific channel) without any corresponding measure of the identity of the person or persons watching television. As a result, it may measure television usage when no one is in the room or when viewers are present but not watching television, because they may be asleep or talking or engaged in some other activities. Audimeter measurements therefore tend to be overestimates of television viewing.

Passive meters—that is, meters designed to detect the presence of individuals in a room where the television is on, without any active participation by those individuals—are under development by A. C. Nielsen. However, although the technological problems associated with such devices appear to have been solved, these meters are still some years away from general use (see the final section of this chapter).

Diaries

Viewing diaries are printed booklets mailed to respondents for use in recording television viewing or radio listening during different parts of the day for a full week. In the case of radio, each respondent receives a personal diary for radio listening designed to be carried in a pocket or purse. The respondent is supposed to record all of his or her radio listening in the home as well as out of the home (e.g., in the car, at the office). Figure 17.2 shows a page from the Arbitron Radio Diary. In contrast, television diaries are household diaries. One is assigned to each television set in the household for use by all viewers when the particular TV set is on and they are watching television. Compared with the use of meters, the diary method of audience measurement is relatively inexpensive. However, the diary data obtained have

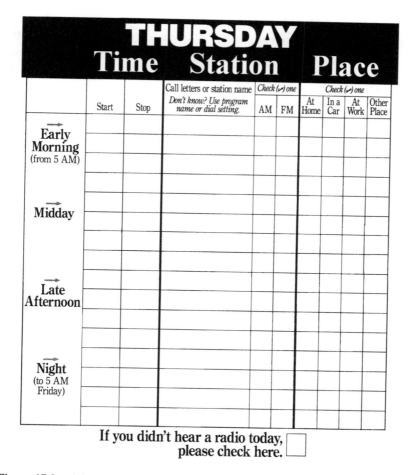

Figure 17.2. A Page From the Arbitron Radio Diary
SOURCE: Reprinted by permission. © 1993, 1994, The Arbitron Company.

to be edited, processed, and tabulated, and the time needed to prepare diary data reports after data collection is about a month—much longer than for meter data.

Ideally, diaries should be completed as media use occurs. However, respondents often fill out their diaries irregularly or at the end of the specified viewing/listening time frame; thus the accuracy of the reporting of television or radio usage depends on respondents' abilities to recall their media usage and/or that of others (e.g., parents reporting their children's television viewing).

The diary method tends to suffer from audience underestimation, because of the reliance on respondent memory. Respondents may forget particulars and may not report all their television viewing or radio listening. Genuine errors may occur through slipshod reporting. Respondents may report their habitual viewing or listening rather than their actual media use. Inaccurate data may result from respondents' confusion in recalling station call letters and channel numbers, or from mix-ups in the cable number lineup. In addition, respondents may prefer to report viewing of various socially acceptable programs or channels instead of acknowledging that they view "adult movies," Infomercials, or daytime soaps. Respondents may deliberately report viewing their favorite stations when they have not, in order to boost its audience numbers.

Telephone Interviews

In the electronic media ratings industry today, telephone interviews are used to collect data of three kinds: actual television viewing or radio listening as it is taking place, named "coincidental" to the specific time of the telephone call; "day-after recall" of radio listening; and radio listening of a preferred station in the past week during various dayparts. In each of these instances, an interviewer will question the respondent about his or her television or radio exposure and probe for further explanations, if necessary. A respondent with particular demographic characteristics may be identified for the interview and all relevant information collected. The identification of a particular respondent, the ability to probe for in-depth explanations, and the collection of other relevant information are all advantages of this method over the diary method, because once a diary is placed in a household, the self-administered booklet cannot dictate who the respondent should be or request further information if responses are missing or incomplete.

Telephone coincidental data, which represent respondents' television viewing or radio listening at the time of the telephone call, generally have a very high accuracy, because no recall or dependence on respondent memory is involved. Respondents are not fatigued by making continuous responses, as in the case of People Meters, but instead respond on only one occasion to report the television use of the entire household or their own radio listening. Ratings derived from telephone coincidental data are considered more accurate than either metered or diary ratings, and the television broadcasting industry regards the telephone coincidental as a standard for establishing baseline data whenever necessary.[2] The main weaknesses of the telephone coincidental are that it cannot be used between the hours of 10:30 p.m. and 7:30 a.m., and it generates only "average minute" data, without cumulative audience information. When radio listening is reported for the previous day or week, reliance on recall is basic and therefore accompanied by the previously discussed problems associated with faulty memory.

Compared with the diary approach, telephone interviews are a relatively costly method of collecting ratings data, because of the need to interview persons one at a time. This is compounded by the length of the calls and the demographic characteristics required for respondents to be interviewed. Depending on the nature and extent of the data collected, reports can be prepared in a week for the telephone coincidental and past-week radio listening, or in 1 to 3 months for day-after recall reports.

Electronic Media Rating Organizations

The organizations currently supplying syndicated broadcast program audience data in the United States include Nielsen Media Research (U.S. national and local-market broadcast and cable television); Arbitron, Willhight Research, and Strategic Radio Research (local-market radio); and Radio's All Dimension Audience Research (RADAR; U.S. network radio).

Nielsen Media Research

Nielsen uses People Meters to generate national television audience estimates called the Nielsen Television Index (NTI), and a combination of Audimeters and diaries to produce local-market television data for the Nielsen Station Index (NSI). The Audimeter-diary mix is used in nearly 30 local markets; the other markets rely only on the diary approach. Nielsen is currently the only electronic media ratings organization producing television audience data on a regular basis. (Arbitron discontinued its television ratings service for local markets effective December 1993.) These data cover only in-home television viewing; they do not include viewing in institutions, college dormitories, hotels, bars, restaurants, offices, or second homes. Clark has reported that a study conducted in November 1989 for ABC, NBC, and the ESPN sports cable network revealed that more than a million viewers watching TV in out-of-home locations were not counted by Nielsen's conventional in-home measurement system. This untallied audience would have increased the three networks' audience share by 2 to 3 points.[3]

Nielsen Television Index

At the national level, Nielsen wires 4,000 TV households randomly selected through multistage area probability sampling consisting of the following stages: counties, census tracts, city blocks, and individual households. If the designated "basic" household cannot be recruited, an alternate household that matches the characteristics of the basic household is substituted. Households are recruited to be Nielsen families for a total of 2 years. NTI provides estimates of network television programs as well as a weekly summary of estimates in the "Pocketpiece." Figure 17.3 shows sections of pages from the NTI Pocketpiece report by individual evening and by program and time period. Nielsen also issues the double-volume *National Audience Demographics Report* 12 times a year. This report provides estimates of program audiences. Figure 17.4 shows the audience composition of a network television program. On-line data are also available directly from the company's computers.

In the process of measuring broadcast television viewing, Nielsen also monitors viewing of cable networks and superstations. About 2,400 households in its 4,000-household sample are cable households, as the current cable penetration is 60%. The total number of households that receive each cable network constitutes the base of a cable network. These bases are smaller than the base for all U.S. TV households. Because each cable network has a different base, ratings between broadcast and cable networks are not comparable, and neither are ratings among the cable networks themselves. Cable reports are customized for each cable network. Figure 17.5 shows ratings for cable programs on CNN.

In 1987, the Committee on Nationwide Television Audience Measurement (CONTAM), an organization formed by the networks in 1963 in response to congressional hearings on the veracity of syndicated ratings, sponsored a study conducted by Statistical Research Incorporated (SRI) to examine the workings of Nielsen's People Meters. The following problems were highlighted in a seven-volume report published in 1989.[4]

First, button fatigue among People Meter household viewers contributed to reported viewing declines over time. The usable data response rate is

A-2   **Nielsen NATIONAL TV AUDIENCE ESTIMATES**   **EVE.MON. NOV.20, 1995**

TIME	7:00	7:15	7:30	7:45	8:00	8:15	8:30	8:45	9:00	9:15	9:30	9:45	10:00	10:15	10:30	10:45
HUT	58.1	59.6	60.7	62.4	64.6	66.3	67.1	67.6	67.5	67.7	67.1	66.8	65.9	64.3	62.3	59.4

ABC TV — MARSHAL (PAE) — NFL MONDAY NIGHT FOOTBALL SAN FRANCISCO AT MIAMI (9:00-11:57)(PAE)

HHLD AUDIENCE% & (000)					7.6	7,320			18.5	17,750						
74% AVG. AUD. 1/2 HR %					10.4	7.6*		7.7*	36.8	17.7*		20.2*		21.4*		19.1*
SHARE AUDIENCE %					12	12*		12*	30	27*		30*		32*		30*
AVG. AUD. BY 1/4 HR %					7.5	7.7	7.6	7.8	16.8	18.6	19.7	20.7	21.2	21.6	20.8	17.7

CBS TV — NANNY — CAN'T HURRY LOVE — MURPHY BROWN — HIGH SOCIETY — CHICAGO HOPE —

HHLD AUDIENCE% & (000)					12.1	11,580	10.9	10,490	12.4	11,930	9.8	9,410	13.0	12,480		
74% AVG. AUD. 1/2 HR %					13.2		12.2		14.6		11.4		18.4	12.8*		13.2*
SHARE AUDIENCE %					18		16		18		15		21	20*		22*
AVG. AUD. BY 1/4 HR %					11.7	12.5	11.0	10.9	12.2	12.7	9.9	9.7	12.4	13.2	13.0	13.5

NBC TV — FRESH PRINCE OF BEL AIR — NBC MONDAY NIGHT MOVIES DEAD BY SUNSET PT 2

HHLD AUDIENCE% & (000)					10.5	10,060			14.9	14,300						
74% AVG. AUD. 1/2 HR %					11.7	9.4*		11.6*	21.2	14.0*		14.9*		15.2*		*5.5*
SHARE AUDIENCE %					*5	14*		17*	23	2**		22*		23*		26*
AVG. AUD. BY 1/4 HR %					8.8	9.9	11.2	12.0	13.8	14.2	14.6	15.1	15.2	15.3	15.5	*5.6

FOX TV — MELROSE PLACE (PAE) — PARTNERS — NED AND STACEY

HHLD AUDIENCE% & (000)					8.9	8,580			4.8	4,600	4.8	4,580				
74% AVG. AUD. 1/2 HR %					11.2	5.9*		8.9*	5.8		5.8					
SHARE AUDIENCE %					13	14*		13*	*7		*7					
AVG. AUD. BY 1/4 HR %					8.9	8.9	8.9	9.0	3.3	4.3	4.6	4.9				

INDEPENDENTS
(INCLUDING SUPERSTATIONS EXCEPT TBS)

AVERAGE AUDIENCE	16.4 (+F)		17.4 (+F)		*0.3		10.8		8.7		8.6		11.8 (+F)		9.8 (+F)	
SHARE AUDIENCE %	28		28		16		16		13		13		18		16	

PBS

AVERAGE AUDIENCE	1.4		1.7		2.1		2.5		2.1		2.4		1.6		1.5	
SHARE AUDIENCE %	2		3		3		4		3		4		3		3	

CABLE ORIG.
(INCLUDING TBS)

AVERAGE AUDIENCE	13.5 (+F)		14.7 (+F)		16.1		16.8		16.8		16.7		13.5 (+F)		12.3 (+F)	
SHARE AUDIENCE %	23		24		25		25		25		25		21		20	

PAY SERVICES

AVERAGE AUDIENCE	1.9		1.7		2.7		3.1		2.9		3.2		3.3		2.6	
SHARE AUDIENCE %	3		3		4		5		4		5		5		4	

U.S. TV Households: 95,900,000

For explanation of symbols See page 6

A-3   For **SPANISH LANGUAGE TELEVISION** audience estimates, see the Nielsen Hispanic Television Index (NHTI) TV Audience Report.

Figure 17.3. Section of the Individual Evening Program Estimate From the NTI Pocketpiece, November 20-26, 1995
SOURCE: Nielsen Media Research. Reprinted by permission.

estimated to be 35%, a rate low enough to challenge the sample's representativeness.[5] Second, the number of multiset homes in Nielsen's sample did not match that of the U.S. population. It appeared that multiset TV households were more difficult for Nielsen field staffers to recruit, and they therefore turned to single-set TV households, which were easier to recruit and install meters in. Finally, the report indicated that children could not be depended upon to record their television viewing; as a result, their viewing was underreported.

CONTAM's recommendations included changing the Nielsen sample every year instead of every 2 years, recruiting more multiset TV households, and requesting that parents or siblings record children's viewing more consistently. Nielsen has reportedly made these changes. However, the major broad-

NTI NAD REPORT — NOVEMBER 1993
TABLE 10A -- EVENING
AUDIENCE BY MARKET SECTION
INDIVIDUAL NETWORK PROGRAMS (TOTAL DURATION)

FRESH PRINCE OF BEL AIR
WEEKS 1234   MINS 120
MON 8.00PM - 8.30PM   CS NBC

10A   EVENING

RATINGS(%)	HOUSE-HOLDS	WRK WOM 18+	WOMEN 18+	WOMEN 18-34	WOMEN 18-49	WOMEN 25-54	WOMEN 35-64	WOMEN 55+	MEN 18+	MEN 18-34	MEN 18-49	MEN 25-54	MEN 35-64	MEN 55+	TEENS TOTAL 12-17	TEENS FEMALE 12-17	CHILDREN 2-11	CHILDREN 6-11
TOTAL U.S.	14.9	10.4	9.5	12.8	11.0	10.2	8.3	6.9	6.8	9.5	8.1	7.4	5.4	3.9	16.3	18.0	11.7	13.2
TERRITORY																		
NORTHEAST	15.4	9.5	9.5	12.7	10.8	10.7	8.5	7.3	6.8	11.4	8.6	7.9	6.2	3.5	19.8	IFR	12.7	13.4
EAST CENTRAL	18.8	14.2	11.0	15.8	13.4	12.7	9.2	7.3	8.1	8.5	9.5	8.0	3.6	4.7	23.3	IFR	19.2	20.9
WEST CENTRAL	12.4	6.0	7.1	8.8	7.4	6.7	5.9	6.8	5.4	12.0	10.7	9.9	6.6	3.0	13.4	IFR	9.8	11.6
SOUTHEAST	17.4	14.4	11.9	15.5	13.8	13.2	10.7	9.2	9.5	10.6	8.2	10.4	8.3	1.3	17.3	IFR	13.2	15.4
SOUTHWEST	14.9	12.6	11.1	17.3	13.7	10.4	8.6	5.6	6.2	4.9	5.5	4.6	4.0	2.1	16.6	IFR	10.0	12.2
PACIFIC	10.8	7.0	7.1	9.0	8.1	8.0	6.7	4.0	4.5	9.0	7.1	7.0	3.4	2.3	8.7	IFR	7.0	8.1
COUNTY SIZE																		
A	14.4	10.5	9.3	13.3	10.7	10.4	7.6	6.2	6.1	10.5	8.3	7.5	7.0	5.1	16.9	18.3	10.4	11.6
B	14.7	11.0	9.4	12.2	10.8	10.6	8.4	6.5	7.3	9.1	8.6	7.8	5.6	4.7	15.8	18.5	12.1	13.4
C & D	15.7	9.6	10.0	12.8	11.6	9.7	9.2	8.0	7.1	9.0	7.4	6.3	6.3	3.3	15.9	17.0	12.9	15.0
CABLE/VCR STATUS																		
ANY CABLE	14.7	10.5	9.2	13.2	11.0	10.1	8.0	5.3	6.2	7.9	7.1	6.8	4.7	4.3	16.9	19.4	12.5	14.5
PAY CABLE	18.1	12.2	10.7	14.9	11.8	11.2	8.8	7.0	7.0	10.5	8.3	7.1	4.3	4.9	16.9	18.1	13.5	15.9
NO CABLE	15.2	10.2	10.1	12.2	11.0	11.0	8.8	9.1	7.8	7.3	8.6	8.4	6.8	3.8	15.3	15.7	10.2	11.1
VCR OWNERSHIP	15.1	9.9	9.1	12.2	10.3	9.7	7.9	6.2	6.3	8.8	7.1	6.8	5.0	3.8	16.3	18.5	11.5	13.4
HHLD SIZE																		
1	8.5	11.0	8.6	IFR	11.0	11.3	10.2	7.1	8.7	IFR	10.1	10.1	6.6	6.3	IFR	IFR	IFR	IFR
2	10.9	10.0	8.5	14.0	11.4	9.3	7.5	6.2	6.1	12.0	9.9	7.5	4.2	3.2	IFR	IFR	IFR	IFR
3+	21.3	10.5	10.3	12.7	10.8	10.5	8.4	8.1	6.7	8.2	7.3	6.9	5.8	4.2	16.0	17.9	11.4	13.1
4+	23.4	10.4	10.1	12.3	10.2	10.2	8.0	10.0	6.9	8.2	7.1	6.7	5.8	7.0	15.8	17.2	10.9	12.7
PRESENCE OF NON-ADULTS																		
ANY UNDER 18	23.0	12.5	11.9	14.6	12.0	11.5	9.2	11.3	7.5	9.7	7.7	7.1	5.7	IFR	16.3	18.0	11.7	13.2
ANY UNDER 12	22.3	13.7	12.1	15.4	11.8	11.6	8.2	IFR	7.9	10.4	8.2	7.5	5.5	IFR	17.1	19.2	11.7	13.2
ANY UNDER 6	20.6	13.1	13.5	16.4	13.6	12.8	8.4	IFR	9.2	12.0	9.4	8.6	6.0	IFR	17.4	18.2	9.8	10.5
ANY 6-11	20.3	10.9	10.7	14.3	10.9	10.8	7.6	IFR	7.2	10.8	7.6	7.2	5.0	IFR	15.5	18.0	12.5	13.2
ANY 12-17	27.7	11.4	10.0	11.1	10.0	10.2	9.5	IFR	6.9	8.9	6.9	6.4	5.6	IFR	16.3	18.0	14.0	15.6
HOUSEHOLD INCOME																		
$20-29,999	15.9	12.1	11.2	13.0	14.0	11.5	9.2	7.1	7.7	9.1	9.6	8.6	6.0	4.7	20.9	IFR	13.9	13.9
$30-39,999	14.5	12.4	10.2	12.0	12.1	11.6	8.2	6.7	6.6	9.2	8.0	7.1	5.8	3.3	17.6	IFR	12.8	16.2
$40-59,999	14.7	9.8	8.1	12.0	9.5	9.2	6.6	2.7	6.2	8.5	7.3	6.8	5.3	1.9	17.8	17.0	12.0	16.0
$60,000+	13.3	7.9	7.0	9.4	7.5	7.3	6.3	5.4	4.8	7.8	5.7	5.2	3.4	1.9	15.0	14.4	9.1	10.8
SELECTED UPPER DEMOS																		
$40,000+ WITH NON-ADULTS	20.8	10.5	8.6	11.6	8.9	9.0	6.7	IFR	5.5	7.4	5.8	5.6	4.5	IFR	16.3	15.7	10.6	12.4
$40,000+ & HOH POM	11.9	7.6	6.2	8.0	6.7	6.7	5.4	3.3	4.8	6.9	4.8	3.9	2.8	1.5	15.0	14.7	7.8	10.0
$40,000+ & HOH 1+ YRS. COLLEGE	13.2	8.6	7.3	9.8	7.8	8.0	6.6	4.5	4.8	8.4	5.9	5.2	3.2	1.3	15.8	14.7	8.3	9.9
EDUCATION OF HEAD OF HOUSE																		
NO COLLEGE	16.0	10.9	10.4	14.1	12.6	11.6	9.5	7.8	8.1	10.5	9.9	9.5	7.4	4.8	16.2	18.5	12.9	14.2
4+ YEARS OF COLLEGE	11.7	8.7	7.1	9.6	8.1	8.1	6.2	3.2	4.3	7.0	5.3	4.7	3.2	1.6	16.9	16.3	8.4	10.0
RACE																		
BLACK	35.4	30.3	25.3	30.4	25.7	26.8	21.7	23.4	16.7	20.4	19.8	20.9	14.2	IFR	28.8	IFR	22.9	24.6

Figure 17.4. Section of Audience by Market Composition for a Program From National Audience Demographics, November 1993

SOURCE: Nielsen Media Research. Reprinted by permission.

CNN AND HEADLINE NEWS MONTHLY REPORT

N I E L S E N   M E D I A   R E S E A R C H

COVG. U.E. = 62981

APRIL 1994
MARCH 28 - APRIL 24

TIME PERIOD	WKS I/C	CNN AND/OR HEADLINE NEWS COVERAGE HOUSEHOLDS			
		HUT %	AA %	SHR %	AA 000
SATURDAY 7:00P- 7:30P	1234	44.5	1.3	3	795
7:00P THE CAPITAL GANG/HL	1234				
SATURDAY 7:30P- 8:00P	1234	46.9	0.8	2	504
7:30P SPORTS SATURDAY/HL	1234				
SATURDAY 9:00P- 9:30P	1234	55.2	0.9	2	556
9:00P LARRY KING WEEKEND/HL	1234				
SATURDAY 9:30P-10:00P	1234	57.2	0.9	2	552

TIME PERIOD	WKS I/C	CNN AND/OR HEADLINE NEWS COVERAGE HOUSEHOLDS			
		HUT %	AA %	SHR %	AA 000
SATURDAY 9:30P-10:00P	1234				
9:30P LARRY KING WEEKEND/HL	1234				
SATURDAY 11:00P-11:30P	1234	51.8	0.5	1	283
11:00P CNN SPORTS TONIGHT/HL	1234				
SATURDAY 12:00M-12:30A	1234	41.7	0.5	1	304
12:00M NEWSNIGHT/HL	1234				
SATURDAY 12:30A- 1:00A	1234	36.9	0.4	1	238

FOR EXPLANATION OF SYMBOLS, SEE BOILERPLATE

PAGE 16   COPYRIGHT 1994 NIELSEN MEDIA RESEARCH - PRINTED IN U.S.A.

Figure 17.5. Audience Estimates for Cable Programs on CNN, Nielsen Media Research, 1994

SOURCE: Nielsen Media Research. Reprinted by permission.

191

cast networks—ABC, CBS, and NBC—still appear to be dissatisfied and are investing an estimated $20 million to create a new ratings system under the auspices of CONTAM, called the System for Measuring and Reporting Television.[6]

Sampling representativeness and methodological biases are important factors influencing ratings results. In 1987, when Nielsen was undergoing a transition from national Audimeters to People Meters, ratings differences were apparent between the two systems. Figure 17.6 compares the national television audience estimates for the same programs produced from Nielsen's People Meters and Nielsen's Audimeters. In addition, data from People Meters used by another service, Audits of Great Britain (AGB), are profiled. In 1987, AGB was a new competitor in the U.S. market. However, because of insufficient industry support, it folded its U.S. operations in 1988. Ratings differences between Nielsen and AGB People Meters were attributed mainly to imbalances in the geographic distribution of the early People Meter samples. Specifically, households in the West, which constituted a larger proportion of the AGB sample, watched less TV than did households in the Northeast, which dominated Nielsen's People Meter sample.

Nielsen Station Index

NSI provides ratings data for local markets. In each of nearly 30 markets, Nielsen installs Audimeters in 300 to 600 households and fields an equivalent number of diaries. Diaries only are placed in households in the other 200 and more local markets. Larger samples are fielded in larger markets. In the metered markets, ratings data are provided from the metered households and demographic data are blended in from the diaries. In the nonmetered markets, ratings and demographic data are all derived from the diaries. In both the metered and nonmetered markets, households are selected from telephone directories supplemented with telephone numbers generated by random digit dialing (RDD) procedures; that is, telephone numbers are randomly generated by a computer in order to capture unlisted telephone households. The households are contacted and recruited to be Nielsen families. Overall response rates range from 35% to 60%, depending on the designated market area (DMA). Increased incentives, cover letters, and reminder telephone calls are used to increase participation among ethnic households, especially African American and Hispanic households. When appropriate, Spanish-language diaries are also provided.

Week one with peoplemeters: how they compare in prime time

The following is a head-to-head comparison of prime time network programing for Monday, Aug. 31, through Wednesday, Sept. 2, using Nielsen's peoplemeter and audimeter data and AGB's peoplemeter sample. AGB provides measurements for the full-length of a program or movie, but does not break down those numbers on a half-hour basis. Such situations are denoted with an asterisk in the chart.

	NTI peoplemeter	NTI Audimeter/diary	AGB peoplemeter*
Monday, August 31			
8-8:30			
ABC ■ NFL	10.7/20	9.7/17	11.9/20*
CBS ■ Michael Jackson Special	16.5/29	17.6/30	13.9/24
NBC ■ ALF	13.5/23	14.9/25	12.0/20
8:30-9			
ABC ■ NFL	14.0/24	13.1/22	
CBS ■ Kate & Allie	12.5/21	14.1/23	11 3/18
NBC ■ Valerie	13.2/22	14.6/24	13 3-22
9-9:30			
ABC ■ NFL	16.3/27	15.1/25	
CBS ■ Newhart	14.4/23	17.3/27	15.5/25
NBC ■ Monday Movie	11.4/18	11.2/18	9.3/16*
9:30-10			
ABC ■ NFL	16.1/27	15.6/25	*
CBS ■ Designing Women	14.8/24	16.2/26	14 8/24
NBC ■ Monday Movie	12.0/19	12 4/20	*
10-10:30			
ABC ■ NFL	17.0/30	16.6/28	*
CBS ■ Cagney & Lacey	11.5/20	12.9/22	11.1/19*
NBC ■ Monday Movie	12.6/22	12.7/22	*
10:30-11			
ABC ■ NFL	17.9/32	16.7/30	*
CBS ■ Cagney & Lacey	10.5/20	11.8/22	*
NBC ■ Monday Movie	12.1/23	12.0/22	*
Tuesday, September 1			
8-8:30			
ABC ■ Who's the Boss	16.3/30	16.2/30	14.2/26
CBS ■ Simon & Simon	7.7/14	6.5/12	6.9/12*
NBC ■ Matlock	10.6/19	13.4/25	11.1/19*
8:30-9			
ABC ■ Growing Pains	18.1/31	18.1/31	16.0/27
CBS ■ Simon & Simon	7.8/13	7.4/13	*
NBC ■ Matlock	11.6/20	14.6/25	*
9-9:30			
ABC ■ Moonlighting	15.1/26	16.1/27	13.7/23*
CBS ■ Houston Knights	11.6/20	11.5/19	10.8/18*
NBC ■ Tuesday Movie	7.7/13	8.6/15	5.8/10*
9:30-10			
ABC ■ Moonlighting	15.3/26	16.9/28	*
CBS ■ Houston Knights	12.3/21	11.5/19	*
NBC ■ Tuesday Movie	6.4/11	7.4/12	*
10-10:30			
ABC ■ Spenser: For Hire	11.3/21	13.3/24	9.7/19*
CBS ■ Night Heat	11.1/20	10.8/19	8 4/16*
NBC ■ Tuesday Movie	6.8/13	7.6/14	*
10:30-11			
ABC ■ Spenser: For Hire	10.6/21	12.9/24	*
CBS ■ Night Heat	11.8/24	11.4/22	*
NBC ■ Tuesday Movie	6.3/12	7.4/14	*
Wednesday, September 2			
8-8:30			
ABC ■ Perfect Strangers	12/22	12.3/23	11.2/21
CBS ■ Mike Hammer	8.7/16	9.5/18	9.7/18*
NBC ■ Highway to Heaven	9.6/18	10.6/20	10.6/19*
8:30-9			
ABC ■ Head of the Class	13.4/24	12.7/22	11.6/20
CBS ■ Mike Hammer	10.0/18	10.5/19	*
NBC ■ Highway to Heaven	10.3/18	12.1/21	*
9-9:30			
ABC ■ MacGyver	11.9/21	12 0/21	11.0/19*
CBS ■ Magnum P.I.	12.0/21	12.7/22	12.3/21*
NBC ■ Bronx Zoo	8.6/15	10.0/17	9.1/15*
9:30-10			
ABC ■ MacGyver	12.3/21	12.2/21	*
CBS ■ Magnum P.I	12.8/22	13.5/23	*
NBC ■ Bronx Zoo	8.9/16	9.7/17	*
10-10:30			
ABC ■ Hotel	8.5/15	9.3/17	7.5/14*
CBS ■ Equalizer	14.2/26	14.2/26	10.1/19*
NBC ■ St. Elsewhere	8 7/16	9 4/17	8 4/15*
10:30-11			
ABC ■ Hotel	8.3/16	8.2/16	*
CBS ■ Equalizer	13.8/27	14.9/29	*
NBC ■ St. Elsewhere	9.1/18	9.6/18	*

Figure 17.6. Comparison of Ratings Produced by Three Monitoring Sources
SOURCE: *Broadcasting and Cable,* September 7, 1987. Reprinted by permission.

Audience estimates from metered markets are available throughout the year on a daily basis, and data from the previous day (overnights) can be downloaded directly from Nielsen's computers. Weekly metered reports are produced in print form. NSI demographic information is reported only four to seven times a year, depending on the market. "Sweeps" periods are television audience survey periods that occur in November, February, May, and July.

Other survey periods are January, March, and October. Reports for nonmetered markets are provided four times a year during sweeps. NSI reports are issued a month after data collection. Audience estimates for each market are reported for two geographic units (metropolitan area and DMA) and two demographic characteristics (age and sex). Figure 17.7 shows a section of the daypart summary. Cable networks that meet the minimum reporting standard of at least one rating in the survey period are reported.

The low response rate for returned, completed diaries compromises sample representativeness. The limited number of weeks surveyed during sweeps leads to "hyping," or the special scheduling and promotion of blockbuster movies and special programs, so that normal viewing becomes distorted. When the NSI data become available a month after the survey period, it is often too late to assist broadcasters in making programming changes.

Nielsen conducts telephone coincidental surveys for specific programs in local television markets when requested to do so by stations. These are often undertaken during nonsweep periods among nonmetered markets. The cooperation rate is generally higher than that of the meter or diary approach. Areas surveyed include the metropolitan area and DMA, and gender and age demographics are also reported. Results are available in a week.

Arbitron

Arbitron uses personal, open-ended diaries to record radio listening among respondents aged 12 and older in more than 250 local markets, or *metros*. Surveys are fielded during 12-week periods: fall, winter, spring, and summer. The largest markets are measured throughout the year, whereas smaller markets are measured once, twice, or three times, depending on their size. The spring report surveys all reportable local markets. Like Nielsen, Arbitron randomly selects households from telephone directories supplemented by telephone numbers generated by RDD procedures, to include unlisted numbers in the sample. All family members aged 12 and older in a household receive radio diaries. The number of usable, completed diaries usually ranges from 550 in the smallest markets to 4,000 in the largest; response rates range from 30% to 40%. Reports are available about a month after the survey period. Audience data are provided for two geographic units (metro and total survey area) and two demographic characteristics (age and sex). Figure 17.8 shows a section of an Arbitron report showing target listener trends.

DALLAS-FT. WORTH, TX

DAYPART	METRO HH	DAYPART TIME(CTZ) STATION	DMA HOUSEHOLD		SHARE TREND					DMA RATINGS PERSONS									WOMEN								MEN						TNS	CHILD		PERCENT DISTRIBUTION		ADJACENT DMA			TV HH RATINGS IN ADJACENT DMA'S		
	R T G	S H R	IN MKT R T G	S H R	FEB 96	NOV 95	JUL 96	MAY 96	2+	12-24	12-34	18-49	18-49	21-49	25-54	35+	35-64	50+	18+	12-24	18-34	18-49	25-49	25-54	W K G	18+	18-34	18-49	21-49	25-49	25-54	12-17	2-11	6-11	MET	HOME DMA	#1	#2	#3	#1	#2	#3

(Table: Dallas-Fort Worth Daypart Summary — MON.-FRI. 9:00A-NOON, NOON-3:00P, 3:00P-5:00P; stations KDAF, KDFI, KDFW, KDTN, KDTX, KERA, KFWD, KHSX, KMPX, KTVT, KTXA, KUVN, KXAS, KXTX, WFAA, WTBS, DSC, ESP, LIF, NIK, TNT, USA, H/P/T.)

#1=WACO-TEMPLE-BRYAN — 273,260
#2=SHERMAN-ADA — 109,130
#3=TYLER-LONGVIEW(LFKN&NCGD) — 222,940

MAY 1996

Figure 17.7. Section of Daypart Summary From NSI Viewers in Profile, Dallas-Fort Worth, May 1996
SOURCE: Nielsen Media Research. Reprinted by permission.

Target Listener Trends

Persons 18-34

	Monday-Sunday 6AM-MID				Monday-Friday 6AM-10AM				Monday-Friday 10AM-3PM				Monday-Friday 3PM-7PM				Monday-Friday 7PM-MID			
	AQH (00)	Cume (00)	AQH Rtg	AQH Shr	AQH (00)	Cume (00)	AQH Rtg	AQH Shr	AQH (00)	Cume (00)	AQH Rtg	AQH Shr	AQH (00)	Cume (00)	AQH Rtg	AQH Shr	AQH (00)	Cume (00)	AQH Rtg	AQH Shr
+WBHR-FM																				
WI '96	13	201	1.0	6.2	18	88	1.4	7.3	19	108	1.5	6.5	17	140	1.3	6.7	8	93	.6	6.3
FA '95	10	209	.8	5.1	11	91	.9	4.4	15	94	1.2	5.7	12	102	.9	4.7	5	78	.4	4.2
SU '95	5	131	.4	1.9	7	51	.5	2.3	7	61	.5	1.8	9	61	.7	2.6	2	39	.1	1.4
SP '95	4	112	.3	1.7	2	30	.1	.7	7	34	.5	2.0	4	40	.3	1.3	1	32	.1	.7
4-Book	*8*	*163*	*.6*	*3.7*	*10*	*65*	*.7*	*3.7*	*12*	*74*	*.9*	*4.0*	*11*	*86*	*.8*	*3.8*	*4*	*61*	*.3*	*3.2*
WI '95	4	130	.3	1.8	4	52	.3	1.5	5	40	.4	1.5	6	56	.4	2.0	2	22	.1	1.6
WFMK-FM																				
WI '96	26	392	2.0	12.4	33	206	2.6	13.4	43	227	3.4	14.8	27	221	2.1	10.6	15	158	1.2	11.9
FA '95	25	366	2.0	12.7	33	231	2.6	13.1	38	219	3.0	14.3	32	235	2.5	12.4	12	149	.9	10.1
SU '95	25	323	1.9	9.7	36	177	2.7	11.6	47	173	3.5	12.1	30	172	2.2	8.6	10	93	.7	7.1
SP '95	26	409	1.9	11.0	33	225	2.5	11.5	48	221	3.6	14.0	29	227	2.2	9.5	11	165	.8	8.2
4-Book	*26*	*373*	*2.0*	*11.5*	*34*	*210*	*2.6*	*12.4*	*44*	*210*	*3.4*	*13.8*	*30*	*214*	*2.3*	*10.3*	*12*	*141*	*.9*	*9.3*
WI '95	24	302	1.8	10.8	30	164	2.2	11.2	42	160	3.1	12.8	36	196	2.7	11.8	10	108	.7	8.1
+WHZZ-FM																				
WI '96	18	371	1.4	8.6	17	155	1.3	6.9	28	223	2.2	9.6	22	242	1.7	8.6	10	166	.8	7.9
FA '95	11	278	.9	5.6	9	127	.7	3.6	16	173	1.3	6.0	13	156	1.0	5.0	5	101	.4	4.2
SU '95	20	347	1.5	7.8	20	192	1.5	6.4	32	215	2.4	8.2	26	198	1.9	7.5	8	120	.6	5.7
SP '95	19	354	1.4	8.1	30	246	2.2	10.5	25	197	1.9	7.3	22	200	1.6	7.2	8	163	.6	6.0
4-Book	*17*	*338*	*1.3*	*7.5*	*19*	*180*	*1.4*	*8.9*	*25*	*202*	*2.0*	*7.8*	*21*	*199*	*1.6*	*7.1*	*8*	*138*	*.6*	*6.0*
WI '95	9	185	.7	4.0	10	95	.7	3.7	12	108	.9	3.7	12	116	.9	3.9	3	61	.2	2.4
WILS-AM																				
WI '96	1	12	.1	.5		4				8				4			1	4	.1	.8
FA '95		3								3				3	.1	.4				
SU '95		27							1	10	.1	.3		16	.1	.3		10		
SP '95	1	9	.1	.4	2	3	.1	.7	4	9	.3	1.2	2	9	.1	.7		10		
4-Book	*1*	*13*	*.1*	*.2*	*1*	*3*		*.2*	*1*	*8*	*.1*	*.4*	*1*	*8*	*.1*	*.4*		*4*		*.2*
WI '95		8								8				4	.1	.3				
WITL-AM																				
WI '96		10				5			1	5	.1	.3		5						
FA '95	**	**	**	**	**	**	**	**	**	**	**	**	**	**	**	**	**	**	**	**
SU '95	1	14	.1	.4	2	14	.1	.6		4			1	4	.1	.3	1	3	.1	.7
SP '95		8				8				4				4	.1	.3				
4-Book	***	***	***	***	***	***	***	***	***	***	***	***	***	***	***	***	***	***	***	***
WI '95		19			2	15	.1	.7	1	11	.1	.3	1	7	.1	.3				
WITL-FM																				
WI '96	31	319	2.4	14.8	39	185	3.1	15.9	49	206	3.8	16.8	43	236	3.4	16.9	13	104	1.0	10.3
FA '95	23	336	1.8	11.7	42	194	3.3	16.7	32	242	2.5	12.1	26	205	2.0	10.1	10	104	.8	8.4
SU '95	29	340	2.2	11.2	47	223	3.5	15.1	41	252	3.1	10.5	38	243	2.8	11.0	15	134	1.1	10.7
SP '95	21	318	1.6	8.9	28	214	2.1	9.8	34	175	2.5	9.9	29	183	2.2	9.5	8	118	.6	6.0
4-Book	*26*	*328*	*2.0*	*11.7*	*39*	*204*	*3.0*	*14.4*	*39*	*219*	*3.0*	*12.3*	*34*	*217*	*2.6*	*11.9*	*12*	*115*	*.9*	*8.9*
WI '95	19	312	1.4	8.5	22	168	1.6	8.2	30	197	2.2	9.2	26	138	1.9	8.5	8	100	.6	6.5
WJIM-AM																				
WI '96	4	60	.3	1.9	5	35	.4	2.0	6	37	.5	2.1	8	40	.6	3.1	2	22	.2	1.6
FA '95	2	68	.2	1.0	1	10	.1	.4	3	28	.2	1.1	3	21	.2	1.2	2	3	.2	1.7
SU '95	2	50	.1	.8	1	10	.1	.3	5	34	.4	1.3	3	24	.2	.9		12		
SP '95	4	79	.3	1.7	4	23	.3	1.4	9	48	.7	2.6	8	44	.6	2.6		8		
4-Book	*3*	*64*	*.2*	*1.4*	*3*	*20*	*.2*	*1.0*	*6*	*37*	*.5*	*1.8*	*6*	*32*	*.4*	*2.0*	*1*	*11*	*.1*	*.8*
WI '95	9	96	.7	4.0	2	20	.1	.7	23	85	1.7	7.0	15	68	1.1	4.9	1	22	.1	.8
WJIM-FM																				
WI '96	5	156	.5	2.9	5	55	.4	2.0	11	61	.9	3.8	8	75	.6	3.1	3	47	.2	2.4
FA '95	5	190	.4	2.5	7	82	.5	2.8	8	71	.6	3.0	6	92	.5	2.3	3	67	.2	2.5
SU '95	3	131	.2	1.2	5	65	.4	1.6	5	51	.4	1.3	3	57	.2	.9	2	35	.1	1.4
SP '95	7	164	.5	3.0	9	67	.7	3.1	11	66	.8	3.2	6	53	.4	2.0	5	53	.4	3.7
4-Book	*5*	*160*	*.4*	*2.4*	*7*	*67*	*.5*	*2.4*	*9*	*62*	*.7*	*2.8*	*6*	*69*	*.4*	*2.1*	*3*	*51*	*.2*	*2.5*
WI '95	5	164	.4	2.2	7	60	.5	2.6	7	69	.5	2.1	6	83	.4	2.0	3	77	.3	3.2

** Station(s) not reported this survey.   * Listener estimates adjusted for reported broadcast schedule.   + Station(s) changed call letters – see Page 13.   4-Book: Avg. of current and previous 3 surveys.   2-Book: Avg. of most recent 2 surveys.

Figure 17.8. Section of Target Listener Trends From Arbitron's Radio Market Report, East Lansing, Michigan, Winter 1996
SOURCE: Reprinted by permission. © 1993, 1994, The Arbitron Company.

The low response rate associated with radio listening diaries is a problem because it challenges sample representativeness. Further, hyping by stations often distorts normal listening patterns. Finally, because respondents are recruited from the same households in this research, the number of households is limited.

Willhight Research

Willhight Research, a Seattle-based organization, collects radio listening data by using telephone interviews about the previous day's radio listening. Established in 1982 to serve the niche of small to medium-size markets, Willhight now provides radio ratings for about 100 markets.

In each market, households are selected using RDD procedures. The sample has a distribution from different geographic (zip code) areas that is proportionate to the population. This is obtained through the use of telephone prefixes that correspond to particular zip codes. Next, the selected respondent in a household is identified according to the criteria of being aged 12 or older and having had the most recent birthday in the household. Selected individuals are called every day for 7 days and are asked to recall the radio stations they listened to the previous day for any radio listening that occurred at home, in a car, or in any other location during specific dayparts. Response rates average 60% and, depending on market size, usable samples range from 500 to 2,000. Reports are available on a monthly basis in both print and electronic formats. Figure 17.9 shows a section from a Willhight Research report.

The main drawback to Willhight's method of research is the inability to reach respondents on a daily basis, which results in reliance on respondent recall of radio listening on the missed days and the errors associated with faulty memory.

Strategic Radio Research

Strategic Radio Research, a Chicago-based company, provides AccuRatings™, a radio listening measurement service that assesses core radio listening, or the radio station "listened to most." Established in summer 1992 with radio audience data for 3 markets, AccuRatings now covers more than 30 markets, which are reported on a quarterly basis with weekly updates.

Survey Area: Missoula/ Lolo, MT (SSA)   Date: April 7 - June 1, 1994   Daypart: Monday-Friday 10am-3pm

A V E R A G E Q U A R T E R H O U R S H A R E (%)

	12+			18+			25 - 54			18 - 34			35 - 54			55+		
	Male	Female	Per	Male	Female	Adult	Male	Female	Adult	Male	Female	Adult	Male	Female	Adult	Male	Female	Adult
KDXT FM	11.9	11.6	11.8	11.8	11.3	11.6	9.9	15.3	12.4	16.4	11.4	14.4	7.4	18.9	13.3	7.6		4.1
KGRZ AM	2.4	1.3	1.9	2.5	1.3	2.0		2.3	1.1		2.8	1.2		.5	.3	10.6	.5	5.7
KGVO AM	18.7	11.9	15.6	19.0	12.1	15.9	19.4	4.5	12.4	9.6		5.6	23.5	7.5	15.3	33.0	39.5	36.0
KLCY AM	1.9	.3	1.1	1.9	.3	1.2	3.4		1.8	.3		.2	6.3		3.0		1.1	.5
KMSO FM	9.1	16.1	12.3	9.3	16.4	12.5	6.2	20.4	12.8	5.1	15.7	9.5	6.4	24.7	15.8	21.3	5.2	13.9
KYLT AM	1.9	3.9	2.8	1.9	3.9	2.8	3.4	6.7	5.0	25.0	21.2	23.5	6.9	11.1	9.0			
KYSS FM	25.1	21.5	23.5	24.2	20.7	22.6	21.0	16.2	18.7	41.3	41.0	41.2	22.1	15.1	18.5	25.2	28.2	26.6
KZOQ FM	22.5	18.7	20.8	22.8	19.0	21.1	26.9	23.2	25.2				10.0	6.5	8.2			
KMBI FM		2.3	1.0		2.3	1.1		.3	.1					.5	.3		8.9	4.1
KUFM FM	5.3	11.3	8.0	5.4	11.4	8.1	8.2	9.1	8.6	.5	7.8	3.5	16.4	11.8	14.0	2.3	17.1	9.1
Total AQH Per.(00)	61.9	51.7	113.6	60.9	50.9	111.8	34.2	29.9	64.1	29.5	20.6	50.1	17.1	18.1	35.2	14.3	12.2	26.5

Figure 17.9. Section of Average Quarter-Hour Shares From Willhight Research Report, Missoula/Lolo, April 7–June 1, 1994

SOURCE: Willhight Research, Inc. Reprinted by permission.

Strategic Radio Research uses short, 6-minute telephone interviews primarily to query respondents aged 12 and older about the radio stations they listened to most in the past week and during different dayparts. Respondents are asked to list all the radio stations they listened to in the past week and their demographic characteristics—age, gender, ethnicity, occupation, education level, and household income. Additional questions about product usage may be included, depending on specific clients' needs, such as questions about brands of soda and beer purchased, cable channels viewed, frequency of movie attendance, and intended purchase of a new vehicle.

Strategic Radio Research interviews one respondent per household in samples of 550 to 8,000, depending on market size. Households are selected using proportionate stratified random sampling procedures based on working blocks of telephone exchanges located within specified geographic boundaries. The sampling frame consists of area market telephone directories supplemented with RDD numbers generated by Survey Sampling, Inc. Response rates range from 36% to 55%. Respondents are selected according to the following priority: a male aged 45 or older, a male aged 12 to 44, and a female aged 12 or older. Interviews are conducted over several days of each week of a survey period during weekday evening hours and at least one weekend day per week. Reports are available quarterly with weekly updates. Figure 17.10 shows a section of an AccuRatings report.

The AccuRatings method has some drawbacks. The data produced represent shares of preferred radio stations, and the past week as reported by respondents does not always refer to the same 7 days, but approximates to core radio listening in general. Also, quota sampling of respondents as opposed to random sampling compromises data representativeness.

RADAR

SRI operates and conducts Radio's All Dimension Audience Research surveys, which provide weekly network radio audience estimates for 48 weeks in a year. Reports are issued twice a year.

RADAR uses RDD procedures to select households. Next, a predesignated respondent is randomly selected from a list of all the respondents in each household. Repeated calls are made to contact the selected household and predesignated respondent. Respondents are asked about the previous 24 hours of radio listening, whether they listened to any radio stations during 3-hour periods, and the location of the listening. This information is obtained every

AccuRatings™

For "How to Read" Information, call
1-800-777-8877

STANDARD DEMO RANKER
PERSONS 18-24 (B= 850)

New York
Winter 1994
January 05 - March 13

Figure 17.10. Section of Standard Demo Ranker for Persons 18-24 From AccuRatings Report, New York, Winter 1994
SOURCE: Reprinted by permission. © 1998 by Strategic Media Research, Inc.

day for 7 days. RADAR response rates of 70% rank highest among the syndicated ratings services. Figure 17.11 shows the location of radio audiences generated from a RADAR report.

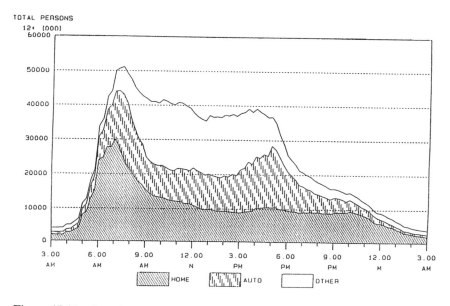

Figure 17.11. Location of Radio Audiences
SOURCE: Generated from RADAR Report, Fall 1993. Reprinted by permission.

When respondents cannot be reached on a particular day, they are asked to recall their radio listening during the previous day or days, and reliance on memory may lead to recall inaccuracies. In the absence of completed daily interviews for 7 days, a problem that arises on a limited basis, radio listening for the obtained days is ascribed to the missing days. Another possible problem is that, knowing that they will be reporting their radio listening, respondents may be influenced to change their listening behavior, thereby distorting their normal listening patterns.

Summary

All of the electronic media audience measurement services discussed in this chapter provide audience estimates of program or station audience size and composition. Depending on the method of data collection, type of sampling, fieldwork procedure, and measuring instrument, audience estimates vary from service to service.

Audimeters measure television exposure but not audiences of the programs; People Meters measure both but demand continual participation from respondents. The diary approach depends on memories, and the telephone interview may also be subject to faulty or biased recall. Response rates for all approaches have systematically declined in recent years, making the recruiting of a representative sample all the more difficult.

Future Prospects

The electronic media audience measurement industry has been developing new audience measurement systems that would require less active participation from audiences and be more respondent-friendly. These include a scanning system that recognizes all members of the household and logs all TV exposure for each family member, a pocket-radio People Meter that senses inaudible codes embedded in radio sound tracks, and a wristwatch that picks up signals from the sound tracks of televised advertisements. Critics, however, have called these new technologies intrusive and Orwellian, suggesting that respondents approached to participate in such surveys will either reject being recruited or be so aware they are being monitored that they will change their behavior as a consequence. Either outcome could lead to data unrepresentative of the vast population of television viewers and radio listeners. The debate continues, and the development of new technology to provide better electronic media audience measurement intensifies.

Notes

1. Statistical Research Inc., *CONTAM Report* (Westfield, NJ: Statistical Research Inc., 1989). See also Ronald Milavsky, "How Good Is the A. C. Nielsen People Meter System?" *Public Opinion Quarterly,* vol. 56, 1992, 102-115.

2. Hugh M. Beville, *Audience Rating* (Hillsdale, NJ: Lawrence Erlbaum, 1985).

3. Kenneth R. Clark, "Nielsen Loses More Points With TV Networks," *Chicago Tribune,* May 10, 1990.

4. Statistical Research Inc., *CONTAM Report.*

5. Milavsky, "How Good Is the A. C. Nielsen People Meter System?"

6. Elizabeth Jensen, "Networks Create Ratings Test System Out of Frustration With Nielsen Data," *Wall Street Journal,* February 4, 1994.

Consumer Purchasing, Starch, and STAS

Does Magazine Advertising Produce an Immediate Effect?

John Philip Jones

The reason this chapter appears in the second section of this book—that devoted to research before the advertising is run—is that it introduces the Starch readership system as a *pretesting* mechanism. Starch research is normally carried out after an advertisement has been exposed in national print media. It is of course still relevant in that use, so this chapter should also be studied alongside Chapters 24, 25, and 26 of this volume, which are concerned with postexposure measurement. However, in this chapter I mainly address the use of Starch for a different purpose—as a prescreening device for print campaigns.

Few analysts today dispute the fact that advertising can trigger immediate sales. However, the research that removed all ambiguity about this effect—pure single-source data analyzed by the Short-Term Advertising Strength (STAS) method (fully described in Chapter 24)—is confined to television advertising for repeat-purchase packaged goods.[1] When I carried out this work, I restricted it to television for totally practical reasons; it was certainly not my intention to treat magazines as a second-class medium fit only to supplement television by extending advertising coverage of light viewers.

In my direct professional experience, I have come across brands that have been built with the exclusive use of magazine advertising. And magazines' unquestionable but not universally recognized creative value deserves to be brought rather sharply to the attention of the advertising community. This is a job that I might well attempt in the future—but that is not my concern here.

This chapter addresses exclusively the question of magazines' *effectiveness* as an advertising medium. As I have explained, in my own research I was forced to concentrate on television, although in reporting on his original 1966 single-source experiment, on which my own research was modeled, Colin McDonald does at least make elliptical reference to other media: "In six out of nine product fields there was sufficient press advertising to look at [purchasing] measurement separately for press and television. We found the same effect tending to occur in both cases."[2]

In discussing my single-source work with advertising practitioners in many countries, I have found an exceptionally strong and increasing interest in the possibility of applying this technique to the measurement of the effectiveness of magazine advertising. There is a good possibility that the single-source research being carried out by A. C. Nielsen in Germany will in the future be extended from television also to magazines. McDonald's new work, employing the Adlab panel (described in Chapter 25), is also being extended into media other than television. And the Norwegian Gallup Institute, working with the Norwegian School of Management, has already begun a bold program to replicate McDonald's research, but on a much bigger scale—a scale large enough to embrace print media, which are very important in Norway. The first findings of this research are available although not yet published, but I have learned enough to be struck by the similarities between what the Norwegians are discovering and my own STAS findings from the United States and Germany.[3]

At about the time I learned of the preliminary Norwegian results, I received rather unexpectedly a battery of unpublished historical data from the Starch organization in New York. I found this material arresting. The Starch information, which was assembled over the 17-year period 1944 through 1960, is nothing less than a pioneer form of pure single-source research applied to magazines. And the beginnings of this research preceded McDonald's experiment by more than two decades! It would be interesting to speculate as to why Starch has not until now opened this archive to the research community. However, because of the importance of the results, it is more urgent to concentrate immediately on some of the remarkable findings.

The Starch Method

The appendix to this chapter will remind readers about Starch's basic system of collecting advertising recognition data. Bearing this in mind, I shall now describe the relationship between Starch's data on advertising coverage (i.e., media exposure/readership) and its information on consumer purchasing. Pure single-source research relates the buying of identified brands by individual consumers to those same consumers' exposure to advertising for those same brands shortly before the purchasing took place. My own STAS effect is measured by the difference (in buying occasions) between purchases of the brand in the households that had received advertising for it during the previous 7 days and purchases in the households that had not. The Starch research does essentially the same thing.

The basis of single-source research is the method familiar from controlled experiments in the hard sciences. It uses matched samples that are identical in all respects except one—the presence or absence of advertising for the identified brand during the period immediately before purchase. The conditions for such controlled experimental research are described by Starch in clear, albeit general, terms:

1. There must be at least two groups of subjects (plants, animals, or people) which are either identical or closely comparable in all important aspects.
2. One of these groups is subjected to a specific amount of the condition or factor concerned, such as the food, or drug, or kind of diet being investigated. This constitutes the exposed or test group.
3. The second group, comparable in all important characteristics, is not subjected to the condition or factor to be investigated. This constitutes the base or control group.

Figure 18.1.   Ad Versus Adless Households

4. Tests or measurements in terms of definite units must be administered to both groups to determine effects.[4]

The Starch work was based on studies of 45,000 advertisements in the *Saturday Evening Post* and *Life* over the years 1944 through 1960. As I shall explain in more detail later in this chapter, Starch used two separate research techniques, both of which can be described as pure single-source methods:

1. Starch compared consumer purchasing by readers of the issues containing advertisements for the brand, with purchasing by readers of the issues not containing such advertisements. I call this the *opportunity-to-see* (OTS) method.
2. Starch compared consumer purchasing by readers of an advertisement for the brand in the issues containing such advertisements with purchasing by nonreaders of such advertisements. I call this the *single-issue readership* (SIR) method.

The two systems produce broadly similar results.

With both these techniques there is no reason to expect any difference in demographics or psychographics between buyers and nonbuyers, and both groups of consumers can be expected to receive the same exogenous, nonadvertising, marketing stimuli—seasonal ups and downs in the brand's sales, the panoply of competitive brands, promotional activity in the market, and so on. The design of the Starch research obeys the scientific "test and control" requirements.

There is a close parallel with the design of my own STAS research, in which I designate the test and control groups the *Ad* and *Adless* households, respectively, as illustrated in Figure 18.1. In my research, the Ad households and the Adless households are not fixed groups. They rotate across the research sample in an apparently haphazard fashion, but they are in fact driven by a single stimulus—whether or not the advertising for the brand that was bought had come into the home during the period before purchase.

During the 7 days before buying a brand, the purchasing households that have received advertising for it are called the Stimulated group or the Ad households, because they have received advertising plus all the other marketing stimuli. The buyers who have received no advertising for the brand—the Baseline group or the Adless households—have received all the other stimuli but not the advertising. There is nothing special about the demographics or the psychographics of the Stimulated or the Baseline groups. Large numbers of households cycle into these groups. But as explained, the process is not stochastic, because the sole discriminator between the Stimulated and Baseline groups is reception of the brand's advertising. There is an independent input that produces a measurable effect. Starch's equivalent (but differently named) households behave in the same way.

The OTS Method

With the opportunity-to-see method, Starch measures advertising's short-term effect by isolating two groups of people: (a) buyers of a brand who have read an issue of a magazine containing an advertisement for it (Stimulated or Ad households), and (b) buyers of a brand who have read an issue of the same periodical not containing an advertisement for it (Baseline or Adless households). The number of buyers in the second group is deducted from the number in the first group to calculate the advertising effect. Purchase data are collected from consumer responses to closed-ended questions.

This method has two features of note beyond its remarkable simplicity. First, it makes no attempt to assess recall of specific advertisements. The independent variable—the presence of advertising in the publication—provides an opportunity to see and no more. This precisely parallels my STAS method. The advertising is independently observed, and the purchasing data are reported by the respondents. Starch's alternative system (discussed below) is slightly more complicated. Second, the research measures *users,* not purchases. It measures penetration, or purchaser level; it does not take account of purchase volume, or even the buying occasions I use for my own STAS research. In the calculations, a Starch purchaser receives a statistical weight of 1. In my research, a STAS purchaser who makes one purchase also receives a weight of 1. However, a STAS purchaser who makes two purchases receives a weight of 2, three purchases receive a weight of 3, and so on. In practice, however, most of the STAS purchases are in the one-purchase group, so that Starch and STAS measure approximately the same thing.

Because Starch collects data from single advertisements and single-occasion buyers, and not incremental purchases from increased advertising pressure, it is not possible to construct an advertising response function. However, because Starch shows a clear (and dramatic) single-exposure effect, judgment suggests that what we are seeing is probably the first observation on a diminishing returns curve.

Starch employed the OTS method to measure the effect of advertising on 73 brands over the period 1959 through 1964. The research covered 707 advertisements for food products, household supplies, drug products, candy, soft drinks, toothpaste, toilet soap, beer, cigarettes, and gasoline. The aggregate sample consisted of 110,000 men and women.

Using the arithmetical method that I use to calculate STAS, with the Baseline indexed at 100, Starch's Stimulated "purchaser" level across all 73 brands and 707 advertisements was 119 (a finding significant at the 99% probability level). For comparison, the average STAS calculated from a single advertisement exposure for my 78 brands advertised on television is an indexed level of 118. I am sure that the reader will be as startled as I was at this similarity.

Starch also made a longitudinal study of 42 brands, averaging purchaser rates in the week before an advertisement for the brand, during the advertising week, and the week after. Using the same STAS system of calculation, the index numbers for all the brands together were 100 before, 115 during, and 100 after. The short-term temporary effect is clear—another parallel with STAS.

Data were tracked over a year (fall 1964 through fall 1965) for Campbell's soup, Dial soap, and Tab soda. In all cases there was a consistent relationship between the buyer rates of the Stimulated group and the Baseline group. With the large brands Campbell's and Dial, the ratios between the two groups remained constant. With the smaller brand Tab, the gap tended to open out over time. This is an interesting point, demonstrating advertising's growing long-term effect (or more precisely its *long* long-term effect), which operates through a process of mutual reinforcement between consumers' satisfaction with the functional properties of the brand and the added values built by the advertising. It produces a number of measurable *brand-related* effects, one of the most important of which is the building of purchase frequency among the brand's corpus of consumers.[5]

TABLE 18.1 Starch Single-Issue Readership Method

1. Calculate the readership of the advertisement for Brand S:

"Seen–Associated"	30%
Nonreaders	70%
Total	100%

2. Calculate the brand buyers within each readership group:

"Seen–Associated"	15.2% buyers
30% × 15.2%	4.56 per hundred readers
Nonreaders	10.8% buyers
70% × 10.8%	7.56 per hundred readers
Total buyers	12.12 per hundred readers

3. Deduct from the "Seen–Associated" buyers those who would have bought without the advertising stimulus (assumed to be the same proportion as the nonreader buyers):

"Seen–Associated" buyers	4.56 per hundred readers
Minus 10.8% of "Seen–Associated" buyers (30%)	−3.24 per hundred readers
Incremental buyers generated by the advertisement	1.32 per hundred readers

4. Percentage incremental buyers generated by the advertisement on the base of all buyers: 1.32 is 11 percent of 12.12.

Using the STAS method:	
Baseline (unstimulated buyers)	
(12.12 − 1.32)	10.80 = 100
STAS Differential Index	12.12 = 113

The SIR Method

The single-issue readership method is an extension of Starch's established "Reading and Noting" research technique (described in the appendix to this chapter). The test group comprises brand buyers who are proven readers of an advertisement for the brand (using Starch's "Seen–Associated" criterion). The control group comprises buyers who are not proven readers of it.

The calculation is reasonably simple. One of its features is the way in which it compensates for the buyers in the test group who would have bought in any event, even without the advertising stimulus. The calculation is in four parts, as shown in Table 18.1; the figures used in the table to illustrate it relate to a brand of toilet soap, coded Brand S.

The SIR method has the practical advantage of being (as mentioned) an extension of Starch's ongoing "Reading and Noting" service. This means that a ready-made evaluative service can, without too much trouble, be offered to the advertising industry. There is also a very real advantage in being able to factor readership into the calculations—a point to which I will return at the end of this chapter. Readers should be reminded, however, of two complications. These do not seriously impede the system, but I believe they impose limits on how far the data can be extrapolated.

The first and rather obvious complication is that the research is based on two separate streams of data, both derived from personal interviews: reported readership of the advertisement and reported brand purchasing. This is a softer data collection method than either Starch's OTS system, in which appearance or nonappearance of the advertisement in the magazine is independently observed, or my own STAS method, in which both types of data are collected mechanically (purchasing via in-home scanners, and television exposure by meters on the television sets, supplemented by a log of the commercials that appear on-air compiled by A. C. Nielsen's "Monitor Plus").

There is, however, one problem concerning collection of all the data from personal interviews that has been proven not to occur with Starch. In any personal interview in which two variables are being examined, it is possible for there to be a contamination between them. Although it is normally assumed that there is one-way causality, with advertising stimulating purchase, it is perfectly possible for the purchase of a brand to trigger greater awareness of advertising for it through the operation of selective perception, and possible also that purchasing might be overstated because of the inclusion of advertising readership questions.

Does this interaction of the two variables distort the figures by exaggerating the connection between advertising awareness and recorded purchasing, or between recorded purchasing and advertising awareness? The answer is no. The Starch organization, conscious of the potential problem of purchasing affecting advertising awareness, made sure that the purchasing questions were separated from the readership ones: They were included as a trailer after readership had been explored. And to examine the possibility of contamination from readership to recorded buying, Starch carried out a practical test. Over five successive issues of the *Saturday Evening Post,* matched samples of respondents were used to collect two separate sets of data: (a) on readership and purchasing, and (b) on purchasing alone. Data were collected from 1,030 respondents on 37 advertisements for 18 brands. The results were that there were virtually no differences in purchasing levels between the two groups.

A second and more subtle problem relates to the nature of "Reading and Noting" itself. This is described as recognition of a particular advertisement in a specific publication. But this all depends on what is meant by *recognition*. "Seen–Associated" describes whether the advertisement has been both seen and associated by the respondent with the brand. Yet laboratory experiments with eye-movement cameras have demonstrated unambiguously that consumers actually see (i.e., their eyes alight upon) a far higher proportion of advertisements than they can consciously recollect in the Starch "Reading and Noting" interviews.[6] Additionally, some recorded readers do not actually look at the advertisement (because they are probably remembering it from a different context).

There is undoubtedly a kind of perceptual screen in each consumer's mind. The consumer sees advertisements (in fact, he or she sees a high proportion of advertisements in any publication), but the perceptual screen keeps a substantial number of them from entering his or her conscious memory. "Seen–Associated" would therefore be more correctly described as "Seen–Screened–Registered in the Conscious Mind–Associated With the Brand."

These two problems are real enough, but I do not believe that they invalidate Starch's method, so long as the figures are aggregated. Individual Starch tests of the same advertisements show consistent results, and the broader the database, the more likely it will be that erratic statistical variations will wash out.

However, I do believe that attempts to extrapolate the Starch findings (e.g., to estimate the incremental sales dollars generated by a dollar of investment in the tested advertisement) drive the figures too far. In comparing advertisement with advertisement, such extrapolations exaggerate small differences in the initial readership and purchasing data. And in any event, quantifying the sales and profit return from advertising expenditure—in either absolute or incremental terms—is a much more complex matter than is suggested by the Starch calculations. One must quantify the value of absolute or incremental sales and deduct the dollar amount of the direct (but not indirect) cost of production of the absolute or incremental volume. Only after this is done is it possible to estimate advertising's absolute or marginal productivity and hence its break-even level.[7]

I shall not discuss Starch's extrapolation into the realm of sales forecasting. Starch used the nonextrapolated SIR method to evaluate 20,000 advertisements, and estimated that on average an advertisement with a "Seen–Associated" readership of 30% generated a purchaser increase of 14% (equivalent to a STAS Differential Index of 114). Compare the figure of 119 for the OTS method—again, we are in the same ballpark.

I have seen fewer than 20 examples of individual brands measured by the two Starch systems, and I do not know how typical these brands are, but the advertising responses do, in fact, seem to vary a great deal. As an example, five advertisements for Campbell's soup achieved (SIR) advertising effectiveness levels (indexed according to the STAS method) of 124, 203, 114, 113, and 106. Note that the "Seen–Associated" readership of these advertisements also differed, with figures of 38%, 64%, 64%, 64%, and 57%, respectively. These two measures should now be considered independently. And this brings me to the really important point about the Starch research.

Starch can locate the advertisements that work best. The effectiveness of print advertising has two separate aspects, which the Starch SIR system enables us to untangle:

1. *Readership,* which can vary greatly among advertisements. Note that with print advertising, readership (i.e., the crude size of the audience) is to a large degree determined by the creative message of the advertisement—its ability to make the advertisement go through the cognitive stages of being "Seen–Screened–Registered in the Conscious Mind–Associated With the Brand." Television advertising does not work in this way. With a magazine, the page is easily turned, but with television, if the set is switched on to the program in which an advertisement appears, the audience tends to see the advertisement. This means that with television, we can more or less rely on STAS as the measure of effectiveness. With magazines, we have to look also at readership.

2. *Intrinsic selling power,* or STAS, which Starch can measure in a similar way to the method worked out for television advertising.

The Starch SIR system can produce simple and comprehensive data to measure both the above variables. The information can be produced reasonably quickly: It is probably sufficient to aggregate the findings of no more than half a dozen Starch tests of a single advertisement to produce a large enough sample. Media can therefore be used selectively and with minimal reach and repetition so as to reduce the media expenditure before Starch produces the test results. I do not think I exaggerate when I say that I consider the system a breakthrough.

Appendix: The Starch and STAS Systems

Starch "Reading and Noting"

Starch conducts personal interviews with a sample of 200 to 400 readers of a specific issue of a magazine or newspaper. These are distributed across 20-30 metropolitan areas. There is a male or female or mixed-sex sample, according to the type of publication and/or brand examined. There are three levels of recognition: The interviewer pages through a journal issue, pauses at each advertisement, and asks the respondent

> whether he or she recognizes the advertisement (this produces the "Noting" score);
> whether he or she associates it with the brand name (this produces the "Seen–Associated" score); and
> whether he or she has read at least 50% of the copy (this produces the "Read Most" score).

STAS

STAS quantifies the effect of advertising on purchasing, as measured by pure single-source research. To date, STAS has been derived exclusively from television advertising. A brand's share of market in the households that had not received advertising for it during the period before purchase is the Baseline STAS. Its share in the households that had received advertising for it is the Stimulated STAS. Stimulated STAS minus Baseline STAS is the brand's STAS Differential. This is indexed on the Baseline, and it represents the net effect on sales of the intrinsic, creative content of the advertisement.

STAS varies widely from brand to brand, but the average for all 78 American brands covered in my original research is a STAS Differential Index of 124. As explained in this chapter, I calculated the effect of all advertisements for the brand entering the home during the 7 days before purchase. Starch covers one exposure only. I can, however, isolate the effect of a single exposure. This single-exposure STAS effect accounts for an average of 73% of the sales effect of multiple exposures. Applying this proportion to my overall average STAS Differential Index of 124 gives the figure of 118 already mentioned in this chapter.

Notes

1. John Philip Jones, *When Ads Work: New Proof That Advertising Triggers Sales* (New York: Simon & Schuster-Lexington, 1995); John Philip Jones, "Single-Source Research Begins to Fulfill Its Promise," *Journal of Advertising Research,* May/June 1995, 9-16.

2. Colin McDonald, "An Effective Frequency Pilot Study," in Michael J. Naples (ed.), *Effective Frequency: The Relationship Between Frequency and Advertising Effectiveness* (New York: Association of National Advertisers, 1979), 99.

3. Thorolf Helgesen, Norwegian School of Management, personal communication, June 2, 1997. Helgesen gave me a summary of his report to the Norwegian Research Society on the recent Gallup research.

4. All references to the Starch research are taken from two unpublished documents, "Measuring Advertising Readership and Results" (1996) and "NETAPPS Measuring Product Sales Made by Advertising" (1960).

5. I discuss the various *long* long-term effects in *When Ads Work,* 62-64. I use the phrase *internal momentum* because it is less clumsy than *long long-term.*

6. John Philip Jones, *What's in a Name? Advertising and the Concept of Brands* (New York: Simon & Schuster-Lexington, 1986), 134-138.

7. I discuss this matter in John Philip Jones, "The Double Jeopardy of Sales Promotions," *Harvard Business Review,* September/October 1990, 145-152.

Part III

Research After the
Advertising Has Run

19

Retail Research, Consumer Panels, Store Checking

John Philip Jones

Retail Research

The retail audit method was invented by Bev Murphy and first implemented by A. C. Nielsen during the early 1930s. I will describe the original Nielsen auditing mechanism here, although since 1990, the data have been collected with the use of scanners. Today both Nielsen and Information Resources Inc. carry out retail research with scanners.

The most important data provided by retail research are estimates of consumer sales, based on a panel of shops. When the original auditing system was used, a simple arithmetical calculation was made in each store: measurement of deliveries of goods over the checking period (in the United States, 2 months), plus inventories at the beginning of the period, minus inventories at the end. Sales out of the store during the period could be measured accurately using this calculation. The traditional retail audit system tabulated the data bimonthly, with six reports per annum.

Scanner systems now capture the same information with greater ease and speed. Information is provided for all brands and pack sizes in a category. By adding the findings from all the shops in the panel, analysts can assemble a large accumulation that is grossed up to estimate total sales in the country, the share of each brand and pack size, and how these change over time. Short- and long-term trends are detailed, as are the specific strengths and weaknesses of brands, varieties, and sizes.

As well as consumer sales, the research provides data on distribution and display and on retail deliveries and inventories. One ever-refreshing feature of retail data is that they are an observed measure of sales, based on aggregated consumer behavior, and are not a monitor of people's memories or opinions, with the notorious problems such research entails.[1]

Some important limitations to retail research should however be borne in mind. First, the classes of stores covered may account for only a limited proportion of the sales of the brands in a particular product field. The retail trade is a dynamic business, and the changes are sometimes greater and subtler than one might imagine. This points to the wisdom of collecting consumer panel data to supplement those from retail research.

Consumer Panels

A consumer panel, which monitors what homemakers actually buy day by day, does not count as large a volume of sales as retail research, but the data collection covers purchases from all types of stores and not just the store types monitored by retail research. A consumer panel therefore has a wider but weaker database than retail research. The two types of investigation complement one another.

But there is another reason consumer panels are important. Measurements of shop sales are the result of an aggregation of a large number of individual consumer purchases. Internal movements inside the aggregates are concealed. The actual people buying in one period could be different, the same, or partly different and partly the same as those in a second period. Retail research cannot provide any means of tracking down these differences; it cannot analyze whether individual consumers continue to buy the same, or less, or more than before. When we study the inner workings of marketing, we need to find out how advertising influences consumers, the people to whom it is primarily addressed. For this, we need consumer panel data. These enable us to examine both consumers' buying patterns and their demographics.

Consumer panels record the detailed purchases of brands and varieties in individual homes, and the information is aggregated to represent the total market. The basic data were originally collected from questionnaires completed by hand (the "paper-and-pencil" method). As in retail research, scanners are now used. These can be either those at the store checkout or handheld scanners supplied to individual homes. Data are normally tabulated weekly.

Store Checking

In their day-to-day work, advertising agencies invariably think of the final consumer (when they are not worrying about the client). On the client side, "consumer orientation" is considered the mark of the more sophisticated type of manufacturer. But both agencies and advertisers should remind themselves that the retail store is the battleground on which much of the competitive struggle takes place. An equally important point is that the most readily accessible information on both consumer purchasing and competitive activity is information gathered from retail outlets.

The best method for measuring retail sales is, of course, properly conducted research, as described in this chapter. However, conclusions that provide serviceable approximations of the truth can be drawn from the simple procedure of store checking.

In store checking, the researcher visits at least one store (preferably a number of stores) and counts (in the case of more than one store, averages) the numbers of facings of the various brands on the shelves. A facing is the front pack on the shelf, excluding the packs ranked behind it. These counts/averages allow the researcher to make a guesstimate of the various brands' market shares, because shelves are filled in such a way that better-selling brands receive more space than do poorer-selling ones. This type of store checking tends to underrepresent large brands slightly and to overrepresent small ones, because the latter are normally given a little more shelf space than their sales justify. The researcher should take this factor into account in making final estimates.

Here is a description of a typical store check carried out in 1985. I am using this ancient study because accurate historical market figures are available with which to check it. The market examined is cat food, and the store visited was Peter's, in the university section of Syracuse, New York. The process took about an hour. The findings were as follows:

1. Brands of cat food occupy about 150 feet of shelf space. This suggests a relatively large category, although much smaller, for instance, than breakfast cereals, because of the relatively smaller size of the user base. The relative shelf allocations suggest that the breakfast cereal category is more than twice the size of cat food.

2. The cat food market is segmented into three parts (canned, dry, and moist cat food) that differ from one another in functional characteristics. Canned is the largest segment; the number of packs on the shelves suggests that it represents a little under half the total value of sales. The display of the dry product indicates that it represents rather more than a third of the total sales value. Moist cat food accounts for the remainder—slightly under 20%.

3. The largest brand in the canned sector appears to be 9 Lives (with more than 20% of the market), followed by Buffet, Kal Kan, and Purina. The combined shares of the four are estimated to be about 60%. The largest brands in the dry sector are Cat Chow, Meow Mix, Friskies, Special Dinner, and 9 Lives, which are not dissimilar from one another in market share, and among them account for about 60%. The moist sector seems to be dominated by Tender Vittles, which alone probably accounts for 60% of sales value.

4. There is a great deal of commonality in pack sizes. It is estimated that at least 70% of sales of canned cat food are in the 6-ounce size. The dry market is dominated by 18-ounce boxes and 56-ounce bags. The moist market is more fragmented by pack size, but a third of sales appear to be accounted for by the 12-ounce size and another third by the 18-ounce size. As in the breakfast cereals market, commonality of pack size is not accompanied by uniformity of price.

A broad confirmation of the accuracy of the above estimates is provided by data published at about the time this store check took place. Sales estimates relating to 1982 were published in 1984.[2] The total value of the cat food market was estimated to be $1.6 billion. The market share estimates that follow are value-based.

The 1982 market shares of the different segments of the cat food market were as follows: canned, 51%; dry, 36%; and moist, 13%. (In 1982, moist was, however, the fastest-growing sector, which means that the store check estimate of 20% may not be unreasonable for 1985.)

In 1982, 9 Lives, Buffet, Kal Kan, and Purina together accounted for 61% of sales value in the canned sector. Cat Chow, Meow Mix, Friskies, Special Dinner, and 9 Lives accounted for 67% of the dry market value. Tender Vittles alone accounted for 67% of sales value in the moist sector.

Government estimates of the value of sales are always some years in arrears. That for breakfast cereals was put at $2.5 billion in 1977.[3] This figure increased by 1985, suggesting that the guesstimate of the relative sizes of the cat food and breakfast cereal categories was a reasonable approximation.

Notes

1. John Philip Jones, *What's in a Name? Advertising and the Concept of Brands* (New York: Simon & Schuster-Lexington, 1986).

2. *Advertising Age Yearbook* (Chicago: Crain, 1984), 248-252.

3. U.S. Department of Commerce, Bureau of the Census, *Census of Manufactures* (Washington, DC: Government Printing Office, 1981).

Campaign Evaluation Through Modeling

Simon Broadbent

It is only when advertising is in the marketplace that we can evaluate its real effectiveness. Good advertising evaluation, paradoxically, does not concentrate on the advertising; rather, it considers the brand advertised. What has advertising added, and how have these values affected consumer behavior?

This chapter concentrates on the clues that sales data give us about the advertising contribution. Unfortunately, the marketplace is also where many other factors interfere with what we see. Some people believe that these disturbances are so great we can never see advertising results. This is unnecessarily gloomy. Econometrics, modeling, and experimentation are the tools we use to disentangle this confusion. These are all branches of statistics—and not the simplest. This kind of evaluation is far from a mechanically applied procedure that the beginner can confidently apply. Rather, we embark on explorations of discovery, with many rocks to avoid on the way. An experienced navigator is recommended. As with statistics generally, there are three stages we go through: data definition and collection, description, and analysis.

There is, however, also an earlier stage: We have to be carefully explicit about the mechanisms and relationships that we believe are controlling what we see. We need a draft model even before we collect data, let alone decide what descriptions are likely to be relevant, or what calculations to carry out. In different words: To interpret measurements we need a theory about effects. If our theory is unsound or incomplete, we can hardly make reliable deductions. As a standard textbook on econometrics states:

> First there is the assumption that the behaviour of econometric variables is determined by the joint and simultaneous operation of a number of economic relations. Second is the assumption that the model, though admittedly a simplification of the complexities of reality, will capture the crucial features of the . . . system being studied, and third is the hope that from the understanding that the model gives of the system we may predict the future movements of the system and possibly control those movements.[1]

Note the caution in "assumption," "simplification," "hope," and "possibly."

Another authority concludes: "Econometric models . . . generally fail to represent advertising processes except possibly over a limited range. . . . Add the problems of collinearity, autocorrelation and simultaneity."[2] These last three terms mean that two so-called independent variables may actually move together, one period's data may depend on the previous period, and changes in, say, advertising may take place at the same time as changes in another causative factor. I would add warnings about weaknesses in the data and the fact that most data are concerned exclusively with short-term effects.

An example will show the sort of problem we may meet. Suppose Friday is the main shopping day in a town: 40% of the week's food sales are made on that day. In the local newspaper, Friday's issue is full of store advertising, coupons, price offers, and so on; of all food advertising, 80% appears on Friday.

A simple analyst might argue that on the other 6 days of the week the 20% of advertising is associated with 10% of food sales each day. When advertising rises on Friday, sales per day increase fourfold. Hence, it might be said, increased advertising "causes" four times as much sales as normal. If it seems to you that this conclusion is too naive ever to be advanced, be aware that many people have analyzed annual sales and advertising in just this way.

We can all see an alternative explanation: that advertisers are fighting for volume share, and it makes sense to place advertisements on the day when sales are highest. Sales timing causes advertising timing, and not vice versa. The regularity of the phenomenon does not prove that the naive assumption was correct, nor will all the statistical testing in the world.

The next step might be to investigate how advertising affects the volume shares on Fridays, not the total volume. A little thought will show that the coupon and price effects on the shares are likely to be confounded with the advertising effect. More thought will suggest that the model supposes that advertising has all its effect within 24 hours, but that some of the sales on other days might also be related to advertising.

Enough has now been said about difficulties, vigilance, and skepticism. Modeling can be helpful; it can provide better numbers than "seat of the pants" analysis. I will now describe the way to approach it.

The Model

First, define what it is you wish to explain. Often this will be your brand's sales, over a certain period of time, in certain defined sales outlets. Most work is done with volume sales, because price is probably a factor causing variation in volume, so revenue is not as helpful a number to analyze. You will probably measure total sales over a number of pack sizes (or whatever variations you make in your product, be it insurance policies, airline seats, automobiles, or whatever).

The time interval used usually depends on your data source. A day, a week, 4 weeks, and a month are the most common. To detect short-term advertising effects, the shorter the period the better.

Sales are the product of your brand's share and total category sales (note that defining your category, or with whom you are really competing, is not trivial). It is sensible to separate brand share as the variable you hope to influence most directly by your marketing activity, including advertising, and category volume as more influenced by broader factors, such as seasonality, weather, and economic trends (though advertising might affect category volume also).

Next, consider what else, besides advertising, might have affected brand share. With experience, you may produce a rather long list. You need to allow for these factors before you deliver your evaluation of the campaign.

For advertising itself, you could try to separate the copy that was run, the media used, the advertisement sizes chosen, the times of insertion, the numbers of opportunities to see (by what audiences?), and so on—not only for your brand, but for its competitors (in what detail?).

In packaged goods, you may also take into account the brand's distribution, its availability on the shelf or elsewhere in the store, its display, and all such store activities. Equivalents may exist in other categories.

You need to know all the other marketing activity that has been undertaken—the features, couponing, pricing, promotions, nontraditional communications, and so on. Again, competitors' actions are likely to have influenced your sales.

There are likely to have been other events—product or packaging changes, editorial mentions in media, or whatever—that also affected sales. Not all of these can be numerically measured.

Fortunately, many successes have been reported with models that use only a few of all these possible variables. They have been successful in that they gave sensible and usable explanations for why sales varied, often accounting for most of this variation.

With advertising, a single number may suffice to describe your campaign (with classification by copy if more than one campaign ran). The number is often total TV ratings (standardized for spot length) or total advertising expenditure (sometimes standardized for media cost inflation). When several media are used, you may analyze them as separate causative factors or add them together on the basis of expenditure. Essentially, you use advertising weight. Quality, or effectiveness, is estimated from the data. (There is an added complication due to time, which will be considered later.)

For competitors' advertising, aggregate expenditure in the category is often a good enough explanatory input, though occasionally you may look at individual brands. For the other variables, percentage of brand distribution (in the sense of front-of-shop availability, and weighted by commodity turnover as is normal) is one commonly used explainer. Price is another, often relative to the category total (or to total competition if your brand has a large share of the category). That is, category price is given by total consumer expenditure on the category divided by the volume sold. A similar figure for your brand, times 100 and divided by category price, gives an index for your relative price. It is equivalent to dividing 100 times your brand's share of the value (money) spent by its share of volume.

If you accept this limited list, you have a time series consisting of your brand's share and other series of possible explainers—often advertising, distribution, and price.

Note that this work is on aggregated data. A separate specialty, not described here, attempts to study individual behavior and to build up other sorts of groups than just the total.

Advertising's Lagged Effects

You could use as your advertising measure the ratings that supported your brand in each period. For long periods, such as a year, this is not unreasonable. For short periods, such as a week, common sense—and evidence—suggests that advertising's effects are not likely to be simultaneous. They probably last a few days or weeks at least.

So you need to replace your series of weekly ratings (0, 0, 200, 200, 0, 0) with something that allows in each week for some effects of previous advertising. The usual assumption is that there is a decay parameter (say, d) such that in a typical week, the effect in the previous week is decayed or reduced by d. Typically, d is between 0.5 and 0.9.

This calculation is done before modeling starts. You may set up several series of lagged advertising effects, called adstocks, for different parameters d, and try each of these out in order to decide on the decay rate.[3] For example, if there had been no previous advertising, the series of ratings above would be replaced by 0, 0, 13, 35, 42, 37, . . . in the case that $d = 0.88$ (which implies that half the total effect has been felt by 6 weeks—a 6-week half-life). If $d = 0.64$ (2-week half-life), the series would be 0, 0, 44, 100, 92, 59, and so on.

First Descriptive Plots

The essential step before modeling is to say exactly how you expect the variables to relate to each other. This does not mean that you must quantify these relationships (you do this later). It means, what sort of relationships? What is your theory, your mental picture? To help you decide this, it is useful to plot the raw data.

There are two straightforward ways to plot the time series: as line plots against time, and as scatterplots (*xy* plots) for one variable against another. In the latter case it is useful to show the period date or number at each *xy* position (for example, *x* might be price, *y* might be sales, and the data label might be week number).

The most important plot against time, showing what you have to explain, is your brand's share as a line plot against time. Are sales roughly steady, but with peaks and troughs? Or is there also a discernible trend (the share is rising or falling)?

Next you look for relationships between your variables: Do sales peaks correspond to high adstock? To low price? Are your adstock peaks at times of low price? Or of high distribution?

So far, it has been assumed you are looking at your brand only. A proper examination will cover at least your major competitors. You will, for example, look to see who loses at your peaks, who gains in your troughs. How does your adstock compare with that of your competitors? Is everyone advertising at the same time? It is possible to make these searches systematic, and to look not at each brand on its own, but at all the major brands (over selected periods) simultaneously.[4] For example, a scatterplot of great importance shows the brands' relative prices on the *x*-axis at two periods (the most recent year and the year before that, for example). It shows their sales shares on the *y*-axis.

So you see which brands are getting relatively dearer or cheaper, and which are rising or falling in sales. A sales rise when price fell may be simply a price effect. But a sales rise when price was steady or rose probably means the brand's base or strength or equity is increasing, and it is often a major advertising objective to do just that.

Further, the relative positions of the brands also show their strength. If brand A sells more than B, and A is at a lower price, this may be easily understood. If A sells more at the same or at a higher price than B, it must be doing something better.

The Simple Model

Before you "fit" the model, as described below, you have to state what it is. A simple linear model, for example, is as follows:

$$Sales = Base + Ad\ Effect + Price\ Effect + Error.$$

Here the base is a constant; ad effect might be

$$\text{Ad Coefficient} \times \text{Adstock}$$

and price effect might be

$$\text{Price Coefficient} \times \text{Relative Price.}$$

Econometricians more often use a logarithmic or multiplicative model (the two are mathematically identical). This model builds in diminishing returns, often a sensible assumption. The log model is

$$\text{Log(Sales)} = \text{Base} * \text{Log(Ad Effect)} + \text{Log(Price Effect)} + \text{Error.}$$

The multiplicative model is

$$\text{Sales} = \text{Base} \times \text{Ad Effect} \times \text{Price Effect} \times (1 + \text{Error}).$$

In all these expressions, the coefficients are going to be estimated in the next stage. The skill lies in deciding what to include, what you can safely leave out, and what interactions are being ignored.

Error is simply the term into which everything falls that you cannot explain in the model. If it is large and variable, this means that a lot of relevant explainers have not been included in the model. If it is small, then the variables you have chosen are associated with most sales changes. But remember the example given above concerning advertising on shopping days. A "good" explanation does not prove causality.

The model you hypothesize may not be the one you conclude is most reasonable. The most likely change is that a variable you thought might affect sales turns out not to have significant effect.

More complex models have been used—for example, with different shapes of response to advertising weight—but the above covers most work. If no effect can be seen with the simple model, complications will probably not give convincing results.

Beginners sometimes think that modeling addresses the request, "Look for all the ways advertising might work in my case." This is not correct. You have to specify the model, you decide "how advertising works"—and you may be wrong.

Remember that the usual adstock model measures only direct, short-term, sales volume effects of advertising. This is not all that advertising is for; it may not be all advertising is doing; the findings probably underestimate the benefits you get.

Regression

Most people nowadays have access to computer packages that accept data like those described above, and by an ordinary least squares method can give estimates for the coefficients. Read a statistical textbook to find out how regression works. It is the most common method used in modeling, though there are other ways of fitting a model than ordinary least squares.

Following are some key terms you will find in any statistical package, along with advice on their meanings:

- *Constant:* Regression always assumes that sales vary around some amount that is fixed and that does not depend on the independent variables. But in commerce, no sales are "constant"; they need continuous support.
- *Dependent variable:* This is sales—but to say so fixes the direction of causality. As I have pointed out, there can be circumstances in which sales cause advertising.
- *Independent variables:* Statistical packages normally assume that the causative variables, or explainers, or measures of marketing activity, are statistically independent. This is very unlikely to be true, and causes great problems. Plot one "independent" variable against another to see whether this is the case. Or use a correlation analysis. Even if current values look independent, the distribution and trade relations you enjoy, and the price you are able to charge when your brand advertises, could not be taken for granted if you were to stop advertising.
- R^2: A number between 0 and 1; the proportion of the variation in sales that is accounted for by the regression. You do not have to get this close to 1 to make the estimates of the coefficients usable.
- *Coefficient:* Each independent variable has a coefficient, the value of which is estimated by the regression.
- *t value:* The package estimates for each coefficient its standard error. The t value is the ratio of the coefficient to the standard error. The package may equivalently give you the probability that the relationship between independent and this dependent variable is not due to chance: 0.90 or 0.95 or greater is often accepted, corresponding roughly to t over 2.0. A small probability or small t means that the coefficient could be zero and that the independent variable may have no "real" effect. But this depends on what other explainers are included. For example, if

advertising helps get distribution, but both advertising and distribution are offered as explainers, you might see advertising with a low t, distribution with a high t. But offer advertising alone and it might now have a high t. A high t is more important in estimating advertising's effect than a high R^2.

- *Elasticity:* A useful concept, rarely calculated in statistical packages, elasticity is derived from the coefficient. It gives the percentage change in sales for a 1% change in the independent variable. Calculate the price elasticity, for example, as the price coefficient times average price divided by average sales.

It is hard to give rules for writing the initial model or choosing which variables to keep in the regression you finally select as your best explanation. Your plots may, for example, show outlying observations; you then decide whether these are due to nonrepeatable circumstances that you wish to exclude; inclusion or exclusion may have a strong influence on the results.

Experience is the way to learn what is normal, what is a good result, and what low t or R^2 may indicate. Examples of adstock modeling are available in the series of volumes titled *Advertising Works.*[5]

Safeguards are as follows:

- If common sense and modeling conflict, use common sense; that is, absurd values of coefficients (such as negative distribution effects) are a sure sign the model is misspecified, but the model may have problems that are not so easily spotted—it just feels wrong.
- Once you have accepted a model, rearrange the data to show the implied result directly. If you can't see it, it's not there.

The object of an analysis of this type is to estimate the size of the (short-term) advertising effect. The estimated coefficient summarizes advertising quality or effectiveness. By comparing this with the break-even advertising elasticity, you see whether an increase in advertising spending could be justified on short-term contribution returns alone—a very demanding criterion indeed.[6] Or, by modeling before and after a copy change, you see whether the short-term advertising effect has improved—again a useful evaluation.

Longer-Term Effects

In this sort of modeling, you are estimating advertising effects as what you observed less what would have happened if you had not advertised. The latter is a construct: You have not seen it, only assumed it (if you used a constant) or estimated it (if you have a different sort of model).

There is no accepted way of estimating effects that are longer-term than the blips seen in a time series after bursts of advertising. Yet many studies lead us to conclude that a brand is more than a box with a product in. People are ready to trust some products more than others, to give them a degree of loyalty despite inducements from competitors, to pay more for them. It often seems likely, and can sometimes be clearly demonstrated, that advertising contributes to these added values, to this strength or equity.[7] It is therefore probable that most time series constant-based modeling today underestimates the contribution of advertising, perhaps severely.

Attempts are being made to model movements in the base itself, and to measure equity directly, and to look for broader effects than simply on volume (for example, in the trade or on pricing).[8]

Experiments

The idea of advertising experiments is seductive. Pick two cities or areas where a brand is in similar situations. In one, change advertising expenditure or run new copy. Compare sales in the test city with the control.

Many tests go wrong, however, giving unreadable results. Part of the reason is that commonsense rules are not followed, such as having two (or, better, three) cities for each treatment, so that if there is unusual competitive activity in one area you can still read the test with data from the other cities. Part of the reason is that the precision of the measurements made is low. This can be considerably improved through econometrics, though this is not done often enough.

The comparison with a control area already removes a major source of variation: If sales go up nationally, for category or seasonality reasons, you will not wrongly attribute this to the test. In fact, the best criterion on which to measure the test is the ratio of sales volume share in the test area to sales volume share in the control. You should construct the test area and control by pooling the separate cities or regions used.

You should look at data for several periods before the test starts. You will rarely find that the ratio then averages one. In fact, exact matching of test and control is impossible. Nor will the ratio be stable.

What matters is that you understand why the ratio varies, which you can do by going through the familiar list (competitors' advertising, relative price, distribution, and so on). However, you now use as independent variables the ratio of these numbers in test and control. You then model the sales ratio and learn the following:

- How large the coefficient of variation of the ratio is before the test runs
- How much this is reduced by allowing for the significant explainers
- An indication of how the explainers affect sales (though with very few observations this is not recommended as a serious finding).

After the test has run for a few periods, you test the hypothesis that sales are explained in exactly the same way as before. If this is the case, your advertising change has had no effect. Technically, you introduce a new dummy explainer, 0 before the test and 1 during it; you then find the coefficient for this new variable.

In a plot of the ratio over time, you look for growth—ideally, a step up, but if not, a gradual increase. That is, your assumption is that advertising works only by a direct, immediate (or short-term) step up in sales.

The importance of the coefficient of variation of the ratio is now clear. You look for an increase in the ratio, but against the variation that naturally occurs. You should not confuse a chance increase with an advertising effect. The smaller the coefficient of variation, the better your opportunity to make a clear decision. Using the other explanatory variables should reduce the amount of variation due to "error" and so increase your chances of reading the test.

A preanalysis (before the test starts) allows you to estimate the coefficient of variation (with or without explanatory variables). Hence you can calculate how long the test will have to run before you can determine an effect with sufficient precision. You should not rush into tests without preanalysis.

Often it is more sensible to run a pressure test (at a higher weight than normally expected, to see whether anything moves, including diagnostic consumer research scores) than a test expected to estimate precisely long-term sales effects.

Econometrics on Survey Data

There is no reason to restrict these techniques to sales data. In advertising, we often use survey data to help us understand what is going on. In a few cases (corporate and political work, for example), opinion research provides the only criteria we have to work with.

This explains the importance of the analysis of regular tracking data on awareness, communication, and other scores. These scores have their own explainers, their own long-term trends as well as blips and so on. Usually, our own recent advertising explains many of the blips, and it is possible to estimate its effectiveness in moving the score (in the short term). New principles are involved, but a powerful tool for evaluation is added to our resources.

Conclusion

In this chapter I have introduced the statistical methods most used as part of advertising campaign evaluation. They do not replace other methods, particularly qualitative work. At best, they tell us what happened, and we need other evidence to tell us why (and to indicate how to improve). Econometrics in advertising is becoming a subject with its own skills, involving the combination of analysis with the rest of the experience gained in a campaign. It is also beginning to be used to investigate a wider range of models than those described here.[9]

Notes

1. J. Johnston, *Econometric Methods,* 3rd ed. (New York: McGraw-Hill, 1984).

2. J. D. C. Little, "Aggregate Advertising Models: The State of the Art," *Operations Research,* vol. 27, no. 4, July/August 1979, 629-667.

3. Simon Broadbent, "Modelling Beyond the Blip," *Journal of the Market Research Society,* vol. 32, January 1990, 61-102.

4. Simon Broadbent, "Using Data Better," *Admap,* January 1992, 48-54.

5. Volumes in the *Advertising Works* series have appeared biannually since 1981, produced for the Institute of Practitioners in Advertising, London, by various editors and publishers. See also N. Barnard and G. Smith, *Advertising and Modelling: An Introductory Guide* (London: Institute of Practitioners in Advertising, 1989).

6. Simon Broadbent, *The Advertiser's Handbook for Budget Determination* (New York: Macmillan-Lexington, 1988); see especially chap. 7 and pp. 109-117, which outline some of the uses of modeling in advertising decisions.

7. John Philip Jones, *What's in a Name? Advertising and the Concept of Brands* (New York: Simon & Schuster-Lexington, 1986).

8. Various examples are available in the *Advertising Works* series.

9. The material in this chapter is expanded upon in Simon Broadbent, *Accountable Advertising* (Henley-on-Thames, UK: Admap Publications, 1997).

Tracking Studies

Paul Feldwick

The term *tracking study* implies any survey that is repeated over time so as to provide trend data. Tracking studies in this sense can include repeated surveys on any topic; there is currently a growing market for tracking studies of customer satisfaction, for example. But in an advertising context (and in this chapter), the term refers specifically to a study that "tracks" response to advertising or other marketing activity over time.

Within this broad definition there are many variations of approach. In particular, there is semantic confusion as to what frequency of interviewing or reporting constitutes a tracking study. In the United States this term is still routinely applied to annual surveys. In the United Kingdom, however, many researchers nowadays would automatically expect a tracking study to be fully continuous.

Having registered the confusion of terms, we can put it aside. The real issue, of course, is not what has the right to be called a tracking study, but what methodology is most appropriate (and affordable) in any given situation.

Frequency

Within our broad definition, a tracking study might be any of the following:

1. An annual survey, sometimes also known as a wave survey. At this level of frequency we might in reality be considering an annual usage and attitude study, with a lengthy questionnaire.
2. A regular (e.g., quarterly) survey.
3. A survey timed to relate to flights/bursts of advertising activity, often known as a *pre/post* survey.
4. Continuous interviewing, but using sample sizes that allow for analysis only every quarter.
5. A "true" continuous tracking study, with fieldwork every week and a sample size large enough to allow reporting on a weekly (probably a rolling 4-week) basis.

The last of these—the continuous tracking study—has become well established in the United Kingdom since about 1980, largely due to its promotion by Millward Brown. It is still comparatively new in the United States, although Millward Brown's American business is expanding rapidly. However, although the continuous tracking study offers real advantages over the others, it is not necessarily the best choice for all types of situations; it is, moreover, necessarily expensive, even if the questionnaire is kept short and the survey syndicated to competing clients.

If we are monitoring something that remains very stable over time, and changes very slowly (such as most usage data, for example), then an annual survey is all that is needed. However, to take a meaningful measure of something that is very volatile and reacts quickly to marketing activity (the best example would be advertising recall), an annual or even a regular quarterly survey would normally be misleading or even useless.

Better than a quarterly survey for such purposes is the pre/post survey, which concentrates interviewing around advertising activity. To evaluate a specific campaign, with a specific communication task, this may be all that is necessary. Continuous interviewing, in itself, irons out odd blips in the data. It is only when the sample size allows continuous reporting, however, that one can begin to relate short-term fluctuations in the data to specific marketing actions.

So a continuous approach is justified, and can be very valuable, when it produces trends that fluctuate in the short term and that can be related to factors such as advertising. It also makes it possible, as the pre/post survey usually does not, to monitor responses to competitive activity on a comparable basis. If, however, a continuous survey is generating data that remain extremely stable from one year's end to the next, one has to ask whether it would be more useful and more cost-effective to replace those questions with more thorough research carried out every year or even two.

Continuous tracking studies have provided some evidence about which types of questions, and in what situations, tend to generate fluctuating responses, and which produce stable responses. Those more likely to show a short-term response to advertising are new or lesser-known brands, rarely advertised brands, peripheral brands, campaigns that say something new, and measures of advertising recall. Those less likely to show such a response are established brands, routinely advertised brands, campaigns that play upon central or evaluative beliefs, and campaigns that reinforce current beliefs.

Whatever the frequency of the survey, advertising tracking study questionnaires have tended to follow the same conventional pattern. The measures usually include some or all of the following:

1. Brand questions
   Spontaneous and prompted brand awareness
   Claimed purchase behavior
   Brand attitude or brand image scales

2. Advertising questions
   Spontaneous and prompted recall of having seen advertising for a brand
   Recognition of an advertisement from a visual prompt (sometimes without the
      brand, so that a further question can be asked about the correct attribution)
   Recall of advertising content
   Attitudes toward the advertising

Such questions are so familiar and even comforting to researchers and marketing managers that they are often routinely applied without sufficient thought. But they all raise questions of interpretation, and it is important to be aware of their limitations as indicators of advertising effectiveness. Each kind of question merits separate discussion.

Brand Questions

Spontaneous and Prompted Brand Awareness

The use of brand awareness measures dates from the linear conversion models of advertising proposed in the late 1950s: AIDA (Awareness–Interest–Desire–Action) and the step conversion model in DAGMAR (Awareness–Interest–Conviction–Search–Action). These measures are based on the commonsense assumption that nobody can buy a product who has not heard of it. Like most commonsense assumptions, this is patently untrue: There are many circumstances in which individuals encounter brands for the first time when they buy those brands.

What is more defensible is the general principle that a known, or recognized, name will be preferred (other things being equal) because of people's liking for familiarity. It can be shown, for example, that with building societies (financial organizations in Britain that make mortgage loans), prompted awareness closely correlates with consideration and indeed with market share. Applied to a new or developing brand, prompted awareness (among the target market) tells us something useful about its developing relationship with the consumer. In most mature markets, however, prompted brand awareness scores are all universally high, at the 80-90% level or higher. They do not at this level provide a very useful discriminator, nor does the tracking of them over time prove very interesting.

It is perhaps because of this that more emphasis is usually placed on *spontaneous* awareness scores, sometimes with the added sophistication that the analysis also records brand first mentioned, second mentioned, and so on. (This is often called *top-of-mind* awareness.) There are some situations where top-of-mind awareness can be seen to be a valuable objective in itself: Where the purchase involves some kind of search—for example, with insurance services—"the first name that comes to mind" will have a real advantage. In other situations, however, the assumption is being made that being top-of-mind indicates consistently something about the customer's relationship with the brand. Although an intuitively appealing thought, this is far from proven. It is easily possible to call to mind brands one would never think of buying.

Gordon Brown (founder of Millward Brown) makes the point that, when monitored in a continuous, weekly, tracking study, it is exceptional rather than normal to find any clear relationship between spontaneous brand awareness and advertising activity.

Claimed Purchase Behavior

Claimed purchase behavior may be a valuable measure in markets where no more robust data exist on penetration or brand share, but it is well-known that claimed behavior is often an imperfect guide to real behavior. It may be that claimed behavior often tells us more about the respondent's relationship to a brand than actual, recent behavior (an idea expanded upon in the idea of the Consideration Scale, discussed below). Such questions are often included as a possible cross-break for analysis rather than primarily to show a trend in themselves.

Intention to purchase questions have been shown by Barwise and Ehrenberg to correlate almost exactly with recent past patterns of purchasing behavior. This is true to the extent that a higher claimed intention to purchase than what is indicated by the current brand share is actually a reflection of a declining share, rather than one that is about to improve.

Brand Image Measurements

To deal with the subject of brand image measurement in full would require another chapter. A huge variety of attribution and scaling techniques exist. The key issues as applied to tracking studies are whether these types of measures are volatile or responsive enough to marketing in the short term to justify frequent measurement and, more fundamentally, whether what is measured is necessarily telling us something valid about the health of the brand and the effect of marketing upon it.

Most continuous tracking studies measure "brand image" in a very simple way. A list of descriptive statements is prepared that may range from the functional ("gets clothes clean") to the more emotional ("a brand I trust"), by way of typical user imagery ("a brand for young people"). Respondents are asked which of these statements apply to each of a number of brands. In practice, the costs of continuous tracking and the need to keep the questionnaire of manageable length mean that the numbers of both attributes and brands are constrained. A slightly more elaborate approach is to use scales for each answer rather than simple ascription; this may produce more sensitive patterns of data at the cost of being more cumbersome to administer.

The value of these types of questions depends primarily on the relevance and sensitivity of the attributes chosen. Techniques exist for identifying attributes that appear to predict buying behavior. These are infrequently used in designing tracking study questionnaires. Perhaps for this reason, and perhaps because "image" is genuinely slow to move, it has been observed that brand image measures on tracking studies usually remain remarkably stable over time. Such movements as do occur can often be explained as a function of changing purchase behavior, rather than as an explanation of it. It has been clearly shown that the number of people rating a brand on any attribute is strongly predicted by the number of people claiming to buy the brand, a fact that needs to be allowed for in the interpretation of any type of "image battery." An increase in sales may therefore be accompanied by a rising trend in positive image ratings, without this necessarily implying that the advertising (for instance) has been a causal factor. There are mathematical techniques for removing these size effects and showing the relative differences between brands.

Brand Relationships

In view of the problems and limitations often associated with interpreting brand awareness, purchase (intention), and brand image, a further type of brand measure has been introduced into some recent tracking studies. This is the attempt to quantify the strength of attachment between the respondent and the brand. It has taken various forms, associated with various research organizations. Many of these techniques were pioneered in Britain, and the research organizations mentioned below are British. Examples of such techniques include the Consideration Scale, a series of statements ranging from "I would definitely consider buying this brand" to "I would never consider buying this brand" (Hall and Partners); the Stochastic Scale, which ranks consumers from "insistors" to "rejectors" (Stochastic Brand Monitors); and, more simplistically, rating of brands on a visual scale between "for me" and "not for me" (TABS).

Given the complexity of actual purchasing behavior, such scales offer a much more sensitive approach to measuring a brand's standing with the consumer than the traditional claimed purchase "yes/no." It is no coincidence that such questions have become popular at a time when there is a universal concern with the measurement of "brand equity." These questions reflect the efforts of tracking study designers to measure the strength of consumers' relationships with a brand in a way that is not merely a tautology for brand share, and that has some predictive or explanatory power. And successful cases have been cited; for example, the research firm BJM claims that its Stochastic Scale measurement showed Tetley overtaking the brand leader PG Tips in the U.K. tea bag market before this actually happened in the marketplace.

Advertising Questions

Not surprisingly, questions specifically relating to advertising show a much more consistent relationship with advertising than any of the brand measures usually do. The debate that continues, however, is how much they really tell us about the effectiveness of the advertising in terms of consumer behavior.

Advertising Recall

There are a number of possible ways of asking people if they remember seeing or hearing advertising: prompting by product field or by media, or by showing the advertisement itself (usually known as recognition rather than recall). The approach currently taken by Millward Brown is to prompt by brand: "Which of these brands have you seen advertised on television recently?" Other researchers (e.g., INRA) ask a similar question, but without a prompt list.

Asking a question like this on a continuous survey will produce a line of data that is generally very responsive to advertising activity. In making value judgments about the results as indicators of the advertising's power to create such recall, two other factors need to be allowed for. One is obvious: that higher levels of ratings achieved (i.e., bigger budgets) will lead to higher recall. The other is that well-known brands, particularly those with histories of famous advertising, may expect to get more people answering positively to this question than is the case with other brands, even if the well-known brands have not been advertising for some time.

To find a way of allowing for these two factors, Millward Brown developed a modeling approach that has become widely accepted and emulated by some other researchers. This explains the level of awareness in any period as a function of three values: (a) the base level, which represents long-term recall and remains static over a long period; (b) recall created by advertising in that period; and (c) recall reflecting advertising in previous periods, which is assumed to decay at a constant rate. This enables researchers to estimate the so-called Awareness Index, defined as the amount of extra "awareness" likely to be produced by 100 gross rating points.

Despite some technical arguments that have been raised, the Awareness Index represents a necessary attempt to process the data if one advertisement is to be compared with another meaningfully. The real question that remains is: How much does recall of advertising measured in this way (or any other way) tell us about the effectiveness of the advertising?

Gordon Brown has argued eloquently that the Awareness Index correlates closely with related recall data, and therefore is a reliable indication that the advertising has been linked with the brand in the consumer's mind. The logic for asking a question prompting with the brand name is that this is what commonly happens at the point of purchase: The customer sees the brand, remembers the advertising, and the memory affects her decision.

However, even if we accept that recall at some level is a necessary condition for advertising effectiveness, no one has argued that it is in itself a sufficient condition. Other things being equal, a higher Awareness Index may be a good thing. But other things need not be equal, may indeed be so unequal that the Awareness Index can be positively misleading. It is possible to have a spectacularly high Awareness Index for an advertisement that fails because it says the wrong things to the wrong people. Choosing between two campaigns on the strength of an Awareness Index alone may not result in a sound decision.

Nevertheless, both clients and agencies will continue to regard good advertising awareness as a sign that they are, at least, being noticed; and extremely poor recall should generally be seen as a danger sign. (However, due allowance needs to be made for small target markets, the delayed buildup of coverage in certain press campaigns, and the fact that a strong association between advertising and brand can be built over time.)

Less seems to have been written on the practice of recognition, though it is commonly used. Here a respondent is shown a reference—usually visual, though it doesn't have to be—with or without the brand name included. Recognition in itself is likely to be an indication that the ad was at least noticed. Recognition without the ability to attribute the correct brand name may be an indication of executional problems.

Content Recall and Attitudes Toward the Ad

Tracking studies that ask about recall of advertising usually take the opportunity to ask for specific recall of content and message, and sometimes add questions on attitudes toward the ad; for example, "It was boring," "It was funny," "I'm fed up with seeing it."

These are similar to the questions routinely used in pretesting advertisements, and as such they undoubtedly offer valuable diagnostic information on what is being retained from the ad, as well as giving some indications of wear-out. The difficulty that sometimes occurs in tracking studies, however, is that across a year the proportion of respondents claiming to recall advertising for a brand may be relatively small. The solution could be to boost the samples around periods of advertising, and conversely to drop such questions altogether during nonadvertised periods. Again, it is sensible to question the assumption that every type of question will benefit from being asked continuously.

Alternatives to Tracking Studies

Tracking studies attempt to show a relationship between advertising and response by relating the two over time. The alternative is to show the relationship by simulating some kind of test and control: those who have seen the advertising and those who have not. A current example of this is the French Axicom system, which discriminates respondents on the basis of media usage into those with high, medium, and low exposure to the campaign. The differences among the groups are then analyzed in terms of brand image, purchase behavior, and so on. In view of the extensive media questionnaire required, this technique offers no cost benefit over more traditional approaches.

However, what should *not* be accepted is the type of analysis Rosser Reeves describes as "usage pull." This involves dividing a sample into those who recall advertising and those who do not, and then taking the difference between the two groups in claimed purchase or brand usage as evidence of an advertising effect. The fallacy here lies in the fact that brand users will almost invariably be more likely to recall advertising for the brand; the correlation is therefore always to be found to some degree, and there is no way of knowing how much is cause and how much is effect. This type of analysis is still to be seen in presentations of tracking study data, and should always be treated with the greatest suspicion.

The Future of Tracking Studies

With the growing demand for advertising to be "accountable," the market for tracking studies has grown and may continue to do so. For some clients the benefit will be more one of comfort than of genuine use. If they can point to a line that has gone up as a result of advertising, the organization may be satisfied, even if in reality the line does not mean very much. (The traditional role of tracking studies in the United States is more often as a "report card" than as an actionable set of data.)

Other clients, however, are taking the view that, for the considerable cost of continuous tracking studies, they expect more useful, actionable data. In response to this we can see a trend to reposition tracking as "brand tracking" rather than "advertising tracking," with questionnaires that place more emphasis on the consumer's relationship with the brand and relate advertising response to this, rather than treating it as an end in itself. An example of this is the Stochastic Monitor, developed in New Zealand and now available in other countries, which brings together measures of communication, behavior, attitude, and image, and looks for relationships among them.

The challenge to researchers is to justify the high price of continuous surveys by offering marketing management useful feedback on what their marketing activity, and that of their competitors, is achieving in the marketplace. For those clients who are not convinced that this is valuable, or who simply cannot afford it, more basic tracking measures such as pre/post studies or annual image studies may still be appropriate.

Television Advertising

Measuring Short- and Long-Term Effects

Nigel S. Hollis

F or most of us who work in advertising, our working lives revolve around brands. How to build them, and how to keep them strong. But what are brands? Just for a moment, let us view them not from the viewpoint of people who work in advertising, marketing, or market research, but from that of the companies that own them. In this context, brands are enduring, profitable assets. Our jobs revolve around keeping brands strong and healthy in order to maintain the future income stream from this resource. But what role does advertising really play in this process?

I think that most of us would argue that advertising is the means by which we can grow new brands and sustain old ones. But it is very hard to prove that advertising has a sustaining role for an established brand for its day-to-day sales. As a way of generating short-term sales, advertising is often shown to come a poor third to trade and consumer promotion.

In the face of this evidence, most people have quite rightly suggested that advertising works in the longer term, but there has been relatively little direct evidence that this is really true. However, if we are to maintain advertising budgets and make the correct decisions about advertising from pretesting or tracking, we need to prove how advertising works, and show that it does.

The Advertising Multiplier

Ultimately, all aspects of the marketing process influence the strength of a brand in some way. Clearly, advertising alone will not support the sales of a brand if the actual product or service offered fails to meet customer expectations, or if the price asked for it gets out of line with its competitive set. Advertising's task is much more subtle than that: It is to leverage the influence of the other elements of the marketing mix, so that the sales that are achieved as a result of those activities are greater than they would have been in the absence of the advertising. In other words, advertising works as a multiplier.

What does this mean? Well, let us consider three different case studies. The first two ads discussed below won the U.K. Institute of Practitioners in Advertising's Advertising Effectiveness First Prize Award; the third received a Certificate of Commendation.[1] In each of these cases advertising worked to leverage other elements of the marketing mix to create a brand that was stronger and more valuable than it would have been in the absence of that advertising.

Crown Solo: Immediate Challenge

In 1989, Crown launched a new gloss paint, Crown Solo, with the "Codex Decoratum" ad by J. Walter Thompson (JWT). The message was clear: Forget all the hassle associated with gloss paint; this one is new, different, and—above all—easy to use.

Solo's share of the white gloss market hit a peak of 18% immediately after the advertising, and Crown's total share rose from 20% to 30%. Would the success of the introduction have been as immediately apparent if the advertising had not spread the news that Solo existed? It seems unlikely.

Would the advertising alone have guaranteed success if Crown's extensive R&D had not resulted in a genuinely superior product? Probably not; it was the combination that was successful.

In fact, the launch of Solo is a classic example of what has been called *immediate challenge* advertising.[2] The biggest changes take place if you tell people something new. If the news is immediately relevant and believable, then you are likely to observe a strong change in purchase intent, image, and sales.

Kia Ora: Interest/Status

In 1983, Kia Ora (from Schweppes) was the third brand in the product field, popular in England, of fruit juice extracts that are diluted with water. Kia Ora was under threat of being removed by the major multiple stores. Schweppes and its agency, BMP (now BMP DDB), developed a strategy to make Kia Ora not just the brand that children wanted, but also the brand that mothers thought their children wanted. The "I'll Be Your Dog" ad was highly entertaining and very memorable.

Sales response modeling demonstrated that the advertising had a powerful effect on sales, but there was an even greater indirect effect on distribution. As a result of the campaign, rather than being delisted from the retail trade, Kia Ora saw its distribution rise from 65% to 85% over a 3-year period, generating far more sales than the advertising alone.

This advertising approach is an excellent example of what Gordon Brown (founder of Millward Brown) has called *interest/status* advertising. The primary role of the advertising was to generate the perception among mothers that Kia Ora was the brand their children would like, even if they did not actively ask for it. Thus it created a status not inherent in the product alone.

Red Mountain: Enhancement

In 1986, Brooke Bond (a Unilever company) was facing a problem. The "cowboy" imagery surrounding the firm's Red Mountain coffee brand led consumers to expect strong, cheap coffee. With this in mind, Brooke Bond and its agency, Still Price Court Twivy D'Souza, initiated a new advertising strategy designed to reposition Red Mountain as a premium-quality coffee for the discerning coffee drinker. The campaign that commenced with the "Dinner Party" ad delivered the message in a creative and involving way.

As a result of this advertising, propensity to purchase the brand increased over a 2-year period and attitudes toward the brand improved enormously. Market share more than doubled, and the brand began to report a profit.

A key part of the advertising's success was the way that it succeeded in changing consumer expectations. The coffee did have a strong, distinctive taste. Before the new campaign this taste was not liked, particularly because people were reminded of it by the imagery surrounding the brand. After the new campaign, people found the ground coffee taste more appealing, because they had by now been conditioned by the new advertising, with its emphasis on quality—even though the product was the same. An important point to note, however, is that trial of the product was facilitated by the distribution of a mini-jar, which made experimentation very low risk. The use of the mini-jar accelerated the natural trial and retrial of the brand that would have occurred anyway, allowing the advertising to frame product perceptions.

This process of guiding product expectations is one of the main ways that advertising can work to benefit a brand. Gordon Brown has called this the *enhancement* mechanism. Enhancement occurs when advertising claims and images are converted into beliefs about a brand during product experience.

In each of the three cases cited above, the advertising clearly leveraged the influence of the other parts of the marketing mix, and this is one of the reasons it is so difficult to prove the influence of advertising. It does not take place in isolation, but actively works through other elements of the mix.

The Advertising Continuum

The above cases were chosen to be fairly obvious examples of the different ways in which advertising works, and they all have the advantage that the effects were fairly obvious too. In the case of most brands, however, the direct influence of advertising is less readily apparent. How obvious advertising effects are in some part depends on how responsive the brand is to advertising, as we shall see later. However, it is also true that the different types of advertising will make their influence felt over different time frames, further disguising their influence (see Figure 22.1a).

The three different advertising mechanisms discussed above—immediate challenge, interest/status, and enhancement—cover a continuum, from those

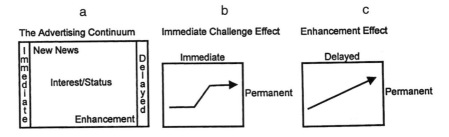

Figure 22.1. Three Advertising Models

whose effects are immediate, and therefore easily measured, to those whose effects may start when the advertising goes on air, but take time for their full influence to become apparent.

The mechanism that can be measured most easily is immediate challenge (see Figure 22.1b). In the life of a brand, the effect of immediate challenge advertising tends to be apparent in the short term but is permanent, at least until the competition catches up, or comes up with their own innovation. It is this sort of effect that purchase-shift tests can easily identify, because people can judge whether the news being delivered is relevant to them or not. However, as we shall see, the purchase intent created may not be as definite as it at first appears.

But what of interest/status and enhancement? We may expect to see some immediate response, but particularly in the case of enhancement much of the influence on perception and sales will come not when people see the ad but when they actually use the brand. Even though an advertising association may well influence loyalty or purchase decisions, it will not necessarily do so at the time of advertising, and the effects may well correlate with the timing of other activities, such as sampling, direct mail, price reductions, and product display.

The effects of this type of advertising tend to be seen as a slow, underlying upward trend in sales rather than a step function or bump (see Figure 22.1c). The effects of the advertising tend not to be just delayed, but "smoothed" across time because of the interaction with usage. This is why when we try to identify the effects of advertising on sales it is important that we look not only at the short-term blips associated with individual bursts, but at the underlying trend as well. Although other aspects of the marketing mix can clearly have impacts on this trend, we have often seen it change quite dramatically as a result of good advertising. However, the exact impact of advertising in this context is very difficult to prove.

Proving Enhancement Exists: An Experiment

Because of this difficulty, Millward Brown decided to conduct an experiment to prove that the enhancement effect does exist.[3] The experiment was conducted to demonstrate the idea that the enhancement of product perceptions could be more powerful than immediate persuasion. Four brands from four different product categories were included in the experiment: cookies, candy, bottled water, and toothbrushes. Each brand was relatively new, had yet to achieve significant penetration, and had received only limited advertising support. To many people, therefore, the existence of the brands was news, and most consumers would be trying them in an exploratory frame of mind. So long as the actual product proposition proved interesting, we would expect to see some significant shifts in purchase intent as well as an enhancement effect once the product was tried.

The research design involved four cells of respondents. Each cell consisted of approximately 230 people matched in terms of age and socioeconomic group. The first pair of cells was needed in order to measure the immediate persuasive effects of advertising. Subjects in one cell were exposed to the advertising and subjects in the other were not. The other two cells mirrored the first except that subjects in both of these cells were also given the product to try under natural conditions. Subjects in all of the four cells were asked about purchase intent in separate telephone interviews 2 weeks after the advertising exposure and/or receipt of the product. The researchers' interest in the advertising was disguised at every stage.

Two types of purchase intent questions were asked. The first was a measure of "definite" intent. The researchers asked, "Next time you go shopping for [category] which of these brands [list] will you buy?" The second measure was much "softer," asking, "Of the brands you have heard of but haven't tried, which one are you most curious to try?"

Comparison of the definite purchase intent response from those who did not see an ad with those who saw the ad showed no persuasion effect. There was no difference in results between the two cells, even at the 90% confidence level. For those seeing the ad, 2 weeks had elapsed. It may well be that more

TABLE 22.1   Millward Brown Experiment: First Part

Curious to Try	Shown Nothing (%)	Shown Ad (%)	Effect of Ad (%)
Candy	10.5	17.3	+6.8
Cookies	9.4	11.8	+2.4
Bottled water	13.9	17.6	+3.7
Toothbrush	9.7	11.5	+1.8
Four brands combined	10.8	14.6	+3.8

people thought they would buy the brand immediately after seeing the ad, but that this definite intent faded away in the intervening period. However, when responses to the question "Which one are you most curious to try?" were examined, a marked difference was found between those shown the ad and those not (see Table 22.1).

The total shift is statistically significant at the 99% confidence level. In the context of a purchase-shift test, these people may well have chosen the advertised brand, because it was immediately on offer. However, in this case the wording makes it clear that there is little conviction attached to the shift: These people are not "persuaded," they are expressing an exploratory interest. In fact, most advertising research suggests that seeing an ad rarely causes people to rush out and buy a brand as a result. However, an ad can generate interest or curiosity that can affect purchasing, if the ideas and associations delivered by the ad come to mind in the right context, when a consumer is making a purchase. This then suggests that a combination of *advertising to arouse curiosity* and *trade and consumer promotion to capitalize on that curiosity* is the right approach to generating trial. Indeed, it is a common finding in new product tracking that consumer promotion has more effect when combined with advertising than when delivered in isolation.

Now what of the enhancement effect? The effect of advertising on product experience was found to be consistently positive in the Millward Brown experiment (see Table 22.2). The individual results for the brand of candy and the toothbrush are statistically significant at the 90% level; the difference for the four brands combined is significant at 99%.

Discussion of Results

So, what do the results tell us? First and foremost, they confirm the existence of delayed effects, in this case enhancement. Advertising claims come into

TABLE 22.2 Millward Brown Experiment: Second Part

Curious to Try	Product But No Ad (%)	Product and Ad (%)	Enhancement Effect (%)
Candy	11.4	17.5	+6.1
Cookies	14.6	19.5	+4.9
Bottled water	10.7	12.7	+2.0
Toothbrush	23.4	31.4	+8.0
Four brands combined	14.6	20.3	+5.7

effect when people are trying the brand and are susceptible to the framing influence that advertising can have. However, the results also place a strong question mark against the abilities of purchase-shift testing to anticipate the potential enhancement effect of advertising.

In the case of the brand of candy, the degree of curiosity created was quite large, and the actual product experience confirmed expectations, resulting in a strong enhancement effect. The persuasion and enhancement effects are both positive and similar in magnitude. However, if we look at the results for the toothbrush brand, we see a very different picture. The advertising seems to have had a meager persuasion effect, possibly because people's initial reaction is to reject the implication that they are buying the wrong brand. In real life this is probably not an unusual reaction, particularly for more considered purchases, about which individuals do not want to admit they may have made mistakes. Little curiosity seems to have been generated by the ad, possibly because most people did not see the relevance of the message at the time they saw the ad. After all, they already had toothbrushes.

However, we can see that once people did have the chance to use the toothbrush, after seeing the advertising, their purchase intent improved dramatically. The increase in the "buy next" score is statistically significant and outweighs the small reaction to the advertising alone. This posttrial effect would be completely missed by a traditional purchase-shift test.

The Role of Creativity in Advertising

The enhancement experiment does prove that advertising can work by mechanisms other than immediate persuasion. However, how can advertisers ensure that when someone does try a brand, the correct ideas and impressions come

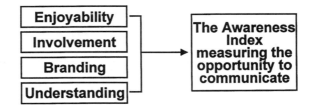

Figure 22.2. Awareness Index

to mind? The truth is that in real life people do not watch television in order to see the ads, think about them, and then make decisions about what brands to buy then and there. Normal people watch television in order to relax and be entertained. Even if they do not actively screen ads out by zapping them, their minds tend to screen them out anyway. If this is the case, and the evidence suggests that it is, what chance does advertising have to influence product experience weeks or months after consumers see an ad?

Even in the case of immediate challenge, or "new" news, advertising, it would be helpful if people remembered which brand they wanted when they got to the point of purchase. Millward Brown believes that it is the role of creativity to stimulate the involvement necessary to get past the consumer's screening process and lodge advertising associations in the long-term memory if advertising is to have an impact on purchase decisions or product experience at a later date. The value of creative "big ideas" is that they actively involve people in what is presented. Advertising is likely to prove successful if what is involving then links to the brand and message.

It has been shown that an ad must combine four elements to ensure that the advertising message or impressions come to mind when people think about the brand: It must be enjoyable, it must be involving, it must be well linked to the brand, and it must be easy to understand.[4] Simple rating scales can measure consumer responses to each of these aspects of an ad, and the results can be combined to produce a measure known as the Awareness Index (AI; see Figure 22.2).

Measuring the Opportunity to Communicate

Over the years, Millward Brown has come to regard the Awareness Index as a measure of the opportunity to communicate a message about a brand. Note that I use the word *opportunity,* because many ads do not even deliver the

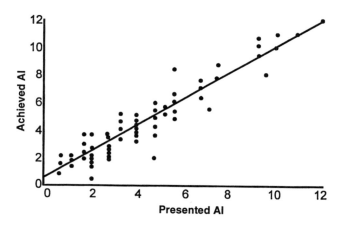

Figure 22.3. LINK Test Validation (United Kingdom):
Presented Versus Achieved Awareness Index Values
NOTE: Data from 234 ads; correlation = 0.93.

messages they are intended to. However, the Awareness Index is not just a convenient summary measure of attention produced by a copy test; it is also one of the key statistics produced by modeling real-life TV ad awareness against television ratings/gross rating points (TVRs/GRPs) from tracking studies.[5]

The definition of the Awareness Index is the increase in claimed ad awareness produced by 100 TVRs/GRPs. The effects of previous advertising, forgetting, and diminishing returns are all factored out in order to identify the effect of current copy on ad awareness. Millward Brown's LINK test is expressly designed to predict this in-market measure and has proved remarkably successful (see Figure 22.3).

Since the modeling of TV ad awareness was first introduced into the United Kingdom in the early 1980s, it has been the subject of much debate. However, at Millward Brown we have seen so many cases where changes in ad awareness anticipated changes in other measures on our tracking studies, that we have become firmly convinced that it is a valid measure of communication. The link to sales effects has been much more difficult to prove. This section presents the results of some new analyses designed to show that there are strong links among TV ad awareness, the Awareness Index, and sales.[6]

First, however, let us consider what the Awareness Index measures. Since the early 1980s, we have modeled the ad awareness of thousands of TV campaigns, and the resulting Awareness Indices range from a low of zero to a

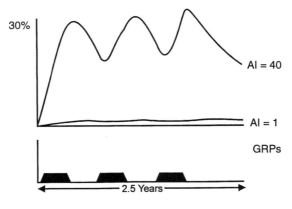

Figure 22.4.   Projected TV Ad Awareness

high of 40%. Figure 22.4 shows the increase in TV ad awareness produced by
three bursts of television advertising, each with a weight of 400 GRPs. The
two lines in the main graph are projections based on two different Awareness
Indices. The lower one is the result of an Awareness Index of 1, and the
proportion of people who say that they remember seeing the brand advertised
recently never rises above 10%. The upper line shows the response to the
highest recorded Awareness Index of 40, but using the same pattern and weight
of spending. In this case, ad awareness peaks at more than 80%. The area
between the two lines represents the extra number of people potentially
influenced by the ad's message or impression. It is the difference in the
opportunity to communicate created by the two ads.

   This gives us an idea of the vast differences that exist among ads in terms
of their ability to make people recognize that they have seen them and to
deliver messages or impressions. But how does this relate to sales?

Identifying Sales Effects Using Sales Response Modeling

Before we can demonstrate the link to sales, we first need to identify the sales
effect for an individual ad. In this section I review briefly the sales modeling
process by which this is accomplished.

   The basic objective of sales response modeling is to measure the sensitivity
of sales to a variety of marketing variables, such as price, distribution,
consumer promotion, and, of course, advertising. In order to create a sales
response model, we must first decide what measure of sales we wish to model.

This can range from volume, value, or share for repeat-purchase packaged goods to new account openings for a bank or inquiries for an insurance service.

Next we decide, in conjunction with the client, which variables are likely to have affected sales over the time period under consideration. The list will vary in relation to the specific brand and category, and we must take into account the environmental factors that affect sales as well as the marketing variables. Modeling the sales volume of a nonalcoholic drink without first allowing for variation caused by the weather will obviously give us some very misleading results. We capture the short-term sales effect for an individual ad by including its individual TVRs/GRPs in the model in the form of "adstocks." This gives us a sales response measure that is independent of the Awareness Index, but against which we can compare the tracking results.

Once we have determined an exhaustive list of variables that might influence sales and found data to represent them in the model, we then fit the variation in sales using multivariate regression. The modeling process itself can be thought of as trying literally hundreds of models with different combinations of variables, in search of a model that has both a good statistical fit and logical fit.

Over the past 10 years, Millward Brown has developed its sales modeling capabilities both in Europe and in North America, examining the sales of many different brands, covering hundreds of different TV commercials and advertising in other media as well. The models used range from simple, early models that included little more than price, distribution, and advertising to state-of-the-art ones like that developed for Millward Brown in the United States.

How Does the Awareness Index Relate to Sales?

Given our assumption that the Awareness Index is a measure of the opportunity to communicate, we should expect to see some relationship between the Awareness Index and the sales response, but we would be naive to expect it to be a perfect one. There are many different variables that determine whether advertising has an effect on sales for a particular brand, and the Awareness Index is just one of them. If nothing else, we would expect the nature of the message and the nature of the advertising to have a strong influence on the type and strength of the sales effect identified.

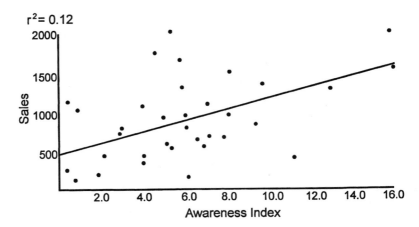

Figure 22.5.   Awareness Index Versus Sales Effect (Value)

That being so, it is hardly surprising that plotting the Awareness Index against the raw sales response shows only a weak relationship (see Figure 22.5). Plotted against the short-term sales response identified for a range of U.K. brands of repeat-purchase packaged goods, the Awareness Index alone explains only a small proportion of the variation in sales response. However, this analysis fails to recognize that all brands are not equally responsive to advertising. A brand's sales elasticity to advertising will depend on the nature of the brand and the category in which it competes.

In fact, brands vary widely in their sales response to advertising. That elasticity depends on five key factors:

1. *Category development:* A brand within a small growing category is likely to be more sales-responsive than one in a large static, or declining, category.
2. *Brand development:* A new brand is likely to be far more responsive to advertising in the short term than a large established brand in the same category.
3. *Competitive context:* The competitive context will obviously have a strong influence. This can cover a multiplicity of variables, but some important ones would be the size and number of competitive brands, the amount of consumer promotion in the category (i.e., the amount of volume sold on deal), and media share of voice.
4. *Strategy effectiveness:* Sales elasticity in the short term is in large part dependent on the message the brand puts across. News that the product has been improved, or is offering 20% extra volume for free, will be more motivating in the short term than an ongoing campaign designed to maintain loyalty.

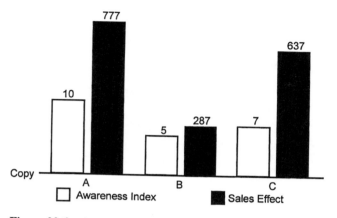

Figure 22.6. Awareness Index Versus Sales Effect
NOTE: Awareness Index and sales effect on different vertical scales.

5. *Communication efficiency:* Last, but not least, we need to consider how efficiently the advertising puts across the desired message or impression. It is this aspect that the Awareness Index is believed to measure.

It has been noted frequently over the years, both in the United Kingdom and the United States, that across an individual brand's history, a good relationship is typically found between the Awareness Index and the short-term sales response. Figure 22.6 shows one example for an established U.S. brand of repeat-purchase packaged goods. The problem we faced was how to make direct comparisons between data for brands like this one and data for other brands in completely different categories. In order to remove the influence of variables other than the advertising, we decided to index the response for an individual execution against that which other executions had achieved for the same brand.

Table 22.3 shows data for the same brand described in Figure 22.6. Looking at the Awareness Indices, we see that these range from 5 to 10, with an average of 7.3. If we divide the actual Awareness Index by this average, we can calculate an index for each campaign relative to the brand's average, as shown on the second line.

Next we repeat this simple calculation for the sales response. As you can see, the indexing does not change the conclusion that the magnitude of the sales response tends to change in line with the Awareness Index. However, the conversion effectively removes the influence of the brand's inherent elasticity

TABLE 22.3   Indexation of Awareness and Sales

Campaign	A	B	C	Average
(a) Awareness Index				
raw data	10	5	7	7.3
index	1.37	0.68	0.96	1.00
(b) Sales Effect				
raw data	777	287	637	567
index	1.37	0.51	1.12	1.00
(c) indexed Awareness Index	1.37	0.68	0.96	
indexed Sales Index	1.37	0.51	1.12	

to advertising, and we can now make an "apples to apples" comparison across brands and categories.

The Influence of the Message Versus Communication Efficiency

The relationship between the Awareness Index and the sales response has definitely improved as a result of the indexing (see Figure 22.7). We can now explain 22% as opposed to 12% of the variations in sales effectiveness with the Awareness Index. But why is the relationship not any stronger?

The indexing has removed most of the first three brand sales elasticity factors listed before. Clearly, however, the "message" component of the advertising still has a significant effect, as well as the communication component, which the Awareness Index measures. At first sight, this supports a concern frequently expressed by certain researchers, that making the message really persuasive is more important than how effectively it is communicated.

However, as discussed earlier, the persuasiveness of the message actually has a lot to do with what can be said about the brand, as contrasted with the quality of the ad. Communicating news is the advertising task most likely to produce a strong response in the short term. An examination of the arrowed outliers in Figure 22.8 reveals that those on the high side of the distribution tended to be executions giving "new" news of some sort.

In fact, we identified three main types of news that typically, but not always, produced a stronger-than-expected sales response. Execution A was a case in

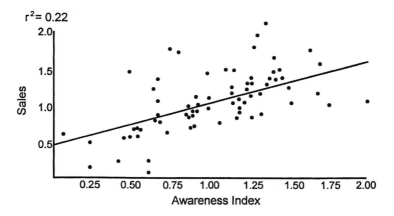

Figure 22.7. Awareness Index Versus Sales Effect—Indexed

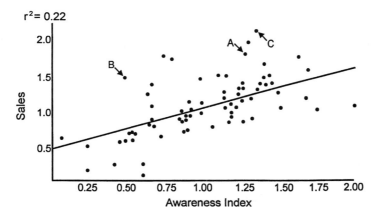

Figure 22.8. Awareness Index Versus Sales Effect—Outliers

point. It announced a new formulation of an established product. The Awareness Index was 20% higher than the brand's average, but the sales response was more than 60% higher. The reformulation was considered to be important and relevant by consumers.

Even if a new claim meets the basic criteria of importance, relevance, and credibility, the data suggest that to achieve its full potential the news must be communicated effectively. The fact that no cases fall in the top left corner of Figure 22.8 suggests that the Awareness Index is an important determinant of the strength of the sales response.

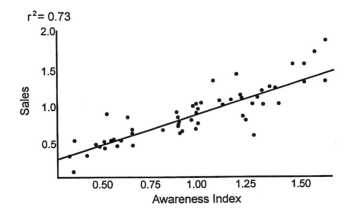

Figure 22.9.   Awareness Index Versus Sales Effect—Adjusted

New product launches are also clearly different in dynamics from the majority of cases. As a brand moves through its life cycle, we might expect its short-term sales elasticity potential to decline. Launch executions will index high relative to subsequent executions for the same brand, because the innate sales elasticity of the brand has decreased, not because the subsequent advertising is less effective. For instance, execution B achieved a relatively strong sales effect but a low Awareness Index. However, this was the launch execution for a new brand. Later executions for the same brand achieved high Awareness Indices, but failed to produce the same sales response because the brand was no longer new.

Finally, advertised promotions are an extreme version of relevant news. Case C is an advertised promotion for an established brand that was giving away an extra 20% of its product free. The news was relevant and very motivating to a substantial number of people.

Immediate challenge or "new" news executions make up about one in five of our data set. In order to achieve a level playing field, we removed all new claim, product launch, and advertised promotion executions from the analysis. Figure 22.9 shows that we can explain 73% of the variations in sales effectiveness by the differences in Awareness Index. This equates to a correlation between sales effect and the Awareness Index of 0.85. The importance of communicating vividly, and linking that communication to the brand, is now clear.

The more effectively the advertising has created branded attention, the stronger the sales response. This might cause concern to advertising agencies, because of a long-standing fear that gaining attention and linking advertising impressions to the brand will favor crude advertising approaches and slogans at the expense of subtlety and creativity. This is not supported by the evidence, however.

Short- Versus Long-Term Response

So far, I have stressed that we are looking at short-term sales effects. In essence, we are looking at the "blips" in sales associated with advertising bursts, not fundamental changes in the strength of the brand. In other words, the majority of the advertising effect is the result of leveraging existing equity, rather than building new equity. Either the advertising reminds people of the brand's existence or it reminds them of its benefits. *The sales response tends to be immediate, but does not last.*

The relationship identified between ad awareness and short-term sales suggests that what we are looking at in tracking studies, and in the LINK copy test, does predict some of the effect of advertising upon sales. However, the phenomenon of advertising is about more than blips in sales. It is often about consistent growth, or maintaining sales. Unfortunately, assessing whether advertising is maintaining sales is difficult, because, as suggested earlier, there is good reason to suppose that it involves some very "smooth" effects.

Brands are in dynamic equilibrium most of the time, and what much advertising probably does is to increase slightly the proportion of consumers who gradually "switch in" to a brand versus the proportion who gradually "switch out." The sophisticated programs designed to "decompose" sales rely on short-term changes in order to attribute the variation to one marketing activity or another.

As we conduct more sales modeling, however, we are beginning to identify more and more cases where the findings clearly indicate that strong communication, combined with a strong Awareness Index, does result in both short- and long-term sales responses. Table 22.4 shows the LINK test results for a relatively new brand of packaged goods. The first column shows the predicted Awareness Index for two different executions; the second column shows a

TABLE 22.4   Predicted Sales Effects

	LINK Test Prediction	
	Awareness Index	*Message Communication*
Ad A	2	okay
Ad B	5	good

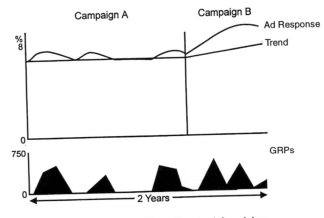

Figure 22.10.   Change in Share Due to Advertising

summary of the communication achieved in the LINK test. Clearly the second commercial would be expected to perform better in-market.

Figure 22.10 shows the short-term response to advertising and the trend in underlying share during the two campaigns. The short-term response to advertising clearly rises and falls in response to bursts. The second ad produced almost double the short-term sales response that the first one did.

Now let us look at the underlying trend in sales for the brand once the short-term variances due to price, advertising, and promotion have been removed. There is a much stronger upward trend during the period when the second ad aired. In fact, the underlying trend in share accelerated dramatically. Given that this gain is not transient, it does not take many months before this type of increase outweighs the short-term increases produced at the time of a burst. Tracking data also showed strong increases in TV ad awareness and positive perceptions of the brand.

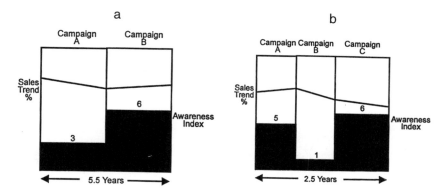

Figure 22.11. Awareness and Sales Trends

This is not an isolated case. Over the years, we have identified several brands for which the underlying sales trends seem to have been strongly influenced by the quality of the brands' advertising. Figure 22.11a shows the underlying sales trend for a U.K. brand of packaged goods, overlaid with the Awareness Index for the brand's advertising. As you can see, the sales trend tends to move in line with the Awareness Index, just as the short-term response did. When the Awareness Index is high, the sales trend tends to slope up, and when the Awareness Index is low, it tends to slope down.

There are several other examples of cases in which we can be fairly sure that advertising has had impacts on long-term trends in sales, but it would be wrong to expect an obvious relationship in all instances. Clearly, other elements of a brand's own marketing mix, as well as competitors' actions, will also affect the trend. For instance, with the brand shown in Figure 22.11b, we can see that although the sales trend does tend to change in line with the Awareness Index, the third set of copy does not completely reverse the downward trend observed during the second campaign. Other factors meant that sales were being lost, and advertising alone could not stem the flow.

In none of the cases we have just looked at can we say conclusively that the change in underlying trend was due to the advertising alone. We need to look for a convergence of sales modeling and tracking results before we can say with any confidence that advertising has played a part.

Nor do I wish to suggest that the Awareness Index is the only determinant of sales effects. As we have seen from the earlier analysis, this is not so. But to the extent that the Awareness Index does measure the short-term opportunity to communicate, and also anticipates the long-term memorability of advertising messages and impressions, it is clear that it is one of the key predictors of both short- and long-term sales effects.

Conclusion

The main point to take away from this chapter is that delayed advertising effects do exist, and that we need to think carefully about how we measure their potential effects from a pretest, or a tracking study, or in sales response modeling. It is a subject worth thinking about, because although "new" news is a powerful advertising mechanism that can produce significant short-term sales effects, by definition it does not last. "New" news soon becomes old, and you cannot always guarantee that you will have news to deliver in the first place.

The longer-term advertising mechanisms, however, are just as powerful but more subtle in their effects, working on people's everyday interaction with the brand to grow belief in the brand's benefits, strengthen loyalty, and generate sales. In the long run, they can have just as much effect on brand equity as the short-term mechanisms, and probably even more, because the equity that they build is solid and cannot be duplicated.

"New" news usually revolves around the differentiation of products and services. Clearly, on the basis of what has been reviewed here, any company that has genuine "new" news should broadcast that news as widely and efficiently as possible. However, it does not take long for competitors to match an innovation or come up with their own. In fact, the brands in many categories today are fundamentally the same. Advertising provides the means to differentiate brands effectively in people's minds in a way that transcends the basic product or service. In this way, advertising really does help to create strong brands that will endure and provide profit for years to come.

Notes

1. Paul Feldwick (ed.), *Advertising Works 5* (London: Institute of Practitioners in Advertising, 1990); Paul Feldwick (ed.), *Advertising Works 6* (London: Institute of Practitioners in Advertising, 1991).

2. Gordon Brown, *How Advertising Affects the Sales of Packaged Goods Brands: A Working Hypothesis for the 1990s* (Fairfield, CT: Millward Brown International, 1991).

3. Andy Farr and Gordon Brown, "Persuasion or Enhancement: An Experiment," paper presented at the Market Research Society Conference, 1994.

4. David Jenkins, "What Are the Components of Recall and Recognition Which Lead to Effective Advertising?" paper presented at the Advertising Research Foundation Copy Research Workshop, September 1992.

5. Gordon Brown, "Modeling Advertising Awareness," *Statistician,* vol. 35, 1986.

6. Nigel S. Hollis, "The Link Between TV Ad Awareness and Sales: New Evidence From Sales Response Modeling," *Journal of the Market Research Society,* vol. 36, no. 1, January 1994, 41-55.

Do Award-Winning
Commercials Sell?

Donald Gunn

This chapter is based on a number of investigations carried out by the Leo Burnett advertising agency. The main findings are derived from a survey conducted by Burnett, with help from more than 120 other agencies around the world, between February and June of 1996, and covering advertising that ran in 1994 and 1995. The results were presented to the delegates at the 43rd International Advertising Festival at Cannes on June 26, 1996.

This project was a direct follow-up to a precisely similar project conducted between February and June 1994 for presentation at Cannes in 1994. This first study covered advertising that ran in 1992 and 1993. When I sum up at the end of this chapter, I will combine the results of the two studies, so that I will present 4 years' worth of evidence.

The 1994 and 1996 studies had two predecessors at Burnett. First, in 1987, Leo Burnett Chicago's Research Department addressed the question of whether award-winning commercials sell, taking as a universe all the Cannes and Clio winners of 1985 and 1986 (minus corporate and public service commercials). The method employed for getting business results was telephone interviews with clients. Answers were obtained for nearly 90% of the commercials; 78% of these turned out to have been associated with marketplace success. Then, in early 1993, Leo Burnett Chicago's New Business Department again addressed this question to provide input for a presentation at a client conference. For this study, the universe was a selection of the most prominent award winners of recent years. The method used for getting results was desk research. For the project in question, results did not need to be obtained on all the cases. The success rate for those cases where answers were obtained was about 80%.

The 1994 and 1996 studies—as will be detailed below—were different from these previous studies in several ways: (a) how the universes were determined, (b) the methods used for gathering the case histories, and (c) the fact that answers were required to be obtained for 100% of the cases.

Objective of the Study

In the advertising business there is a substantial body of opinion that is dismissive of if not scornful toward creative awards. A number of advertising practitioners—both at client firms and in agencies—take the view that awards (the prizes that advertisers' organizations give to individual ads and campaigns) are basically a frivolity, as well as wholly irrelevant, indeed probably counterproductive, to the main business at hand: the selling of products and services.

These practitioners assume and believe, and also broadcast the view, that winning awards and selling products are for the most part, and in some fundamental way, mutually exclusive. They clearly suspect that the motives involved in creating an ad that wins awards are different from those involved in making an ad that is designed to sell. This makes a mockery of the value that advertising's creative people place upon awards, which to them represent the highest recognition by their peers.

The disbelief and skepticism exist at three levels, starting with the most extreme:

1. Award-winning commercials do not sell.
2. Award-winning commercials are less likely to sell.
3. Just because a commercial wins awards, that does not make it any more likely to sell.

The basic objective of the our study was therefore quite simple: to find out, once and for all, whether such quite commonly held views are right or wrong. Our hope and belief (as opposed to our objective) was that we would find out that these tenets of disbelief are totally and utterly wrong.

The Commercials Reviewed

The universe for the 1996 study—the body of commercials reviewed—was the 200 "most awarded" commercials in the world in the two preceding years—1994 and 1995. We identified these commercials as follows. We began with the "winners' reels" from all the major advertising award contests in the world for 1994 and 1995. We tabulated all of the winners of these contests—45 contests in total—in order to identify the 200 most awarded commercials/campaigns in the world for the years in question.

Markets and Agencies

The 200 commercials/campaigns that made up our 1996 universe came from 26 different countries and from a total of 129 different agencies (see Table 23.1). Among them, these 200 commercials had won a grand total of 1,483 major creative awards.

Methodology and Responses

We obtained the case histories for the 200 commercials in our study as follows. The first stage consisted of phone calls (all done by me) to appropriate persons at all of the 129 agencies, to explain our project and to ask for their help. We identified the best person to deal with at each agency—normally it was the CEO or the executive creative director—with the input of Leo Burnett chief executives and creative directors, market by market.

TABLE 23.1 Countries Represented in the Study

Country	Number of Commercials
Argentina	7
Australia	9
Belgium	1
Brazil	11
Canada	2
Chile	2
Colombia	1
Czech Republic	1
Denmark	1
Finland	2
France	9
Germany	6
Great Britain	37
Hong Kong	3
Italy	3
Japan	6
Netherlands	9
New Zealand	3
Norway	9
Portugal	1
South Africa	5
Spain	12
Sweden	6
Switzerland	3
Thailand	2
United States	49

The initial phone call to each agency was followed up by a formal letter that reconfirmed the parameters of the project and gave reassurances of confidentiality. With this letter, we sent questionnaires—one for each commercial/campaign in the study. The questionnaire had five key sections:

1. What were the objectives the advertising was designed to achieve?
2. Did it achieve these objectives (in your and your client's opinion)?
3. If yes, provide quantified details in support.
4. If no, identify probable reasons.
5. Correct/complete the list of major awards the advertising has won.

Some of our respondents wrote their replies directly on the questionnaires; the majority, however, sent longer responses.

Some of the agencies replied quite quickly, whereas others needed a certain amount of reminding and cajoling. But by the week of June 24, 1996, we had succeeded in getting answers for all 200 cases: 179 came directly from the agencies in the manner described previously, 7 were obtained from clients, and 14 were obtained via desk research—either from retail audits and published data or from trade, industry, and marketing press sources. In 3 of these last cases, the agencies wanted to help us, but the clients were not in favor of participating in the study. Otherwise, we undertook desk research when we became worried that the agencies in question, busy as they were, would not get around to answering before the Cannes deadline.

Examples

In the first stage of the project, we gathered the business results in order to establish the purely numerical case. How many of the world's 200 most awarded commercials of 1994 and 1995, based on measured results against defined objectives, had been associated with marketplace success?

But for the seminar to be presented at Cannes, we obviously needed to show film and give examples. So for 56 of the case histories (prime candidates) we went back to the agencies to seek their permission to show their commercials and to quote from the business information they had provided. Permission was granted for all 56 cases.

For this report, I also feel the need to include some examples—to give a flavor of the quality of the information gathered in the two studies as well as the diversity of the case stories. However, I do not feel that I am at liberty to make totally free with the confidential information that was provided, so I have camouflaged the cases somewhat in the examples that follow, and brand names are omitted. Many, but not all, of these examples were among the 28 stories we featured at Cannes.

A brand of jeans in Europe. This brand's hugely popular commercials have won Lions at Cannes just about every year since the campaign started in 1986, from which year until 1994 sales had sextupled. In 1995, sales forged ahead another 15% (that's 3 million pairs of jeans) against zero overall market growth. Considering that 66% of Europeans aged 15-29 already own an average of 2.3 pairs of the brand in question, this represents a notable achievement.

An in-car CD player based in the United States. A modest-budget campaign ran in print and on TV, and the commercial's attitude and language (or lack of it) seemed to make an impact on the young male target audience, which is very averse to hype. Share of the CD player category shot up from 15% to a peak of 25% during the campaign period, taking the brand to number one in the category for the first time.

An ocean cruise line. Advertising in North America, this company eschewed the standard portrayal of onboard glamour and glitz round-the-clock for a much more individualistic and sensory interpretation of the benefits of a cruise. Capacity reached record levels in 1995, with competition generally flat or declining. Also, business from first-time cruisers and younger (25-34) customers moved ahead significantly.

A brand of athletic shoes in North America. In 1991, only 17% of this company's sales were to women. Since then, TV and print advertising has forged emotional ties, demonstrating that the manufacturer understands that a young woman's participation in athletics is much of who she is and who she can become. Between 1991 and 1993, sales to women rose 40%. And for the period of our survey—fiscal year 1994-1995—dollar share for young women indexed 128 versus the successful year before.

A brand of household batteries in a big Latin American market. The job of the advertising was to find a way to differentiate the product in a market totally dominated by Duracell and Energizer—with much bigger budgets and well-defined creative concepts. Sales were up 38% in the first 6 months the new advertising ran.

A meaty snack product in the United Kingdom. New advertising starring an outrageous character as a personification of the product broke in July 1993. Sales were up 33% in the first half year, and the proportion of the population having ever tried the product grew by 40% in 15 months. This campaign had the second-highest "Advertising Impact" score ever achived in the United Kingdom, and was an IPA Advertising Effectiveness winner.

A young fashion footwear brand in a market in Africa. These shoes had been manufactured in limited quantities for a niche market, but in 1993 production capacity was doubled. With a "shoestring" budget, the agency devised a much-talked-about campaign, comprising (a) graffiti on outdoor sites, (b) three print ads, and (c) three low-cost commercials. Since the advertising, shipments are up by 500%.

A chain of photo shops in a European market. This chain introduced a new, bigger size of paper (exclusive to them) for photographic prints. The advertising dramatized the difference in an intrusive but also empathic way. In the first year, sales increased 24% (with 85% of prints made in the new size), and the retailer achieved a record market share of 60%—12% higher than the previous year.

A state lottery in the United States. Sales had actually been declining before new advertising helped reverse the trend in fiscal year 1992-1993. The campaign has gone from strength to strength. In 1995-1996, awareness of the advertising's tag line hit an all-time high. Sales were up 28.5%, and profits to the state lottery's fund for education totaled a record $1.26 billion.

A brand of jelly—the market leader in a South American country. This brand introduced a new "instant" version, aiming to do so without significant cannibalization of the main brand. The advertising successfully created a separate appeal and personality. Indexed brand sales rose from 100 to 137 with the new variety added, and market share rose from 52% to 59%.

A major bank in a Scandinavian market. This bank had pension insurance as a "sleeper" somewhere in its product portfolio. New advertising dramatized the target consumer's need for a "golden parachute" in a hilarious but also persuasive way, which also showed the product (and the people offering it) as easy to understand. Sales increased by no less than 500%, and the product has become market leader.

A national milk board. This organization launched a new campaign in 1993 starring a multitalented cow named Lovely. The cow has become a national icon, and major gains have been achieved in all key attributes, ranging from "important nutritionally" to "acceptable social drink." After more than 20 years of declining milk sales, the curve is now flattening out.

A major European newspaper. At a time when national frontiers in Europe were changing rapidly and even bewilderingly, this newspaper came up with a timely promotion, offering "New Maps of Europe" to its readers. During the promotion, peak daily sales of 1.2 million copies were achieved—a figure never reached before by any newspaper in the market since 1945.

A powdered detergent in a major Latin American market. In this market, Levers had had the powdered detergent category to itself for years. In 1993, a local company dared to launch a brand directly against Omo, the market leader. The advertising was a direct parody of Omo's testimonial approach. Despite drastic blocking tactics, the new brand has successfully broken in to become second in the market, with a peak market share of 18%.

A national meat marketing brand. This brand saw its advertising positioning of beef as an essential source of iron contribute to a fundamental change in consumer perceptions. Consumption of beef rose in 1993-1994 for the first time since 1988 (a surprising phenomenon considering the frequently negative attitudes toward red meat in Western societies). The value of increased sales that year was U.S.$196 million—for a media investment of U.S.$4 million.

A national soft drink brand in a Scandinavian market. This brand had seen its franchise eroding in the face of aggressive spending and marketing by Coke, Pepsi, and Fanta. New advertising broke in 1993, wittily positioning the product as an alternative to the "lifestyle" brands. The ad budget is less than half of the leader's, but sales and share were up for 1993, after 7 years of consecutive decline. And by 1995, share was back at approximately the 1987 level.

A U.K.-based conglomerate advertising to the investment community in the United States. Parodies of movie classics served to inform the target consumer about the corporation's portfolio of business and its inherent strengths. A toll-free telephone number that allowed viewers to receive information on the investment opportunity generated more than 25,000 calls in 1993 and 1994. The U.S. shareholder base has increased from 22% to 25% of the corporation's total.

A casually chic jeans and fashion clothing brand. This brand's highly original and often controversial advertising is created in Sweden. Sales tripled in the first 4 years of the campaign—between 1991 and 1994. And even from the high level thus achieved, 1995 sales were up 43% over 1994—with the brand now selling in 54 markets and the ad campaign running in most of them.

A national radio station. In support of the wide range of programs offered by a national radio station, the concept "rediscover the power of the spoken word" was dramatized in a highly original and unexpected way. A 10% sustained increase in listenership was achieved, with 48% campaign awareness even 6 months after the advertising when off the air. And 32% of respondents said that the advertising had made them more interested in listening to the station.

A sports watch in a European market. A much-awarded campaign for a sports watch broke in March 1995. Turnover in the brand's key European market (the one where the campaign was created) was up 14.5% for the year to February 1996 (versus 4.4% decline in the global watch industry's turnover). This was achieved despite increases in price, and with distribution becoming more selective.

A car model in a top European market. This car was far from being the most glamorous and top-of-mind in the illustrious range the manufacturer offered in a top European market. In an economic climate where corporate belts were tightening, new advertising positioned the model as a business car and gave it a reason for being. The model tripled its market share, and the ad was voted the most highly appreciated car commercial of the year (1994) by the public.

Summary of Findings

The key finding of our 1996 study was that 174 (87%) of the 200 most awarded commercials in the world in 1994 and 1995 were associated with marketplace success. Within these 174, 119 were successful in terms of "hard data" objectives. The objectives of the advertising had been specified increases in sales value or sales volume or share, and these objectives were achieved or surpassed. The other 55 were successful against attitudinal or awareness or image-related goals. Again, these had been the objectives that were set for the advertising to achieve. This group included nearly all the public service and all the corporate commercials.

At the top end of the study was a group of cases—more than 50, over 25% of the total—for which the level of business success was not just good, not just very good, but could more appropriately be described as astonishing.

Comparing the 1994 and 1996 studies, we see that the results are remarkably similar. The key finding, when we combine our two studies, is that 346

TABLE 23.2 Analysis of Findings,, 1994 and 1995

		1994 Study	*1996 Study*	*Total*
AA	Highly successful versus "hard data" goals	47	54	101
A	Successful versus "hard data" goals	70	65	135
B	Successful versus qualitative goals	55	55	110
C	Not successful	28	26	54
Total		200	200	400

(86.5%) of the 400 most awarded commercials in the world in 1992, 1993, 1994, and 1995 were associated with marketplace success.

Unsuccessful Cases

We attempted to identify "the most probable reasons" for lack of success in the 54 cases where the creative did not work in the marketplace. These reasons included the following:

- The strategy was wrong.
- Circumstances changed, rendering the strategy wrong.
- The product was wrong—or did not meet the expectations the advertising generated.
- The goals set for the advertising were unrealistic.
- Insufficient media weight: The client switched priorities and therefore budget to another brand or assignment.
- Insufficient media weight: The client "fell out of love" with the ad.
- The ad was a "test commercial" that stayed on the back burner.
- One ad was made for a contest (which it won) organized by a business magazine, but it had no real media exposure.
- The ad was a "made-for-award-shows" commercial (there were 3 such "ghost commercials" in the sample).

Conclusions

Before summing up, I should touch on the issue of the accuracy of our data. Would agencies have told us if their advertising had not worked? I have personally worked on all of the information gathering and all the analysis, and

I am extremely confident that the overall level of the case history material is accurate.

First, I was dealing on a confidential basis with very senior people at the world's best advertising agencies (26 of whom, by the way, *did* tell me that the advertising had not worked). My own belief is that good advertising people at this level are inherently honest and are more interested in getting at the truth than in being proved personally right.

Second, for 56 of the cases (the candidates for use as examples at Cannes), I went back to the agencies for clearance to use the results and detailed numbers they had provided. So they knew that their data were liable to be quoted before 2,000 or so delegates at Cannes, including people from their own markets or with intimate knowledge of their categories. There was not a single case in the 56 where anyone backtracked on previous claims or wanted to reduce any numbers.

Across the total universe of 200 cases, there may have been the odd exaggeration here or the odd omission there. But, having seen the quality of the case history returns and the material provided, I believe these to be fairly minimal.

The hypotheses we were disputing were (a) that award-winning commercials do *not* sell, (b) that award-winning commercials are less likely to sell, and (c) that just because a commercial wins awards does not make it any more likely to sell. Our study aimed to find out, once and for all, whether these quite commonly-held views about our business are right or wrong. And we can now address these views quite simply as follows: In any given market category over a given period of time, what tends to be happening on average is that about one-third of the brands are going up, one-third are going down, and one-third are holding. The 86.5% success record found in this study is more than 2.5 times better than 33%. Thus the evidence is overwhelming that well-focused commercials that are based on the right message and, in addition, deliver that message and translate it freshly, charmingly, engagingly, and intelligently work better than commercials with the right message but which lack these creative qualities. Commercials with award-winning qualities are 2.5 times as likely to be associated with business success as are average commercials.

Single-Source Research

John Philip Jones

Single-source research is a method for measuring the sales effects of advertising. It was developed originally on an experimental basis in the United Kingdom in the mid-1960s. The 1970s and 1980s saw continuous attempts to apply the technique in the United States, with only limited success. The situation improved in the early 1990s.

Many people responsible for brands are uncomfortable with certain types of quantitative research, and the research industry has tended not to be user-friendly. Single-source research—despite its cost and the complications involved in implementing it—is in essence a simple technique, and its findings are easy to understand.

Single-source research is not new. However, the pure method used by A. C. Nielsen (which I will describe shortly) is so unusual as to be almost unique. It is greatly more valuable—but also much more difficult to employ—than the diluted method (which I will also describe), which has been used fairly widely over the course of the past 20 years.

277

Market research is carried out in three phases: Surveys are planned, fieldwork is carried out, and the data are analyzed. Information is collected in two ways: (a) by monitoring, observing, and picking up data mechanically (e.g., with scanners and other types of electronic meter); and (b) by asking people (e.g., buyers of a product category) to provide information and opinions. The market research industry is split approximately evenly between these two methods. Advertising effects can be evaluated reliably only through the use of monitoring devices (method a). The intervention of consumers (method b) introduces many inaccuracies that can prejudice researchers' ability to produce robust conclusions.

Sales of a brand are the product of many marketplace variables. The most important of these are consumer satisfaction with the functional properties of the brand in comparison with its competitors; the advertising, as the source of the brand's added values; the price, which is expressed mainly through its trade and consumer promotions; the brand's distribution and display in the retail trade; marketplace parameters, notably seasonality; and—a very important variable—the activities of competitive brands.

The major difficulty in evaluating the influence of advertising (on its own) lies in determining how to isolate it. How do we untangle advertising's effects from all the other factors impinging on sales? And even if we manage to establish an apparently clear statistical correlation between advertising and sales—for example, between exposure of households to a brand's advertising (based on a large statistical sample of such households) and sales of the brand measured from (another) large group—how do we know that there is a direct cause-and-effect relationship between the two?

There is a well-known trap for the unwary concerning the direction of causality. Does A cause B, or does B cause A, or are they both caused by C (something else entirely)? (For more discussion of this matter, see Jones, Chapter 9, this volume.)

One way the market research industry has met the challenge of such statistical confusion is by borrowing a tough mathematical technique from the econometricians, who use it for the analysis of microeconomic and macroeconomic data. This technique takes statistics from separate and unconnected sources—such as consumer panel or retail scanner figures measuring the sales of different brands and estimates from Leading National Advertisers (LNA) of the advertising budgets and patterns of media expenditure for those brands —plus a number of other measures, and compares and analyzes the different data sets. Taking the sales of a selected brand as the end result (known technically as the dependent variable), the researcher analyzes all the other sets of information to determine the relative importance of each of them as causes (described technically as independent variables). This is done using the statistical device of multivariate regression, and it is often possible at the end of the analysis to construct a mathematical model that quantifies the relative importance of each of the individual influences on the sales of the brand. The role of advertising can be isolated in this way, and as a part of this process it is possible to calculate a brand's advertising elasticity—that is, the percentage by which the sales of the brand are likely to increase as the result of a 1% increase in advertising expenditure alone.

This type of analysis has great practical value and has been carried out on hundreds of occasions. However, it is very complicated and requires mathematical skills of a high order. Line managers—the very people who should be using the information—are often unable to understand it. Further, a model is occasionally incomplete; it may fail to explain the complete picture of a brand's sales because of missing elements the model cannot detect because they have not been included in the original statistical inputs.

An alternative system to multivariate regression is controlled experimentation in the marketplace. Two (or more) regions are selected, and the brand is marketed in identical ways in those regions, except for variations in the advertising, such as changes in copy, in budgetary weight, or in patterns of media exposure. Controlled experiments of this type have been run extensively, but they are generally very expensive to implement, take a lot of time, and are difficult to monitor. They also often yield fuzzy and indeterminate results, because the differences between the areas are often greater than the differences between the specific advertising variables being tested.

In Britain, a technique known as the Area Marketing Test Evaluation System (AMTES), which combines regional testing with econometric evaluation, was developed by Beecham (now SmithKline Beecham) and has been used successfully for a number of years. AMTES has not been employed much in the United States, and this lack of popularity has been difficult to understand (although it may be due to suspicion of any techniques developed in foreign countries).

The general fault of the econometric systems is their mathematical complexity: the inevitable consequence of the way in which they attempt to describe a complex world. The problem with marketplace experimentation is expense, plus the practical impediments to finding comparable regions. In the face of these difficulties, the ingenuity of market researchers eventually succeeded in producing a third system that is both original and simple, and one that holds the promise of replacing both econometrics and market experimentation as a device for measuring accurately advertising's contribution to sales.

This was the genesis of single-source research. The technique focuses attention on the fieldwork stage rather than the analytic stage, and it does so by bringing together at the very beginning of the research the data that must be compared and related to one another to establish statistical relationships.

In single-source research, all the information is collected at the same time from the same people. It brings together a household's exposure to marketing stimuli (e.g., a brand's advertising) and purchases of that brand within the same household.

Single-source research is, however, a label that has come to be interpreted imprecisely. It is now generally applied to research that can be carried out in a number of different ways and with varying degrees of rigor. In particular, the phrase "a household's exposure to marketing stimuli (e.g., a brand's advertising)" is capable of more than one meaning.

At a looser extreme, household exposure to advertising can be measured in a simple way by looking at consumers' purchasing of identified brands and at these consumers' total exposure to specific media. This is the type of information provided by Mediamark Research Inc. and Simmons Market Research Bureau—information widely used for media targeting. It represents a significant step beyond a reliance on demographics. At the looser end, also, are the types of single-source research that concentrate on area testing. Typically, in this system areas are subjected to varying amounts of advertising for a brand, and these variations in the quantity of advertising that consumers are likely to receive are related to the volume of consumer purchases. In this chapter, I shall call systems like these *diluted single-source research.*

These systems are different from the method employed when the single-source technique was first explored in the marketplace. This exploration took place in the United Kingdom in 1966, and the person most associated with that work is Colin McDonald. McDonald's original system is called *pure single-source research.* Pure single-source research determines each household's reception of advertising for specific identified brands and then relates this to the purchasing of those same brands by the same household shortly after the advertising. There is a tight relationship within each household and for each brand between advertising exposure and purchasing.

The data collection system for all single-source research (pure and diluted) is described technically as disaggregated. From this disaggregated foundation—from this large collection of statistical observations, or little bits of knowledge, each relating to separate homes—the figures can be clustered to throw light on the variables of interest. The individual observations from pure single-source research are much more relevant to the effects of advertising than are those from the diluted method.

In single-source research, the different types of data are collected together within the same household. The various data sets do not have to be related to one another after the event, at the analysis stage (as in multivariate regression), because this has already taken place at the fieldwork stage. The clusters of statistical observations simply have to be assembled in a commonsense fashion to throw light on the problem being examined; for example, is there any difference in the purchasing of a brand between those households that receive advertisements for it and those households that do not?

Following the first use of pure single-source research by McDonald in the United Kingdom in 1966, new types of single-source research were introduced in the United States during the two succeeding decades, and the meaning of *single-source* underwent some mutations. The concept became diluted. Papers presented at various conferences devoted to this type of research sponsored by the Advertising Research Foundation have used at least 14 separate definitions, all different from that given in this chapter.

By the 1980s, single-source research began to lose its focus on advertising and therefore its unique advantage: its ability to measure advertising effects. It became increasingly associated with scanner data (i.e., sales figures) collected at the checkout counters of food stores. The term also came to mean data relating to a substantial number of variables. Indeed, advertising descended in importance as promotional actions of different types began to take more prominent places in the data collection—reflecting the fact that promotions were becoming quantitatively much more important than advertising at that time.

This chapter, however, goes back to the origin of single-source research, which is rooted in the relationship between the identified advertising for specific brands and the purchasing of those brands. The system used to implement pure single-source research was introduced by A. C. Nielsen in the early 1990s.

The effect of advertising on purchase can be isolated through a device named Short-Term Advertising Strength (STAS). STAS is based on purchase occasions as measured by the Nielsen Household Panel. Purchase occasions are recorded in the household sample from data collected by handheld scanners in the home. Television exposure is monitored by meters attached to the television sets. And the commercials appearing on-air at the times the sets are switched to specific identified channels are registered by an independent monitoring system (with the proprietary name of Monitor Plus). These three methods of collecting data are complex and expensive to set up and operate, but they provide all that is necessary to calculate the STAS for any brand.

- The brand's share of all purchase occasions in the households that had received no television advertising for it during the 7 days before buying is the *Baseline STAS*. Other analysts might describe the Baseline STAS as the brand's "natural" or "brand equity" sales level.
- The brand's share of all purchase occasions in the households that had received at least one television advertisement for it during the previous 7 days is the *Stimulated STAS*.
- The difference between the Baseline STAS and the Stimulated STAS is the *STAS Differential*.

The STAS Differential is invariably indexed, so the numbers generally calculated represent the percentage by which the Stimulated STAS is above or below the Baseline STAS (indexed at 100). For each brand, the STAS measure is an average of all the weekly periods across the year. This means that with virtually all brands, a number of purchasing occasions are included. This is a procedure that gives STAS a considerable statistical solidity. (For further discussion of STAS, see Chapter 25.)

Is STAS a Uniform Measure for All Types of Buyers?

John Philip Jones

S hort-Term Advertising Strength (STAS) is a research technique developed during the early 1990s for measuring the immediate selling power of an advertisement (it is discussed also in Chapters 18, 24, and 26 of this volume). STAS is the ratio of brand share in the households that have received advertising for an identified brand during the 7 days before they buy it and the brand share in the households that have received no such advertising. These groups are called the *Ad* and *Adless* households, respectively. My work on this concept in both the United States and Germany produced a single STAS Differential for each brand in each country, representing an average for all the households in the two groups, the Ad and the Adless.

I stress the importance of the short period of 7 days as the advertising "window" for two reasons. First, advertising close to day of purchase is more effective than advertising that appears earlier. Second, 7 days represents the average grocery shopping cycle in the United States; reflecting this, my recommended media strategy is to plan a minimal level of weekly exposure, to be repeated for as many weeks as the budget will allow.

To calculate a STAS Differential, one must divide the sample of homes in the research panel into four unequal subsamples:

1. Homes that receive advertising for the brand and buy it
2. Homes that receive advertising for the brand and do not buy it
3. Homes that do not receive advertising for the brand and buy it
4. Homes that do not receive advertising for the brand and do not buy it

For each brand (i.e., each STAS number), the composition of these four groups is of course different from that for any other brand/STAS.

The need to divide the sample in the way just described has made me sensitive to the danger of working with inadequate subsamples if we are to break down in any way the STAS average for a brand. This is why I regarded my total samples as minima. In the United States, I employed 1 year's data from a panel of 2,000 homes. In Germany, I used 2 years' data from a panel of 1,000.

Colin McDonald, who first developed the pure single-source technique in the United Kingdom in 1966, has found a way, however, of broadening the empirical basis of STAS calculations. He managed in 1995 to find and use a powerful battery of consumer purchasing and media exposure data collected by the Taylor Nelson research organization for the Central TV Company in Britain. The data came from a panel of 1,000 homes and collected continuous information relating to 23 product categories over the 4½-year period September 1985 through March 1990. The data bank is known as the Adlab panel.

McDonald looked at a number of variables not covered in my research, notably the following:

1. He examined households switching into a brand compared with households repeating a brand purchase. (I lumped both of these together in my computation of market share.)
2. He varied the lengths of period during which advertising exposure was counted. (As explained, I looked at a uniform window of 7 days.)
3. He calculated STAS by brands with differing shares of voice within the purchase interval. (I have throughout disregarded the purchase interval as less useful, in my opinion, than the 7-day window.)

4. He looked at variations in STAS among heavy, medium, and light television viewers. (I combined these groups.)

5. He looked at variations in STAS among heavy, medium, and light buyers of the brand examined. (Again, I combined these.)[1]

I must emphasize that in my work in developing STAS, I tried very hard to produce a simple and comprehensible measure of short-term advertising effectiveness that can be employed by clients and agencies to guide operational policy in the marketplace, and the degree to which my work has been used in this way has not been totally disappointing. In the United States, the lessons drawn from my work regarding media strategy are now being used by a possible majority of major advertisers.[2] In Germany, STAS is used by clients of A. C. Nielsen to differentiate more effective from less effective campaigns. And GfK—the German research organization affiliated with Nielsen's main American competitor, Information Resources Inc.—after at first being bitterly antagonistic toward my work, has now adapted STAS to its own purposes.[3]

McDonald's analyses of the Adlab data provide additional knowledge that might lead to improvements in the precision and operational efficiency of STAS. I shall concentrate here on the last two pieces of work on my list of McDonald's analyses: those relating to weight of television viewing and the weight of brand purchasing.

Variations in STAS by Weight of Media Exposure

McDonald's starting point is the calculation of the Purchase/Viewing Index (PVI), which is the ratio of a brand's share among high television viewers to its share among light television viewers. Out of a sample of 52 brands, 42 have a PVI of more than 10 percentage points either side of the average. For the majority of these brands, heavy viewers buy more than the average amount; for a minority of brands, light viewers buy more. There is a statistical association (with a correlation coefficient of 0.55) between the size of a brand's PVI and the size of its STAS, showing a likelihood that brands biased toward heavy purchasing by specific media-exposed groups will also have a higher STAS.

TABLE 25.1   Proposed Operational Policy for Various Levels of STAS

Quintile	Average STAS Differential	Operational Policy
First	198	maintain campaign
Second	130	maintain campaign
Third	112	beta (i.e., large brands, maintain campaign; other brands, search for alternative campaign)
Fourth	100	search for alternative campaign
Fifth	82	search for alternative campaign

What does this mean? In my judgment, the last STAS calculation is less important than the basic data on media exposure. What is really useful to advertising practitioners is the ability to differentiate the above-average buying by the high (or the low) television viewing groups on a brand-by-brand basis. If it can be demonstrated, for example, that heavy television viewers are likely to buy the brand significantly more than light television viewers are, this is a conclusion directly relevant to a brand's media strategy. In this particular case, it is likely to direct the brand's television schedule toward high-rating prime-time programs. McDonald's analysis—in its simplest form—can contribute to the efficiency of advertising practice.

It is also possible to calculate a STAS Differential for each viewing group, but this means that we have to divide our basic sample into 12 subsamples. For heavy viewers, for medium viewers, and for light viewers separately, we must divide the sample into the 4 subsamples listed on p. 284. This is likely to make some of the statistics rather fragile. However, setting this important point aside, three STAS estimates can be generated to compare with the average. There are circumstances in which this will be worth doing—such as when the bottom viewing/buying group is likely to generate a STAS Differential significantly below the average—and when this happens the campaign may well have to be abandoned. However, I believe strongly that such an eventuality is likely to be rare.

We should also bear in mind the limits or boundaries that we should set in using the STAS data operationally. Table 25.1 proposes such limits. The STAS figure in the first column is the average STAS Differential for each quintile of the 78 American brands I analyzed, ranged from the highest to the lowest average STAS.[4]

I believe that in all five quintiles, the operational policy should remain the same even if differing viewing groups generate STAS levels 10 percentage points either side of the average (e.g., 108 to 188 for each quintile). Even if the spread were much greater—say, 20 percentage points either side of the average—the only quintile that would be difficult to evaluate would be the third one.

The really difficult decision point would be where the STAS levels are for brands at the top end of the third-quintile range. When an individual STAS Differential is, say, 120, then it is a tricky judgment call whether or not to abandon the campaign if the STAS for an important media viewing group is 20 percentage points below this 120.

Variation in STAS by Weight of Brand Buying

McDonald's conclusions based on this second analysis are not dissimilar from those based on his analysis of television viewing patterns. He has published a diagram showing STAS variations for heavy and light brand users, calculated during a 7-day window of advertising exposure. This diagram indicates an average spread in STAS of about 15 percentage points between heavy and light users of various brands.[5]

This difference should be taken into account during the process of strategic targeting. However, I believe that in most cases—as with variations due to differential buying by different viewing groups—the differences are not going to be large enough to cause a change in operational policy. Table 25.1 and the discussion of its implications will similarly apply.

McDonald's analysis of the different STAS levels by weight of brand purchase shows a much greater spread of numbers if the data are analyzed during a brand's purchase interval (generally a longer period than 7 days). Because I have good reasons for selecting a 7-day advertising window (discussed at the beginning of this chapter), I do not believe McDonald's analysis of purchase interval data to be totally relevant, despite its intrinsic interest.

McDonald's work with the Adlab panel is ongoing. Advertising and research practitioners, especially those in Britain, are following his conclusions with great interest as they are revealed.

Notes

1. Colin McDonald, "How Frequently Should You Advertise?" *Admap,* July/August 1996, 22-25; Colin McDonald, "Short-Term Advertising Effects: How Confident Can We Be?" *Admap,* June 1997, 36-39.

2. Myers Report Industry Research, *The Myers Report* (New York: Myers Report Industry Research, December 16, 1996).

3. Klaus Kindelmann and Raimund Wildner, "What a Revised STAS Can Tell Us About Advertising's Short-Term Effects," in *The 1997 European Advertising Effectiveness Symposium, Paris* (Brighton, UK: Advertising Seminars International, June 1997).

4. John Philip Jones, *When Ads Work: New Proof That Advertising Triggers Sales* (New York: Simon & Schuster-Lexington, 1995), 23.

5. McDonald, "Short-Term Advertising Effects," 38.

Part IV

Advertising Effects, Including Some Unexpected Ones

How Much
Advertising Works?

John Philip Jones

This chapter is based on the findings of pure single-source research, a technique also discussed in Chapters 18, 24, and 25 of this volume. A very brief description of pure single-source research is that it measures each household's reception of advertising for specific advertised brands and relates this to the purchasing of those brands by those same households shortly after the advertising. We must isolate, identify, and prove reception of advertising for the brand within a defined period before buying takes place (I use a period of 7 days before purchase). This means that we must record buying on a purchase-by-purchase basis, with the use of scanners. The basic measure of advertising's short-term effectiveness is Short-Term Advertising Strength (STAS), which is the difference between a brand's share of purchase occasions in the households that have received advertising for it and its share in the households that have not.[1]

The baseline level (brand share without advertising) is called the Baseline STAS. The share in the households that have received advertising is called the Stimulated STAS. The difference between the two levels is known as the STAS Differential.

Can Advertising Generate Immediate Sales?

The answer to the question posed in the above heading is yes. Before the arrival of scanner data, the only type of advertising that was seen to drive sales immediately was direct response. The problem that made it impossible to isolate the immediate effectiveness of advertising for repeat-purchase packaged goods was the research methodology. Research data collected over infrequent intervals smoothed all short-term sales fluctuations, some of which were driven by advertising. The fact that these fluctuations were concealed led many analysts to doubt their existence. Some analysts began to believe that the sole purpose of advertising was defensive, and that in most circumstances it worked slowly and cumulatively.

At the time when the advertising industry had to rely on retail audit data collected six times a year, annual sales estimates moved from year to year in a seamless way, and bimonthly figures changed direction only in response to seasonal movements, which were always regular and predictable. From bimonthly data it was often possible to detect the effects of sales promotions, especially by examining closely changes in market share. But the immediate effects of advertising were very rarely detectable, although long-term trends could be seen.

There was a real downside to this type of analysis. It inevitably led to the conclusion that promotions are the tactic of choice to generate immediate sales lifts; advertising was seen as a device that pays off only in the long term. Theories about brand images and brand equity were developed to explain this doctrine of advertising's long-term effectiveness, and the research industry duly responded by devising a battery of measures to evaluate advertising's long-term operation in terms of cognitive and affective variables. These provide useful diagnostics, but they were—and still are—generally overinterpreted. The belief that we should look for advertising's influence exclusively in the long term has also led to the rather remarkable view—widely albeit tacitly believed—that advertising is capable of working in the long term without having any effect in the short term (the "sleeper effect," or "advertising as time bomb").

Weekly increases in sales are driven by seasonal uplifts, sales promotions, and advertising for the brand. Weekly decreases are driven by seasonal downturns, sales promotions, and advertising for competitive brands. From all the cases we have seen of this type of sales volatility, there is a universal

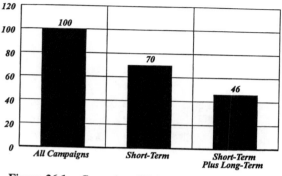

Figure 26.1.   Campaigns With Positive Sales Effects

pattern of sharp and erratic sales ups and downs (See Chapter 3 by Bogart, in this volume).

How Many Campaigns Boost Sales?

Some 70% of campaigns increase sales immediately. In many cases this boost is small—and temporary. Long-term effects, as measured by market share improvement over a year (or maintenance of share in the case of a small number of large brands that are under pressure), are generated by 46% of campaigns (see Figure 26.1).

Short-term effects of campaigns are very variable. This is apparent when the brands are ranked by the size of the STAS Differential and divided into deciles. A fair interpretation of the decile analysis shown in Figure 26.2 is as follows:

- 20% of campaigns work with a first order of effectiveness.
- 30% work with a second order of effectiveness.
- 30% are not very strong either way.
- 20% have a negative effect (i.e., they are incapable of protecting the brand from the marketing activities of competitive brands).

The year-end effects are more muted than the short-term effects. In each decile the sales are less positive. A comparison of Figures 26.2 and 26.3 provides clear evidence of competitive forces operating within the market to subdue the short-term sales effects over the course of a year. The main reason brands do not maintain their STAS Differentials against competitive pressure

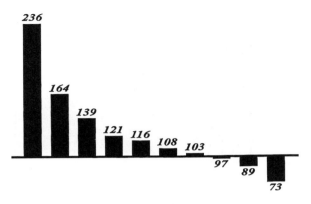

Figure 26.2.   Range of STAS Effects

is a lack of media continuity. When a brand is not advertised, it is vulnerable to the short-term influences of the promotions and advertising for all other brands in the category.

Is There a Threshold of Advertising Pressure for a Short-Term Effect?

One of the reasons many media schedules have tended to lack continuity is that continuity has been sacrificed to obtain "flights" or "bursts" of concentration demanded by a once-prevalent doctrine that advertising has to cross a threshold of multiple exposures in order to generate any effect all. As I shall demonstrate, pure single-source research has shown that such a threshold does not exist, and that it is economic and desirable to run advertising continuously so long as a schedule reaches a reasonable majority of members of the target group at least once in any week.

The STAS analysis provides reliable data on the amount of media exposure necessary to increase short-term sales (see Figure 26.4). A conclusion from the research that has startled the research community is that one exposure generates the highest proportion of sales, and additional exposures add very little to the effect of the first. The advertising response function is concave-downward, demonstrating diminishing returns in the clearest possible way. Effective frequency is provided by a single exposure. It is wasteful to concentrate media money into flights to provide an average of more than one "opportunity to see."

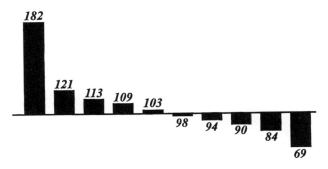

Figure 26.3. Range of Year-End Sales Changes

Given that one exposure within an advertising flight generates much the largest quantity of sales, high-pressure airtime flights are wasteful. And because such high pressure is not much more effective than minimal pressure (i.e., enough to ensure that most members of the target group are exposed to advertising for the brand once), STAS can be assumed to measure the creative quality of the campaign and not the amount of media expenditure during the period before purchase.

Data From Other Countries

Pure single-source research employing the STAS measure has been carried out in both the United Kingdom and Germany.[2] The range of STAS effects is remarkably similar between the United States and the two European markets. The three countries are compared in Table 26.1 (the figures for the United States in the table repeat those in Figure 26.2). In the table, the only important difference among the three countries relates to the top end of advertising effectiveness. Especially among the 30% of most effective campaigns, the STAS is more positive in the United States than in Britain, and Britain is in turn ahead of Germany. It is not known why this should be, but I suspect that it is due at least partly to the more effective use of advertising pretesting in the United States than in Europe.

The two pieces of European research also provide data on the shape of the advertising response function. These confirm, *mutatis mutandis,* the prevalence of diminishing returns, as was found in the United States.

One of the oldest and best-known advertising aphorisms, variously attributed to William Hesketh Lever in Britain and John Wanamaker in the United

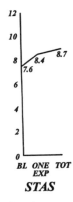

Figure 26.4.   The Effect of One Advertisement—All Advertised Brands

TABLE 26.1 Range of STAS Effects in Three Countries

Decile	United States	United Kingdom	Germany
Top	236	184	154
Ninth	164	129	127
Eighth	139	119	116
Seventh	121	114	108
Sixth	116	110	106
Fifth	108	107	101
Fourth	103	102	100
Third	97	98	98
Second	89	93	92
Bottom	73	73	83

States, is that half of all advertising is wasted, but the author does not know which half. Pure single-source research from the United States and Europe suggests strongly that Lever and Wanamaker were correct in broad terms. They were both highly experienced advertisers, besides being intelligent and successful men. It is interesting that their purely instinctive conclusion about advertising effectiveness has received empirical support almost a century later.

Notes

1. John Philip Jones, *When Ads Work: New Proof That Advertising Triggers Sales* (New York: Simon & Schuster-Lexington, 1995).

2. See, respectively, Colin McDonald, "How Frequently Should You Advertise?" *Admap,* July/August 1996, 22-25; John Philip Jones, *When Ads Work: The German Version* (Frankfurt am Main: Gesamtverband Werbeagenturen, 1995).

27

Reduced Advertising and Its Impact on Profitability and Market Share in a Recession

Alexander L. Biel

It is no surprise that when economies become soft, businesses naturally search for ways to cut expenses. Marketing budgets in general, and advertising budgets in particular, are vulnerable targets, because they can be cut at relatively short notice. However, little is known about the consequences of changes in such spending on share of market and on profits. Do budget cuts really help short-term profitability? And what, if any, are the risks of ad budget reduction?

Of course, not all marketers retreat when the economy recedes. Here's what Toyota's head of marketing in the United States, George Borst, said to *Wall*

NOTE: This chapter is an adaptation of an article that appeared in *Admap,* May 1991. Used by permission.

Street Journal reporters at the beginning of the 1990-1991 recession: "We see this as a time to *strengthen* the brand image of Toyota. . . . Toyota has posted a healthy increase in its fourth quarter spending." Mr. Borst went on to comment: "You really need to spend when the chips are down. . . . *you can really lose a lot if you let the momentum get away from you.*"

What can be learned from those marketers that take a more proactive position? What happens to their market share and profits? A series of collaborative studies undertaken by the Ogilvy Center for Research & Development and the Strategic Planning Institute provide some answers to these questions. These studies all utilized the unique PIMS database. This chapter is based on the empirical studies made by these two organizations.

The acronym PIMS stands for "profit impact of market strategy." PIMS is the only database that includes both marketing and financial information on the same businesses. At the time of this analysis, the database included a minimum of 4 years of data on each of 749 consumer businesses. These encompass durables and nondurables, including packaged goods businesses, as well as service organizations. The businesses are based in Europe as well as North America. Businesses with large shares of their markets contributed data, as well as businesses with small market shares. Some of the units in the database earn very high profits; others yield quite low rates of return. These businesses represent a substantial, respectable, and reasonably diversified sample of consumer businesses.

Advertising's Contribution to Share of Market/Profitability

The first issue to be explored is the contribution of advertising expenditures to share of market and profitability under normal conditions, because this sets the scene for an analysis of the impact of a recession.

Specifically, does it pay for a marketer to spend money on advertising under *any* conditions? Today, when so many marketers are questioning the value of media advertising, and instead turning to promotions and other marketing stimuli, this is the crucial starting point.

The first study focused on all 749 of the consumer businesses in PIMS. In order to gauge advertising's contribution, a measure of spending was required. To remove the "brand size" effect (i.e., large brands spend more than small

TABLE 27.1   Relative Advertising Expenditures and Share of Market

A:S vs. Direct Competitors	Average Share of Market (%)
Much less	14
Less	20
Equal	25
More	26
Much more	32

brands), advertising-to-sales (A:S) ratios versus competition were chosen. This made possible the classification of consumer businesses into five groups based on their A:S ratios versus those of their direct competitors. The research clearly demonstrates a link between A:S ratios and market share (see Table 27.1).

How Advertising Works

In an effort to gain better insight into how advertising works, we probed the data further. The research established that advertising drives share of market by increasing both the salience and the relative perceived quality of the advertised brands of goods or services (this is shown in Figure 27.1). Although advertising is in no way a valid substitute for improvements in product or service quality, it can arguably *amplify* and *reinforce* perceptions of quality where that quality does exist. Consequently, it is hardly surprising that increases in perceived quality are linked to increases in market share.

So far, we have concentrated on share of market, because share is a very good indicator of brand strength at the consumer level. And, indeed, the well-established link between share and profits was certainly confirmed in these data, as Figure 27.2 demonstrates. However, that still does not completely address the accountability issue. Some brands that have a sizable share of market earn pitifully small profits. Although these are admittedly exceptions, it is important to document the direct relationship between advertising spending and actual profits.

The data in Table 27.2 indicate that marketers with A:S ratios that are much lower than those of their direct competitors earn an average return on invested capital of 17%, before taxes and interest expenses. Those whose advertising-

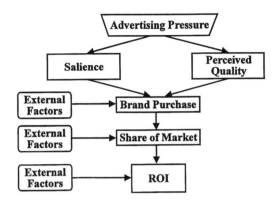

Figure 27.1.   How Advertising Works

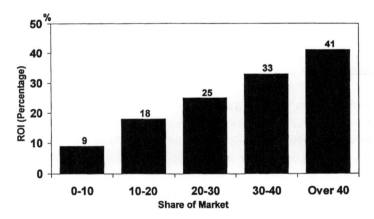

Figure 27.2.   Market Share and Return on Investment

to-sales ratios are somewhat less or equal to those of their direct competitors earn a return on investment (ROI) of about 22%. Businesses with A:S ratios that are somewhat higher than those of their direct competitors earn 25%. But those that spend *much* more relative to their direct competitors average a return of 32% on their invested capital. In other words, those with much higher A:S ratios earn ROIs that are *nearly double* those of businesses spending much less relative to sales.

Because the PIMS database covers businesses over time, it can also be used to study the impact of recession on advertising. This is my second study..

TABLE 27.2 Relative Advertising Expenditures and Return on Investment

A:S vs. Direct Competitors	Average ROI (%)
Much less	17
Less	22
Equal	22
More	25
Much more	32

Advertising During Recessions

Although the recessions that make the newspaper headlines are generally seen as all-encompassing and national in scope, this definition obscures the fact that "normal" national economic conditions are really an averaging of good times in some industries and bad times in others—growth in some parts of the country and decline in others.

During a national recession, of course, everyone gets hurt. But some sectors feel the pressure far more than others. Conversely, of course, during a period of expansion some markets reap greater benefits and others lag behind. A more useful, empirically determined definition of recession is one that relates annual growth at one specific time to the longer-term growth trend of a specific market.

For purposes of the second study, a specific market was considered to be in recession when short-term growth lagged long-term growth by at least 4 percentage points. On the other hand, when a market exceeded its long-term growth rate by more than 4 percentage points, it was considered to be in a period of expansion.

Using this definition, how do consumer businesses fare under different market conditions? To understand what happens during changing conditions, it is useful to look at changes in rates of return for those businesses enjoying the fruits of market expansion compared with those suffering the privations of a shrinking market. Figure 27.3 shows that, as might be expected, there is a substantial market effect on a firm's return on invested capital. It is, of course, hardly surprising that the study found that when a market contracts, the profits of most businesses in that market are hurt. In this study, the average consumer business lost just under 2 percentage points of profit, dropping from a return on invested capital of 21.9% to 20.0%.

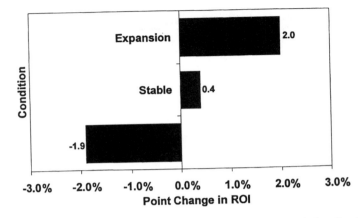

Figure 27.3. Changes in Return on Investment Under Different Market Conditions

It is also no great surprise to learn that when the market expands, the average consumer business in the PIMS database enjoys an increased ROI, moving up by 2 percentage points. In fact, one might well expect rates of return to increase even more sharply during a period of market growth; the fact that they do not may be explained to some extent by the difficulty that some businesses face in meeting increased demand.

Within this framework, what is the relationship of changes in advertising spending to changes in return on invested capital? To answer this question, the study looked at the specific spending policies employed by the businesses in the database. Of the 339 observations of the strategic business units in the sample that experienced recessionary periods, one-third cut their spending on advertising by an average of 11%, whereas two-thirds of the businesses actually spent at higher rates than before. Of those businesses raising their advertising investments, the majority limited the increase to no more than 20% more than they had previously been spending. (The average business in this group increased spending by a modest 10%.) However, a minority of those businesses raising their expenditures made substantial increases, averaging 49% and ranging from more than 20% to 100%.

This provided three groups of businesses of roughly the same size with three very different coping strategies. How did they perform? (See Table 27.3.) As previously noted, when a market shrinks, the average business suffers a drop in profits. However, the important point here is that this happens to those that cut their budgets as well as those that increased their spending. Indeed, it

TABLE 27.3 Changes in ROI Related to Changes in Advertising Spending During a Recession

Spending	Changes in ROI (%)
Decrease	−1.6
Modest increase (<20%)	−1.7
Substantial increase (20-100%)	−2.7
Average change—all businesses	−1.9

is interesting to note that businesses yielding to the natural inclination to cut spending in an effort to increase profits in a recession find that it really does not work. Those businesses cutting back fare no better in terms of ROI than those that modestly increase their ad spending: The budget cutters lose an average of 1.6 percentage points, whereas those increasing their spending by an average of less than 20% drop 1.7 points of ROI, a difference that is not significant.

What about those firms that *substantially* increase their advertising budgets in a soft market? They experience a somewhat larger drop in ROI: The most aggressive marketers reduced their return on invested capital by 2.7%. However, those advertisers that increase spending—whether modestly or aggressively—achieve greater market share gains than those that cut their advertising investments. This, in turn, puts them in a better position for reaping post-recession profitability benefits.

These findings led us to dissect the relationship between changes in ROI and changes in advertising pressure. As demonstrated in our first study, advertising spending and ROI are linked, but only indirectly. Salience and quality drive buying behavior, which of course is reflected in sales, and therefore in share of market. But market share, of course, is affected by market conditions as well as advertising pressure.

It was found that the businesses in the PIMS database enjoy a *higher* rate of share growth during downturns, but a *lower* rate of share increase during stable periods and periods of market growth (see Figure 27.4). One explanation for this is that weaker businesses—businesses with lower shares of their markets—may be less able to defend themselves during downturns, while their larger competitors become more aggressive in order to make up sales that are threatened due to lower growth of the total category.

To identify the relationship of changes in spending to changes in share of market, we again analyzed the data in terms of the spending strategies of the

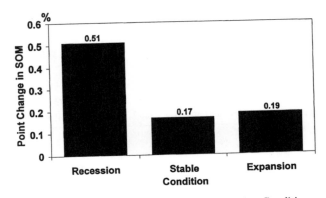

Figure 27.4. Changes in Share Related to Market Conditions

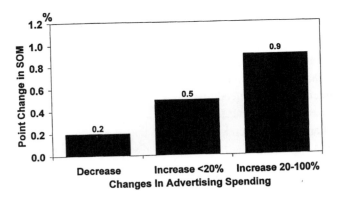

Figure 27.5. Changes in Share Related to Changes in
Advertising Spending During a Recession

various businesses employed. We learned that those markets reducing their
budgets during a recession attain lower share gains than do their more
aggressive counterparts (see Figure 27.5).

On the other hand, marketers that increase spending are able to realize
significant gains in terms of market share. Whereas those reducing their
spending managed to gain only two-tenths of a share point, firms that modestly increased their budgets by up to 20% earned increases of five-tenths of
a share. But those bullish marketers that averaged a 50% increase in advertising expenditures managed to wrest almost a share point from the competition.

It is worth noting that although there appear to be opportunities to win share by becoming increasingly competitive during a recession, when markets expand, share gains are harder to come by. Marketers that decrease their spending during an expansion of the market lose share, albeit slightly; on average, they drop a tenth of a share point. Those that increase their spending by upward of 20% as their market expands increase their average share, but by only half a percentage point. In other words, *the possibility of gaining share through increasing advertising pressure would appear to be greater when the total market is soft.*

It is important to remember that the changes in both share of market and ROI found in this study were achieved during the recessionary period itself. Other research indicates that the main—but by no means the entire—impact of advertising on sales is achieved in the year the budget is spent. However, the main impact of share gains is translated into gains in profitability in subsequent periods.

Although the data reported here are of course correlational, and do not necessarily prove causality, they nonetheless suggest that there may be some attractive share-building opportunities during periods when business in general contracts. Indeed, the data suggest that aggressive marketers may well find that recessionary periods offer unique opportunities to build share and position themselves advantageously for the market's recovery.

As noted above in the discussion of our first study of consumer businesses, a clear relationship has been established between share of emarket and return on investment. These data suggest that the advertiser who is able to build share is likely to enjoy a better return on invested capital than is the marketer with a lower market share.

But what happens if a recession continues to deepen? Interestingly, a study conducted in the United Kingdom addresses this issue. It was commissioned by the Billett Consultancy and conducted by Taylor Nelson AGB. It compared ad spending and share changes for 127 brands of repeat-purchase packaged goods in 46 different product categories. Again, the sample was heterogeneous, with categories ranging in size from £800 million down to £40 million. The time frame for the analysis was the first 6 months of 1991 compared with the first 6 months of 1992, when the national recession had deepened. The brands were broken down into three equal size groups (terciles), ranked according to the increase or decrese in their advertising budgets.

Again, and not atypically, some categories rose and others dropped. In those markets that continued to recede, brands in the top tercile in advertising expenditure change—those showing an increase—gained 1.7 share points. To accomplish this, they boosted their spending by 27% on average. But those brands in the lowest tercile of advertising expenditure change—those brands that most *reduced* their spending—found that their average share of market had declined 2.1 points.

The analysis has concentrated on consumer marketers simply because more data are available in that area. There has been less recent research on the impact of advertising in the business-to-business field. However, in 1982, Kijewski presented a study of more than 1,000 industrial marketers that revealed remarkably similar patterns compared with those described in this chapter. During the market-specific recessions analyzed, 25% of business-to-business advertisers spent aggressively. The spending increases ranged from 28% to 80%, and averaged just under 40%.

For their efforts, these advertisers enjoyed share gains averaging 1.5 percentage points, and ROIs of 25%. Interestingly, the ROIs were not statistically different from the ROIs earned by those that cut budgets or only modestly increased spending. However, the average gain in share of market was significantly higher than that of budget cutters as well as those increasing their spending less aggressively.

Before I summarize these three very consistent and extremely broad-based studies, some additional observations are in order. The first relates to our market-specific definition of recession. During a national recession, three additional phenomena are often observed:

1. Consumers generally tend to stay at home more; in turn, they are likely to increase their consumption of media.
2. Media rates often become more attractive due to the softer advertising market that accompanies recession.
3. The marketer that increases advertising pressure during a downturn is also likely to enjoy a greater share of voice than would be the case if the market were expanding.

Of course, the first two of these conditions were not present in our study, because industry-specific recessions were the target of the analysis. However, it is arguable that these findings are likely if anything to be somewhat *understated* because of their absence.

Finally, it should also be noted that the macroanalytic level of the PIMS database does not enable us to look beyond advertising weight. It does not allow an examination of advertising quality. This discussion has been based on averages. But clearly, more effective advertising will produce returns at the higher end, and less effective advertising will underperform these averages.

Summary

First, and not surprisingly, virtually *all* businesses earn reduced profits when their markets are in recession. Less obvious is the fact that marketers that modestly increase their investment in advertising pay no greater penalty in terms of ROI than those that cut spending.

But businesses that cut their advertising expenditures lose no less in terms of profitability than those that actually *increase* spending an average of up to 20%. In other words, cutting advertising spending to increase short-term profits *does not work.* Even worse, however, those advertisers that cut spending lose the opportunity to gain share.

Conversely, and even more important, the data also reveal that a moderate increase in advertising in a soft market can improve share. The evidence shows that a larger share of market generally leads to higher profits in subsequent periods.

For the aggressive marketer, an even more opportunistic view emerges. By significantly increasing advertising and absorbing a short-term reduction in ROI, companies can take advantage of a recession to increase market share significantly. By doing this, they position themselves to reap the longer-term benefit of enhanced profit as the market starts to expand again.

Margin and Price Effects of Manufacturers' Brand Advertising

Robert L. Steiner

A brand's retail price depends on the costs and margins of its manufacturer as well as those of the wholesalers and retailers that distribute it to household consumers. What complicates predicting the effects of advertising is that it can have very different effects on the costs, margins, and prices of these firms. For example, advertising may raise the manufacturer's selling price because it increased the firm's margin by more than it reduced its costs. Yet the brand's retail price may have been lowered because the manufacturer's advertising reduced retailers' markups by more than it increased the manufacturer's selling price. Even within the manufacturing sector, advertising typically exerts a contrary effect on the margins of the brand advertisers and those of the producers of competing unadvertised goods.

Our examination must also move beyond advertising's effects on individual manufacturers and retailers to deal with the more important social question: What is its impact on the industry as a whole? Finally, certain advertising-induced changes in industry structure do not show up immediately. These longer-term effects must be identified and distinguished from short-run effects.

I begin this chapter with some nontechnical definitions of the key concepts needed to probe these matters. I will then describe the analytic framework that will be used in the balance of the chapter to identify the effects of manufacturers' brand advertising on margins, costs, and prices in a number of commonly encountered industry structures and for the consumer goods economy as a whole.

Demand Schedules, Elasticity, Competition, Margins

Demand Schedules

A demand schedule (demand curve) indicates the quantity that buyers will take at each price, holding constant the prices of other goods. I will be referring to three demand schedules: the quantity the brand's manufacturer sells at each factory price (DM), the quantity of the brand that consumers will buy at each retail price (DK), and the quantity the typical retailer who stocks the brand will sell at each retail price (DR).

Elasticity

Economists use the concept of price elasticity of demand to measure the sensitivity of an item's sales to small changes in its price. The price elasticity of demand is defined as the percentage change in the quantity demanded of an item in response to a small percentage change in its price. We say the price elasticity of demand is "unity" when a small percentage increase (decrease) in the item's price causes the same percentage decrease (increase) in the quantity sold. When small percentage changes in price cause more than proportionate changes in the quantity demanded, the brand is said to have an elastic demand schedule; when the proportionate change in quantity is less than that in price, the demand schedule is said to be inelastic.

Competition and Elasticity

Elasticity is positively related to competition. At one extreme, in perfectly competitive markets such as exist in a true commodity industry, sellers face infinitely elastic (horizontal) demand schedules. The interactions of supply and demand produce a market price that all sellers accept. They do so because they can sell any quantity they like at the market price, but would make no sales at prices above that level. The classical preconditions for a perfectly competitive market require that there be a host of sellers providing a homogeneous product who sell it to a host of buyers under conditions in which both buyers and sellers have perfect information.

At the other extreme there are occasionally markets in which a single brand has a monopoly. The seller could be a manufacturing firm or a retailer that is the exclusive vendor of a brand in its market area. The seller of a monopolistic brand will face a downward-sloping demand curve, because as a brand's price is reduced, buyers will purchase larger quantities of it.

In the consumer goods economy almost all brands exist in an environment that is between the polar extremes of perfect competition and pure monopoly, which economists refer to as *imperfect competition*. In this state the goods of rival sellers are partial but not complete substitutes for each other; that is, they are similar but not identical. In imperfect competition, sellers lose some but not all of their revenues when they raise prices above those of their competitors, so they face downward-sloping demand schedules that are less elastic than those of sellers in perfectly competitive markets.

On the other hand, given an identical schedule of consumer preferences for a brand, the manufacturer in an imperfectly competitive market faces a more elastic demand schedule than in a monopoly. Unlike the monopolist, which by definition has no competitors, the firm in an imperfectly competitive industry gains or loses sales to rivals in response to changes in the firm's price. Likewise, DR is always more elastic than DK unless the retailer is a monopolist, in which case DK = DR. As competition heats up or abates in monopolistically competitive markets, sellers' demand curves become, respectively, more or less elastic.

Margins

Per the Lerner theorem, in equilibrium for the profit-maximizing firm, elasticity is the reciprocal of the margin. Margin is defined as price minus marginal cost divided by price. Marginal cost is the change in the firm's total cost as a result of producing one more unit. When marginal cost is constant as output rises, the firm's marginal and variable cost schedules are the same. In the definition of margin, fixed costs—those that do not vary with output (e.g., overhead)—are not included. But over time a firm's overhead will be raised or lowered as its output increases or decreases. So in this long-term sense, all costs are variable.

In sum, the more competitive the market, the higher the elasticity of demand faced by sellers and the lower their margins.

Analytic Framework, Single- and Dual-Stage Models

The Single-Stage Framework

Writing in 1950, E. R. Hawkins observed that "economic theory in general has been written as though the producer sold directly to the consumer. . . . The middleman has not been in the picture at all." [1] Almost a half century later it unfortunately remains true that when economists wish to analyze the economic effects of advertising they are frequently still trapped in the "single-stage" framework implied by the foregoing.

In single-stage models, the manufacturer is positioned as the firm and the wholesale/retail markets that intervene between manufacturer and consumer in the real world have been dispensed with by the implicit assumption that they do not matter. In this single-stage world the manufacturer's or factory price (PM) is presumed to be a reasonable and unbiased proxy for the price consumers pay (PC) for a brand.

The manufacturer here might be likened to a mail-order house that deals directly with consumers. The demand schedule faced by the mail-order house is the brand's consumer demand curve (DK). Alternatively, in the single-stage paradigm, manufacturers may be viewed as selling to consumers through an inert distribution system in which retailers buy and sell as perfect competitors. The manufacturer's demand curve (DM) is then "derived" from the brand's consumer demand curve (DK) through subtraction of the intervening costs of distribution (including a perfectly competitive rate of return) at each quantity. Assuming constant costs in distribution, the demand schedule faced by the manufacturer selling through an inert distribution system, like that of the mail-order manufacturer, depends solely on consumer preferences.

If, as the result of successfully advertising its brand, a manufacturer now sells twice as many units at a 10% higher factory price than before, the single-stage interpretation is that this must exactly reflect the new schedule of consumer preferences (the brand's new DK curve). But it will be shown that the manufacturer's demand curve cannot be proxied forward to the consumer level and that consumer prices have risen by less than 10% and may even have fallen. Indeed, if retail prices had risen by 10%, consumers would have far less than doubled the quantities they demanded.

The failure of single-stage models to explain the difference in the behavior of demand at the two levels, and other real-world phenomena, is the inevitable consequence of such models' underlying assumption that little predictive power is lost by eliminating the markets that come between manufacturers and consumers. But as any consumer goods manufacturer knows, the quantities of a brand he can sell and the price at which he can sell it are heavily dependent on what happens in the channels of distribution. It is common experience that retailers are far from being inert price takers. They constantly attempt to bargain down the manufacturer's price. Even when they succeed, they may end up buying a competitor's brand instead. Moreover, retailers can stimulate a brand's sales substantially by featuring it on special display, or they can retard its sales by placing it on the bottom shelf. Retailers can also elect to price the brand attractively or to apply a high markup that causes many consumers to pass it by.

Manufacturers and retailers see competition as both a horizontal and a vertical process. Manufacturers in a product category vie to increase their share of market valued in factory selling prices, whereas retailers in a metropolitan area vie to increase their share of market valued in consumer (retail) prices. Simultaneously, the brand manufacturer and its retailers both strive to increase their respective shares of the brand's retail price—that is, each tries to obtain a larger portion of the total available margin in the vertical system.

Manufacturers in a Dual-Stage World

None of the foregoing dynamics can even be described, much less analyzed, in a single-stage framework that assumes either that manufacturers sell directly to consumers or that they deal with consumers through an inert distribution system. We therefore will analyze consumer goods industries in a simple dual-stage model. In the first stage, manufacturers sell to firms called retailers, which, as in a typical chain store organization, combine the whole-sale and retail functions into single integrated firms. In the second stage, retailers sell the goods to household consumers. This structure dispenses with the separate wholesaler level that occurs in some industries, although not with the wholesalers' function. Compared with a triple-stage model, it greatly simplifies the analysis without sacrificing much accuracy—so long as the industry's wholesaling sector is reasonably competitive or relatively small.

The demand function faced by a real-world consumer goods manufacturer is determined not only by the schedule of consumer preferences for the brand but by three dual-stage effects that play no role in a single-stage world. These are as follows:

- *Retail penetration:* The total share of the retail market in a product category accounted for by all dealers that stock a brand. If a brand has a 95% retail penetration, it is stocked by stores that together account for 95% of retail sales in the category.
- *Dealer support:* The measure of the merchandising efforts put forward by the brand's retailers. These include both advertising the brand in newspapers and other local media and in-store support, such as product display and push by salesclerks.
- *Retail gross margin:* The brand's retail gross margin (RGM) is the difference between its consumer price (PC) and the manufacturer's price (PM) divided by PC. Thus the retailer's share of a brand's consumer price is its RGM, and the manufacturer's share is 1 minus RGM. *RGM is the scoreboard on which the status of retailer/manufacturer competition is recorded.*

It is intuitively obvious that when advertising increases a brand's popular-ity, the manufacturer benefits further because more stores will now want to stock it and retailers in general will accord it more promotional support than before. But in addition to increased retail penetration and dealer support, the successfully advertised brand's manufacturer typically also benefits from the retail gross margin effect. In the section below headed "The Intensively Advertised Industry," I explain why advertising forces down the brand's RGM. When that occurs, the manufacturer's demand curve shifts outward. The fall in RGM means that at any factory price the retail price is now lower. So on his new demand curve, the brand's manufacturer sells more units at the old factory price and, up to a point, can raise his factory price and his margin without raising the brand's retail price above its preadvertising level.

A good way to see this is to describe conditions facing manufacturers and retailers in an unadvertised industry and then record the changes that occur by the advent of successful manufacturers' brand advertising. A century ago such transformations were common in England and in the United States as the new phenomenon of manufacturers' advertising swept across the consumer goods economy. A more recent example took place in the 1960s in the toy industry, which could not advertise effectively until the advent of television permitted commercial messages to be delivered to children.

Retailer Margins in a Dual-Stage World

In addition to any effects from the vertical bargaining between manufacturers and retailers, the margins of retailers in a category are determined primarily by the vigor of competition among rival stores. Intrabrand competition (competition on the same brands) is the most direct form of competition among retailers. As such, it is a more important determinant of their margins than interbrand competition among stores, which takes place between the category's different brands.

To illustrate: Retailer A is under much greater pressure to reduce his price on Brand X if Retailer B cuts that brand's price than if Retailer B cuts the price of Brand Y. The more so if Retailer A does not stock Brand Y.

The Unadvertised Industry

To visualize conditions in a prototypical unadvertised industry, think of a 7th Avenue apparel category, such as women's dresses, awash with the brands of around 5,000 U.S. manufacturers plus those of foreign producers. In such industries manufacturers do make differentiated items. But because "consumers have no strong preference for one brand over several others . . . the manufacturer . . . is a beggar at the retailer's office."[2] These conditions empower the industry's retailers by simultaneously sheltering them from vigorous price competition with other dealers and enabling them to bargain down manufacturers' selling prices. They arise in product categories where consumers are more disposed to switch brands within store than stores within brand.[3]

In unadvertised industries, consumers generally enter retail stores with a generic demand for goods of a particular class. Retailer A finds it makes little difference whether he stocks Brands X, Y, and Z or Brands Q, R, and S with the same general attributes. Few consumers will walk out of the store if Retailer A fails to carry Brand X, or if he prices it above what other retailers are asking for it.

In industries with a multitude of little-known brands, each individual brand will be thinly distributed, making it time-consuming for shoppers to compare the prices different dealers are asking for different brands and for the same brand. Nor do retailers typically offer unknown items at reduced, sale prices in their newspaper ads. They long ago learned that such ads do not pull store traffic, in part because consumers do not know from their own experience whether or not the advertised price is really a bargain. Manufacturers and retailers refer to items whose prices consumers have difficulty judging as *blind.*

Thus the preconditions for a competitive intrabrand or interbrand market are not met. Consider the case of typical unadvertised Brand X. Few stores sell it. The lack of manufacturer and retailer advertising, in combination with high search costs, ensures that consumers lack information. On this account, the product homogeneity criterion is also not fulfilled, for consumers do not readily recognize that Xa, Xb, and Xc are the same manufacturer's Brand X on sale in three different retail stores.

Retailer demand schedules (DR) will reflect this lax competitive climate, and because elasticity and margin are negatively correlated, retailers should have high margins. And so they do. In apparel categories and numerous other unadvertised industries, the "keystone" pricing formula has long held sway: Retailers simply double the manufacturer's price to set their own price, resulting in a retail gross margin of around 50%.

The RGM, of course, considers only the invoice cost of the goods (the manufacturer's selling price in a dual-stage world). Retailers also have non-invoice variable costs in connection with handling, financing, and selling the goods. These costs normally total less than 10% of retailers' selling prices. They tend to be negatively associated with the rate of brand turnover, and are therefore relatively high in unadvertised industries. When both invoice and noninvoice variable costs are considered, retailers' margins are estimated at around 40% in the typical unadvertised industry.

It is straightforward that manufacturers' margins in unadvertised industries will be thin. To the intensive horizontal competition among the numerous small market share manufacturers is added the vertical bargaining clout of retailers. When individual brands lack a franchise with consumers, retailers have free rein to play off one manufacturer against the next in search of a better price and more favorable terms. Therefore, there is an inverse association between margins at the two stages—high ones for retailers and low ones for manufacturers.

As seen through single-stage glasses, the unadvertised industry appears to maximize consumer welfare except where manufacturers have very high costs because they are operating well below minimum efficient scale (MES). As previously noted, in single-stage analysis factory prices are used as a proxy for retail prices. This methodology filters out the high cost of distribution, which typically causes consumers to pay about twice factory prices in unadvertised, noncommodity product categories.

The Intensively Advertised Industry

Patent medicines and soaps were among the earliest convenience goods to be advertised intensively by manufacturers; bicycles share this distinction for expensive, durable products. A number of contemporary observers, including the economists Alfred Marshall in the United Kingdom and Emily Fogg-Meade in the United States, have reported that the onset of manufacturers' advertising set off savage retail price-cutting.[4]

When a brand becomes famous through advertising, or for any cause, all the previously unsatisfied conditions for intensive competition in the retailer/consumer market become fulfilled. There are now a host of consumer buyers for the newly popular brand, and a host of retail sellers emerge to satisfy the demand. Through advertising by the manufacturer and by retailers, word of mouth, experience in using the brand, and lower search costs, consumers now have abundant information. The lax intrabrand competition that characterizes the typical unadvertised industry quickly disappears. Consumers shortly come to understand that the Pears soap—or Lydia Pinkham's Vegetable Compound or the Columbia bicycle—on sale in different stores was the same item. High-price dealers must then drop their prices, because consumers are understandably loath to pay Dealer A more than Dealer B for what they recognize is the same thing. Ironically, it is this ability instantly to recognize a brand wherever it is sold, rather than the kind of carefully researched product information found in *Consumer Reports,* that is principally responsible for disciplining the markup retailers apply to a brand's factory price.

Dealers also find that it is advantageous to feature famous brands in newspaper ads at sale prices that are well below their everyday levels. Part of the payoff is that shoppers attracted to the store are likely to purchase some higher-margin items as well. Retailer price advertising stimulates intrabrand competition and dampens dealer margins. This intuitively obvious statement is reinforced by well-conducted studies that compared retail prices in states that did not restrict retailer price advertising of the goods with those that did. Cady examined prescription drugs, and Benham and Benham looked at eyeglasses.[5]

Recent empirical studies have also validated what consumer goods manufacturers and retailers have long known, that there is a strong negative correlation between the weight of brand advertising and retailer margins, because manufacturer's advertising increases competition among the brand's retailers.[6]

Successful advertised brands soon develop a "reputation premium" that requires unadvertised goods of similar type to be offered at a substantial discount from the advertised brand's retail price in order to sell in acceptable volume.[7] Therefore, after intensified intrabrand competition has forced down the retail margins and the prices of advertised brands, interbrand competition on retail counters then depresses the margins and prices of competing unadvertised brands. This process occurs faster and further in categories where retailers stock the same general assortment of brands than in those where individual brands are very selectively distributed, a practice that raises consumer search costs.

As consumers become more brand-loyal, a brand's consumer demand curve (DK) almost certainly becomes less elastic. But the fall in the elasticity of demand at the manufacturer's level (DM) in a dual-stage world is of a far greater magnitude. Compared with little-known brands, consumers are far more disposed to switch stores within brand than brands within store, should the retailer fail to stock a leading advertised brand or choose to price it above the market. This conduct by consumers now empowers the manufacturer of a successfully advertised brand, for as a brand becomes progressively stronger, it becomes less substitutable for retailers. Small factory price increases no longer cause a loss of retail penetration and dealer support, as they do with an unadvertised brand.

I noted earlier that the manufacturer also enjoys the elasticity-reducing and margin-increasing benefits of a fall in his brand's RGM. The following is an oversimplified illustration. If a brand's preadvertising factory price was \$5 and its retail price $10, a 50% RGM, and the postadvertising RGM falling to 25%, the manufacturer could raise its factory price to $7.50 without raising its retail price above $10.

In the horizontal arena, there is yet another competitive effect from the falling RGM, which occurs because the advertised brand's RGM will be substantially below that of competing unadvertised brands. This means the latter items must now lower their factory prices even to sell at the same retail price as the advertised brand. But because of their lesser reputation, the unadvertised items will no longer be viable competitors unless their retail prices are well below those of the competing advertised brands. The combination of the RGM effect and the reputation premium exerts a substantial squeeze on the margins of unadvertised brand manufacturers, even as it elevates margins for the famous advertised brands.

So in the advertised industry, there is an inverse association between the margins of manufacturers of the leading advertised brands on the one hand and the margins of the retailer resellers of these brands and those of competing unadvertised producers on the other.

With respect to costs, advertising reduces retailers' short-run noninvoice costs by increasing turnover rates of advertised items. The effect at the manufacturer's level is mixed. It largely depends on the industry's life-cycle phase and on whether advertising is needed to achieve minimum efficient scale. MES is largest in industries requiring massive capital investments and complex manufacturing and assembly operations that give rise to a long "learning curve." These conditions are found in many consumer durables and in some nondurable products.

In some mature, intensively advertised categories, increased spending by rival brands no longer increases aggregate industry demand. If MES is also low, as with certain over-the-counter drugs, this combination can produce supracompetitive retail price levels, because even razor-thin retail markups are insufficient to offset the towering mean factory prices.

The Volume of Advertising and the Advertising Response Function

The above-described dynamics that underlie the intensively advertised industry explain why there is so much more brand advertising in our economy than single-stage models would predict. To maximize profits, the brand's manufacturer must jointly optimize for price and advertising budget.[8] To do that, the firm will continue to expand its advertising budget until the last dollar of advertising at the optimal price generates just a dollar of additional contribution margin, the latter being the difference between the extra revenue produced by the advertising and the marginal cost (excluding the cost of advertising) incurred to obtain it. Due to the three dual-stage effects, the response to advertising as experienced by the brand's manufacturer is much higher than it would appear in single-stage models, where retail penetration, dealer support, and retail gross margin are unaffected by the volume of advertising.

Studies of the advertising response function fail to discover the true function faced by the manufacturer because they have measured the response in the laboratory or, if in the marketplace, either in units or valued in the prices consumers pay. The first fails to capture any of the dual-stage effects, and the second two ignore the RGM effect.

When a brand's RGM is falling, its factory price is rising relative to its retail price. Therefore, when output is properly valued in the prices the manufacturer receives, the manufacturer can experience a period of increasing returns to advertising, although the returns appear to be diminishing when the response is measured in units or in retail prices.[9]

Three Other Industry Structures

In both the unadvertised and the intensively advertised industry structures there is a substantial difference between consumers' willingness to switch brands within store and their willingness to switch stores within brand, causing margins in the manufacturing and retailing sectors to be inversely related. In other industry structures these propensities are roughly equal, and margins at the two stages tend to be positively associated.

Mutual Dependence

Bowman has shown that manufacturers are often impelled to adopt resale price maintenance in industries where manufacturers and their retailers are "insecure partial monopolists" and the profits of each are dependent on those of the other.[10] For example, a brand with a modest advertising budget may be moderately popular, and its manufacturer may experience conflict among the three dual-stage effects. When a certain amount of retail price-cutting breaks out, the insecure manufacturer fears that many retailers will drop or at least downplay his brand because they will be able to switch numerous shoppers to a competing item with a higher margin. At the same time, the insecure retailers fear that if they do not meet the cut prices, the brand's consumer franchise is strong enough to cause many of their clientele to seek the item at a price-cutting store.

The mutual insecurity prompts a vertical deal. In exchange for guaranteeing the dealers a satisfactory margin, the manufacturer is able to maintain his own margin and his retail penetration and dealer support within the traditional-store segment, whose retailers are disinclined to engage in competitive price-cutting practices. As a result, average retail prices will not decline and will in all likelihood advance above the previous level.

In another scenario, a vertical deal can result from the exercise of strong countervailing bargaining pressure by dominant retailers against the manufacturers of brands with well-established consumer franchises.

The Mixed Regimen

When consumers are quite prone to switch both brands within store and stores within brand, and there are no vertical restraints, retail price levels will be below those in the other three structures that have been described. This "mixed-regimen" scenario usually requires that there be a group of leading advertised brands that are actively challenged by the private label offerings of the dominant chain store retailers. In essence, competition between the two kinds of brands holds both manufacturers' and retailers' margins at modest levels, an outcome that is unlikely to occur in other industry structures.

Consumer acceptance of the store brands selling at relatively low retail prices keeps the lid on the factory prices of the leading advertised brands. Adding the typically thin RGM of advertised brands to their relatively low factory prices produces a moderate level of advertised brand retail prices. At the same time, the advertised brands' reputation premium continues to ensure that competing private-label goods are sold at considerably lower retail prices. Private-label brands will lose substantial market share should their retail prices rise too far toward those of the advertised brands. And, as we have recently seen in cigarettes, detergents, disposable diapers, and cold cereals, if advertised brand factory prices become too high, the brands lose share to private labels and are then forced into major reductions in factory price.

The low consumer prices in the mixed regimen also reflect lower costs throughout the vertical system. The mass merchandisers that market their own-label brands and account for most of the retail sales of the leading national brands are very efficient operators. Moreover, if there are scale economies to be had in manufacturing, these will be reflected in lower costs and factory selling prices for the advertised brands and for the competing store brands, which are typically produced by a handful of private-label manufacturers that supply the leading chains.

"True" Commodity Industries

The four structures so far described are found in noncommodity industries, where manufacturers make physically differentiated, competing goods. But there are industries—including milk, sugar, eggs, gasoline, aspirin, and certain hardware and apparel categories—where all producers make goods that are homogeneous within grade, or virtually so. Yet we must classify as "true" commodity industries only those in which consumers recognize the product homogeneity across brands and across stores, often with the aid of grading (for example, Grade A extra-large eggs). These categories will have little or no advertising, because advertising cannot survive when it cannot successfully differentiate brands. In the absence of collusion, intensive competition brings about low margins at both stages.

When consumers are unaware of existing physical homogeneity, the industry behaves as though that condition did not exist, and it should therefore be classified under the appropriate noncommodity structure. Thus acetylsalicylic acid (Bayer Aspirin) and acetaminophen (Tylenol) are properly classified as intensively advertised industries. In certain apparel categories dominated by store brands, laboratory tests established that the rival brands were identical, but consumers appeared ignorant of this fact, so the category behaved like a typical unadvertised one.[11]

Short- and Long-Term Assessment

The above analysis has indicated that in noncommodity categories that are either heavily advertised or virtually unadvertised, margins of firms at the two stages will be inversely related. The same inverse relationship obtains in the manufacturing segment of intensively advertised industries between the margins of the leading advertised brands and those of unadvertised manufacturers' brands and private labels.

Depending on minimum efficient scale and the life-cycle phase, intensive advertising may or may not generate net cost saving in the industry's manufacturing sector. In the retailing sector, costs will be lower when individual brand turnover is faster and in industries where efficient mass merchandisers account for the lion's share of retail sales.

Based on the above and the foregoing analysis of the benefits of strong national-brand/private-label competition, we can conclude that retail price levels in noncommodity industries will be lowest where the mixed-regimen structure is in place. If the minimum efficient scale is reasonably large, retail prices tend to be lower in heavily advertised industries than in unadvertised ones, otherwise not; prices may often be highest in the mutual-dependence scenario, with its vertical restraints. Margins and prices will be at low, competitive levels in true commodity industries, absent collusion. Here, advertising plays no role.

Although we have seen that advertising does not always bring the lowest prices to consumers, it is essential to consumers' welfare due to its often pivotal role in the development of an array of innovative new products—a topic that is beyond the scope of the present chapter. Moreover, the foregoing price analysis has focused on the short run.

Over the longer haul, manufacturers' brand advertising has made a cost-reducing contribution of a different sort by facilitating a more efficient vertical allocation of functions in the consumer goods economy. Historically this has involved the upstream migration of the product information and reputation or certification functions from small-scale, clerk-serviced retail stores to the brand's manufacturer. Thanks to such capital-intensive innovations as the rotary printing press in the 19th century and the electronic media in the 20th century, these functions are now more efficiently provided through manufacturers' advertising messages rather than at the retail level.

This transformation of functions stimulated the growth of a series of new, capital-intensive forms of retailing that were designed to resell differentiated brands with which consumers had become familiar through advertising, as well as commodity products, at far slimmer markups over factory price than could the traditional merchants of the day. Some of these new retailing forms (e.g., supermarkets and discount stores) were self-service, whereas others, such as the original department store and contemporary Home Depot-type outlets, were not.

In all events, between the information provided by the manufacturer and the services provided by the mass merchant, consumers receive a somewhat different but not inferior bundle of services, along with lower prices, compared with what they had at the small-scale, traditional retail store.[12]

Notes

1. E. R. Hawkins, "Vertical Price Relationships," in Reavis Cox and Wroe Alderson (eds.), *Theory in Marketing* (Chicago: American Marketing Association, 1950), 179.

2. Richard B. Heflebower, "Mass Distribution: A Phase of Bilateral Oligopoly or of Competition?" *American Economic Review*, vol. 47, no. 2, 1957, 279.

3. Robert L. Steiner, "The Inverse Association Between the Margins of Manufacturers and Retailers," *Review of Industrial Organization*, vol. 8, 1993, 717-740.

4. Alfred Marshall, *Industry and Trade* (London: Macmillan, 1920); Emily Fogg-Meade, "The Place of Advertising in Modern Business," *Journal of Political Economy*, vol. 9, 1901, 218-242.

5. John Cady, *Restricted Advertising and Competition: The Case of Retail Drugs*, Domestic Affairs Study 44 (Washington, DC: American Enterprise Institute, 1976); Lee Benham and Alexandra Benham, "Regulating Through the Professions: A Perspective on Information Control," *Journal of Law and Economics*, vol. 18, October 1975, 421-447.

6. Robert L. Steiner, "Does Advertising Lower Consumer Prices?" *Journal of Marketing*, vol. 37, no. 4, 1973. See also Steiner, "The Inverse Association"; and Mark Albion, *Advertising's Hidden Effects* (Boston: Auburn House, 1983).

7. Dorothea Braithwaite, "The Economic Effects of Advertisement," *Economic Journal*, vol. 38, no. 149, 1928, 16-37. See also Neil Borden, *The Economic Effects of Advertising* (Chicago: Richard D. Irwin, 1942).

8. Robert Dorfman and Peter O. Steiner, "Optimal Advertising and Optimal Price," *American Economic Review*, vol. 44, no. 5, 1954, 826-836.

9. Robert L. Steiner, "Point of View: The Paradox of Increasing Returns to Advertising," *Journal of Advertising Research*, vol. 27, 1987, 45-63.

10. Ward Bowman, "Resale Price Maintenance: A Monopoly Problem," *Journal of Business*, vol. 25, 1952, 141-155.

11. Rachel Dardis and Louise Skow, "Variations for Soft Goods in Discount and Department Stores," *Journal of Marketing*, vol. 33, 1969, 45-50.

12. Robert L. Steiner, "The Nature of Vertical Restraints," *Antitrust Bulletin*, vol. 30, 1985, 81-135.

Editor's Note: The Steiner Effect and the Steiner Paradox

The preceding chapter is important for a number of reasons. First, Steiner's subtle and elegant analysis of the effect of manufacturers' consumer advertis-

ing on retail margins describes a phenomenon that has a widespread effect
that impinges on consumer welfare. The way in which consumer advertising
depresses retail margins is a major factor that causes consumer prices to go
down and acts as a countervailing force to the advertising-related pressures
that drive prices up. (These include the way in which manufacturers' consumer
advertising tends to raise manufacturers' own margins.)

Steiner was the first analyst to uncover advertising's contrasting effects on
retailers' and manufacturers' margins. His article "Does Advertising Lower
Consumer Prices?" which was published in October 1973 in the *Journal of
Marketing,* launched all the work on margins that was later carried out on both
sides of the Atlantic, notably that done by the American analysts Farris and
Albion.[1] In 1979, the British academic W. Duncan Reekie published interesting data from the United Kingdom and Australia on the effects of manufacturers' advertising on retail margins alone, but did not examine manufacturers'
margins.[2]

Michael Lynch (of the U.S. Federal Trade Commission) has used Steiner's
name to describe the effect of consumer advertising on margins; in Lynch's
words, "I call this negative correlation between gross margins at the retail and
manufacturing levels the 'Steiner Effect.' "[3] This label is entirely appropriate,
and I have used it in my own writings on the subject.

In a different type of investigation—on the effect of *retailers'* advertising
on retail margins—Lee Benham of the University of Chicago in 1972 compared the prices of eyeglasses in the states in which optometrists' services
could legally be advertised and those states where such advertising was
forbidden. Benham demonstrated with exquisite clarity that prices were
significantly lower in the states where eyeglasses were advertised.[4] (Benham
also demonstrated that most professors of economics and of marketing were
unable to predict this outcome!)

In his chapter, Steiner describes another phenomenon related to consumer
advertising and the distributive trade, a phenomenon also first disclosed by
his own analyses. In his discussion in the section headed "The Volume of
Advertising and the Advertising Response Function," Steiner states, "When
output is properly valued in the prices the manufacturer receives, the manufacturer can experience a period of increasing returns to advertising, although
the returns appear to be diminishing when the response is measured in units
or in retail prices."

Advertising normally yields diminishing returns to incremental pressure,
at least in the short term. Steiner's example describes the (perhaps common)

circumstances in which a brand is newly introduced, and when its distribution is building. The increasing returns that he isolates are driven by increasing retail distribution and dealer support, together with reduced retailer margins— all a response to successful advertising for the brand in question. I have found evidence of this effect in my own work, and I have described it as the *Steiner Paradox.*[5]

In his chapter, Steiner uses the term *retail penetration.* This concept is precise, but readers should note that in my own writing I describe the phenomenon as weighted (or dollar) distribution. My own use of the word *penetration* is confined to consumer purchasing, and I am naturally anxious to avoid confusion on this point.

Notes

1. Paul W. Farris and Mark Albion, "The Impact of Advertising on the Price of Consumer Products," *Journal of Marketing,* vol. 44, no. 3, 1980, 17-35.

2. W. Duncan Reekie, *Advertising and Price* (London: Advertising Association, 1979).

3. Michael P. Lynch, *The "Steiner Effect," a Prediction From a Monopolistically Competitive Model Inconsistent With Any Combination of Pure Monopoly or Competition,* Working Paper 141 (Washington, DC: Federal Trade Commission, Bureau of Economics, 1986).

4. Lee Benham, "The Effect of Advertising on the Price of Eyeglasses," *Journal of Law and Economics,* vol. 15, 1972, 336-352.

5. John Philip Jones, *Does It Pay to Advertise? Cases Illustrating Successful Brand Advertising* (New York: Simon & Schuster-Lexington, 1989), chaps. 1, 2.

Macroeconomic Effects

The Influence of Advertising on Overall Sales Levels

John Philip Jones

The macroeconomic or aggregate effects of advertising—as opposed to its influence on individual brands—have long been the subject of controversy. This issue has informed a number of debates about social welfare, such as whether advertising encourages the growth of what some people consider to be inessential and even pernicious expenditures at the expense of supposedly essential ones. In this chapter I examine a number of facts concerning the macroeconomic effects of advertising.

The two overarching factors dominating this issue are (a) the absence of growth in most consumer goods markets in economically mature countries and (b) the existence of dense clusters of competing brands in most product categories, most of which are heavily advertised, but the effect of whose advertising tends to be negated by the countervailing efforts of rival brands.

Market Maturity

In the United States, Canada, Japan, Australasia, most Western European countries, and other developed economies, there is little growth in total demand (sometimes known as primary demand) in most categories of consumer goods, except for a minority of special cases. In some of the latter demand is driven by technological innovations (e.g., computers); in others it is driven by changing lifestyles (e.g., the growth of diet soft drinks, bottled water, and muesli and related breakfast cereals). Yet others are very small in absolute size (e.g., dental rinse, eyewash and eyedrops, artificial sweeteners).

The fundamental reason for lack of growth is the large size most categories have reached already. In the United States, 90% of female homemakers buy breakfast cereals, and almost a third of these serve them on average more often than once a day.[1] The average American per capita consumption of soft drinks is more than 500 cans per year.[2] It is really difficult to see how these consumption levels can be much increased.

The situation is generally irreversible. It is very rare indeed for stagnant markets to resume the growth of earlier periods except in unusual circumstances (e.g., following fiscal changes, like a major reduction in sales tax, which may cause new growth in the demand for consumer durables by encouraging consumers to replace old but still serviceable equipment).

As incomes increase and consumer consumption does not, the result is that people tend to save an increasing proportion of their income. This tendency was detected by Keynes in the 1930s and formed an important part of his analysis of the secular causes of unemployment. What economists term the *increasing marginal propensity to save* is responsible for a gradual reduction in effective demand, because not all saving is converted into productive investment. This circumstance, in turn, calls for public investment to restore demand to the level needed to maintain full employment.

There is a mathematical reason why it is especially difficult for large individual brands to grow: the enormous size many of them have reached already. The growth in absolute terms that is called for by a steady annual percentage increase is something that becomes progressively, and eventually

TABLE 29.1   Changes in Volume Usage of 150 Major Consumer Goods,
                 1989 Compared With 1988 (in percentages)

Categories	Volume
All categories	100
Strongly growing categories (8% growth or more)	15
Modestly growing categories (3-7% growth)	28
Stable categories (1-2% growth, no change, or 1-2% decline)	34
Modestly declining categories (3-7% decline)	13
Strongly declining categories (8% decline or more)	10

SOURCE: Data provided by Mediamark Research Inc.

insupportably, larger than the increase of the year before. It is one thing to sell 10,000 extra units; it is another thing altogether to sell an extra 10 million.

Another point relating to market stagnation is that changes in consumer tastes, and the health scares that regularly enliven the lives of the American educated classes, have caused a decline in a number of important markets, such as cigarettes, coffee, dairy products, and hard liquor. Such declines (shown in Table 29.1) have to be balanced against the numbers of still-expanding categories before we can draw an overall conclusion about market trends. Table 29.1 shows data for 1988-1989; since that period, the balance of growing and declining categories has, if anything, become more negative.

The plateauing of most American consumer goods categories had taken place by the early 1980s.[3] Similar data are not available for other economically developed countries, but judgment suggests that these probably lagged a decade behind the United States.

Advertising's Weak Macro Effects

Ten Product Categories in Britain

High and in some cases increasing advertising expenditures are apparently unable to influence market size. Table 29.2 displays 10 important categories of repeat-purchase packaged goods on the British market. In these, the value of sales shows a downward trend; the advertising trend is erratic but upward overall.[4] It is clear from this table that the significant and often increasing expenditures on advertising have been unable to generate category growth, or even to arrest decline.

TABLE 29.2 Ten British Product Categories: Manufacturers' Sales and Advertising (both at 1990 prices)

| Year | Manufacturers' Sales | | Advertising | |
	£ (billions)	Index	£ (millions)	Index
1985	9.0	100	148	100
1986	9.1	101	168	114
1987	8.9	99	194	131
1988	8.9	99	221	149
1989	8.7	96	212	143
1990	8.4	94	180	121
1991	8.3	93	180	122
1992	8.4	94	188	127
1993	8.2	92	176	119
1994	8.1	90	173	117

A good deal of additional data exist that confirm that advertising is unable to drive markets upward. Following are some selected but typical examples.

British IPA Studies

The first eight volumes of authoritative cases describing advertising effects published by the British agencies association, the Institute of Practitioners in Advertising (IPA), contain 156 papers. Of these, 133 cases robustly demonstrate brand advertising to be outstandingly successful. Out of these cases, 110 (83%) indicate nothing about the influence of advertising on aggregate market size. Advertising's influence was felt exclusively on individual brand shares.[5]

Jean-Jacques Lambin

In 1976, the Belgian analyst Lambin published details of 10 cases in which he estimated the advertising elasticity of *category,* as opposed to brand, sales. By so doing, he isolated advertising's macro effect. In only 4 of the 10 cases (2 covering soft drinks and 1 each covering hair spray and transportation) was it possible to find a statistically significant advertising elasticity relating to markets as a whole. These were at a very low level of significance (25%). And the elasticities themselves were also small: In 3 of the 4 cases, they were below what is apparently the average advertising elasticity for brands in competitive markets.

Even more important, Lambin admitted that the 4 cases were examples of developing markets, "where product-related social, economic and technological forces are favorable to the spontaneous expansion of demand." [6]

Julian L. Simon

In 1970, the American economist Julian L. Simon published an examination of advertising and the propensity to consume, using an interesting and original array of empirical sources. Simon admitted the imperfections of most of his data, and the result of his evaluation was that he found the overall macro effect of advertising to be indeterminate; there was no clear effect either way. In other words, during the late 1960s, when consumer goods categories were still growing, Simon was unable to detect any evidence of macro effects from advertising.[7]

This conclusion is no great distance from Neil Borden's in the first serious examination of the economic effects of advertising, which was published more than half a century ago: "Basic trends of demand for products, which are determined by underlying social and environmental conditions, are more significant in determining the expansion or contraction of primary demand than is the use or lack of use of advertising." [8] Borden's conclusion relates specifically to the more mature markets, in which advertising arguments tend to be extremely discriminating (i.e., brand specific) rather than motivating (i.e., selling general product benefits). As I have noted, mature markets are the rule and not the exception in the United States in the 1990s.

Cigarettes

Lester G. Telser published in 1962 a rigorous analysis of the relationship between sales and advertising expenditures for Camel, Lucky Strike, Chesterfield, and other brands of cigarettes. Cigarettes have been an exceptionally advertising-intensive category, and Telser examined massive data from the earliest days of the brands he covered (Camels having been first sold in 1913). He concluded that "the levels of advertising were high enough to place the companies at the point where there were diminishing returns to advertising."

This conclusion is not really surprising in view of what is now known about the prevalence of diminishing returns to incremental advertising pressure.

Because Telser believed that Camels in particular "were supplying consumers with more advertising than they want," he provided oblique but persuasive evidence that advertising had reached levels at which it was no longer contributing to increased cigarette consumption.[9]

An interesting parallel conclusion can be drawn from the more recent progress of sales in the cigarette category. In this, overall consumption began to decline only in 1981, a decade after the major reduction in advertising expenditures that followed the removal of cigarette advertising from the television screen in early 1971. (Even since 1981, the decline has not been continuous.) The period 1971-1981 was a time of massive and uniformly unfavorable publicity about the effects of smoking on health. Not only does the stability of cigarette consumption provide evidence of the lack of responsiveness of demand to negative persuasion, but it also shows that advertising has little macro effect in a downward direction. In the same way that high levels of advertising do not increase category sales, reduced advertising does not depress them.

The specific relationship between advertising and cigarette consumption has been the subject of at least 19 econometric studies in a number of countries. A British academic named Duffy, of the University of Manchester, examined these reports, compared their findings, and reached the following general conclusion: "The balance of evidence suggests that aggregate cigarette advertising has had little or no influence upon total cigarette consumption in the U.S. in recent decades."[10] After examining data from Britain, New Zealand, West Germany, Spain, Australia, South Korea, and Greece, he arrived at broadly similar findings from these countries also.

Bar Soaps in Sweden

During the 1960s, the Unilever operating company in Sweden detected a flattening in total sales of toilet soap—a stagnation in average consumption per capita at a level below that in other developed countries, notably the United States. A special advertising campaign was mounted to try to get the total market moving again. It failed.[11] This is a typical experience for generic advertising campaigns, although there are some exceptions, one of which—for avocados—is discussed below.

The wide-ranging evidence cited above all points in a single direction—that advertising is incapable of generating primary demand. Any contrary evidence from mature categories to demonstrate that advertising is capable of stimulating overall demand is thin. I have referred to generic advertising, which embraces commodity/product group/industry campaigns, such as those for tea, milk, meat, fur, antifur, telephone usage, and seat belt usage. Such campaigns might be expected to boost primary demand, yet in practice, such advertising is "never credited with any big effects." [12]

As already discussed, advertising's generally weak macro effect is due partly to elevated consumption levels in developed categories and partly to the mutual cancellation of the effects of advertising for competitive brands. The latter will now be examined.

The Influence of Competition in Negating Advertising Effects

In order to find evidence bearing on the influence of competitive advertising, we need to find categories in which there is no direct competition, or at least no competitive advertising. I am aware of only one strong case: the generic advertising for avocados. [13]

The main point about most agricultural products is that they have no head-on competition. Demand in the category is narrowly confined and is therefore sluggish in the short term. However, supply is controlled by nature, and can fluctuate widely without human intervention, strictly according to weather conditions. Heavy supplies of avocados reduce price and demand is slow to pick up; short supplies boost price and demand is slow to contract. Described technically, the demand for avocados is rather inelastic—a phenomenon described diagrammatically by a steeply falling demand curve.

The main avocado producers in the United States, California farmers, had suffered during the 1950s from the slowness of demand in responding to price reductions. Every heavy crop had a disastrous effect on prices and consequently on farm incomes.

The 1959-1960 season produced an enormous supply of fruit, which had the expected effect on prices and incomes. As a result, the farmers got together to set up a cooperatively funded advertising and publicity campaign aimed at helping to stabilize the market. The intention was to increase primary (i.e., total) demand, not just demand for particular varieties or fruit from certain regions. This was to be done, first, by encouraging existing users to buy more

TABLE 29.3 Average Value of California Avocados ($ per acre)

Period	Value
1950-1951 through 1954-1955	588
1955-1956 through 1959-1960	413
1960-1961 through 1964-1965	529
1965-1966 through 1969-1970	938
1970-1971 through 1974-1975	1,756

(e.g., by showing recipes in the advertising), and second, by bringing new buyers into the market. Boosting demand in this way could be expected to be a slow process.

As with all agricultural products, the size of the avocado crop is governed (as I have mentioned) by the forces of nature, and because the fruit is perishable, it cannot be stored to carry stocks forward from year to year. All avocados grown during the season have to be eaten or thrown away. This is why a heavy crop brings down prices. However, if advertising pushes up demand, the price will increase without any response in increased output within the same season. This characteristic of the market enables us to freeze the effect of advertising on price.

Theory would therefore lead us to expect sharply increasing prices as a measure of advertising's success in boosting consumer demand. The evidence confirms that this is what happened. Table 29.3 shows the figures for a sequence of five periods of 5 years each (averaged in order to even out short-term fluctuations). There was no advertising and promotion during the first two periods; the campaign began in 1960.

From the period of lowest prices, and using the average price during this period as a base index of 100, average returns per acre increased to an index of 128 during 1960-1965, to 227 during 1965-1970, and to 425 during 1970-1975. These increases are uncorrected for inflation, but they are greater than any increase that inflation alone would have brought about. This is especially true of the huge increases in 1965-1970 and 1970-1975. Essentially, the only change that took place in the marketing of avocados before the price rise was the advertising and publicity campaign, so that the price increase can be reliably attributed to this campaign. The number of households purchasing avocados increased during the period, and so did the average household purchases of the fruit. Significantly, purchases went up most among older households—those to which the advertising campaign was mainly directed.

Here then is a clear case of advertising's ability to stimulate primary demand. However, the following factors make the avocado example a special case:

1. The boost in demand for avocados took place during the decade from the mid-1960s to the mid-1970s. In this period there was still a good deal of growth in consumer goods expenditure in the United States.
2. The campaign itself was planned and executed with far greater subtlety and finesse than is the case with most generic advertising, which tends to be monolithic and very direct.
3. The growth in avocado consumption was from a low base level. The market (narrowly defined) was nowhere near maturity.
4. Although there is no direct competition for avocados, there is indirect competition—from different types of food eaten as dips, hors d'oeuvres, and salad ingredients. The demand for avocados is narrowly restricted in the immediate present, but it can be stretched over time by successful advertising, which encourages the gradual acceptance of avocados in place of indirect substitutes. This factor of partial substitutability therefore enables us to understand the responsiveness of avocado demand to the unquestionably successful advertising campaign.

The avocado case emphasizes the importance of competitive advertising as a factor inhibiting category growth. It does this by demonstrating the reverse relationship—that such growth can be stimulated by an effective campaign exposed in the absence of competitive advertising. But the avocado case is highly unusual. The normally large amount of competitive advertising activity in consumer goods categories, added to the irreversible maturity of most such categories, means that the avocado case should not cause us to modify the general conclusion that advertising *has generally little effect at the macro level,* no matter how much it may influence the demand for individual brands.

Notes

1. John Philip Jones, *How Much Is Enough? Getting the Most From Your Advertising Dollar* (New York: Simon & Schuster-Lexington, 1992), 26.

2. John Philip Jones, *Does It Pay to Advertise? Cases Illustrating Successful Brand Advertising* (New York: Simon & Schuster-Lexington, 1989), 143.

3. Jones, *How Much Is Enough?* 26.

4. Harry Henry, "Does Advertising Affect Total Market Size?" *Admap,* January 1996, 16-19. The product categories covered were breakfast cereals, instant coffee, tea, biscuits, cheese,

cakes/buns, frozen fish products, bread, butter, and frozen vegetables. Of these, the only category that showed any responsiveness to increased advertising pressure was breakfast cereals.

5. Simon Broadbent (ed.), *Does Advertising Affect Market Size?* (London: Advertising Association, 1997).

6. Jean-Jacques Lambin, *Advertising, Competition and Market Conduct in Oligopoly Over Time* (New York: American Elsevier, 1976).

7. Julian L. Simon, "The Effect of Advertising Upon the Propensity to Consume," in *Issues in the Economics of Advertising* (Urbana: University of Illinois Press, 1970), 193-217.

8. Neil Borden, *The Economic Effects of Advertising* (Chicago: Richard D. Irwin, 1942), 433.

9. Lester G. Telser, "Advertising and Cigarettes," *Journal of Political Economy,* October 1962, 471-499.

10. M. Duffy, "Econometric Studies of Advertising, Advertising Restrictions and Cigarette Demand: A Survey," *International Journal of Advertising,* 1995.

11. These observations are based on my own personal experience dating from the period 1967 to 1972, when I was responsible for the advertising for the largest brand of bar soap in Sweden.

12. Andrew S. C. Ehrenberg and Neil Barnard, "Advertising and Product Demand," *Admap,* May 1997, 14-18.

13. Steven A. Greyser, "California Avocado Advisory Board," in Steven A. Greyser (ed.), *Cases in Advertising and Communications Management* (Englewood Cliffs, NJ: Prentice Hall, 1981), 23-61.

Name Index

Subject Index

About the Authors

Alexander L. Biel is a distinguished international market research and marketing consultant, as well as an acknowledged expert on brand equity and advertising evaluation. He was educated at the University of Chicago and Columbia University. After serving as Associate Director of Research at Leo Burnett, he held a series of senior posts at Ogilvy & Mather in Europe and North America. He was Executive Director of David Ogilvy's Center for Research & Development (later the WPP Center for R&D). He is the author of more than 70 articles and papers on marketing topics, and his 1993 book *Brand Equity and Advertising* (with David Aaker) is in its fourth printing. He is a nonexecutive director of Research International and President of Alexander L. Biel & Associates.

Leo Bogart (Ph.D., University of Chicago) is a marketing consultant and columnist for *Presstime Magazine.* Previously, he was Executive Vice President and General Manager of the Newspaper Advertising Bureau. He has directed opinion research for Standard Oil Company (New Jersey; now Exxon), marketing research for Revlon, and international research for McCann-Erickson. Among his books are *Strategy in Advertising, Commercial Culture,* and *Polls and the Awareness of Public Opinion.* He has served as President of the American and World Associations for Public Opinion Research, the Society for Consumer Psychology, the Market Research Council, and the Radio and Television Research Council. He and George Gallup were the first persons to be elected to the Market Research Council Hall of Fame.

Simon Broadbent began his work in media research and advertising in 1962, after 7 years at universities and three jobs in the industry, the last as a marketing manager. He has worked for Leo Burnett in London and Chicago, and is a founding partner of the Brand Consultancy. He currently chairs the U.K. Advertising Association's Economics Committee. His academic background and training in engineering have formed his main interest, in which he is one of the world's leading experts: measurement of the effectiveness of advertising. He helped start the Advertising Effectiveness Awards run by the Institute of Practitioners in Advertising, and also edited the first three books on the subject: *Advertising Works, Advertising Works 2,* and *20 Advertising Case Histories.* He has published books on media and media research (*Spending Advertising Money*), on the decision concerning how much an advertiser should spend (*The Advertiser's Guide to Budget Determination*), and on campaign evaluation and planning (*Accountable Advertising*).

Fiona Chew received her Ph.D. in communications from the University of Washington, and is currently Associate Professor at the Newhouse School of Public Communications, Syracuse University. She is an active consultant on various national and international telecommunications projects. She has assessed the impact of television and mass media on audience perceptions, and was involved in a four-country project that investigated the impact of a five-part television series on health. She was also coinvestigator for a Kellogg Foundation research grant project that evaluated the long-term national impact of a television program. Her other projects include assessing the perceptions of news viewers for MacNeil/Lehrer Productions and evaluating the appeal, comprehensibility, and after-school use of science programs for Children's Television Workshop. She is a former television/film producer of educational programs, has worked for a consumer market research organization, and was a research director at a major-market public television station. Her research interests focus on message analysis and effects, health communication, and information needs. She has published in the major journals in her field.

W. Edwards Deming (1900-1993) was an engineer, a statistician, and one of the world's leading marketing thinkers—a guru whose ideas have exercised enormous influence. He began to study Japanese industry after 1945 and contributed to its spectacular growth. He conceived the philosophy of total quality management, the widely applied management system aimed at the highest-quality production accompanied by reductions in costs. The drive toward these objectives is provided by cooperative work among employees at all levels, totally focused on and committed to the same goals. He was a believer in the idea that the person who does no research has nothing to teach.

Andrew S. C. Ehrenberg has been Professor of Marketing at South Bank University, London, since 1993. He was trained as a mathematician, and he spent 23 years at the London Business School and has held academic appointments at Cambridge, Columbia, Durham, London, New York University, Pittsburgh, and Warwick. He was in the advertising industry for 15 years, at research companies and at an agency. He is a former Chairman of the Market Research Society (U.K.) and was Gold Medalist in 1969 and 1996. He is an expert in the empirical study of consumer behavior with theory to match, as well as in advertising, promotions, and pricing. With his colleagues he has published 10 books and monographs and more than 300 papers, which have appeared in *Nature, Journal of the Market Research Society, Admap, Journal of the Royal Statistical Society, Journal of Advertising Research, Journal of Marketing Research,* and *Journal of Marketing.* He is an active speaker and consultant on both sides of the Atlantic.

Paul Feldwick, a graduate of Oxford University, is a leading British advertising analyst and planner. Head of Account Planning at BMP DDB, London (the agency where Stanley Pollitt pioneered the account planning concept in the 1960s), he also has global responsibilities with DDB Needham Worldwide. He is a key participant in the Institute of Practitioners in Advertising (IPA) Advertising Effectiveness Awards and editor of two volumes of the collected prize-winning papers, *Advertising Works 5* and *Advertising Works 6.* A Fellow of the IPA and of the Market Research Society (U.K.), he is a well-known writer and speaker on advertising and research topics.

Donald Gunn is Director of Creative Resources Worldwide at Leo Burnett Company. He graduated from Cambridge University in 1962 with a B.A. in social anthropology, and was appointed Account Executive trainee at the British advertising agency the London Press Exchange (acquired by the Leo Burnett Company in 1969). He changed positions from Account Director to Copywriter in 1968. He has served as Creative Director at Leo Burnett in South Africa, the Netherlands, and France, and has also served as Regional Creative Director in Europe on the Philip Morris account. In 1984 he was transferred to the Leo Burnett head office in Chicago to become Director of Creative Resources Worldwide, and he has been carrying out this role based in London since 1995.

Nigel S. Hollis, a British-born market researcher, is Group Research & Development Director for Millward Brown International, based in Connecticut. (Millward Brown is probably the most important research company in the world that specializes in brand and advertising tracking.) He began his market research career at Cadbury Schweppes in the United Kingdom. He joined Millward Brown in 1983, and had a key role in the development of Millward Brown's successful TV LINK pretest. In 1988 he transferred to the United States and, before moving to his current position, worked on a variety of client businesses, mostly related to the analysis of tracking research. He has published in the *Journal of Advertising Research, Admap, Planung und Analyse,* and *Journal of the Market Research Society* (U.K.). The topics of his research include brand equity measurement, ad banner effectiveness on the World Wide Web, and sales response modeling.

John Philip Jones is a British-born American academic and a graduate of Cambridge University (B.A. with honors and M.A. in economics). He spent 27 years in the advertising agency business, including 25 years with J. Walter Thompson in Britain, Holland, and Scandinavia, managing the advertising for a wide range of major brands of repeat-purchase packaged goods. In 1981, he joined the faculty of the Newhouse School of Public Communications, Syracuse University, where he is now a tenured full Professor and former Chairman of the Advertising Department. He is also Adjunct Professor at the Royal Melbourne Institute of Technology, Australia. His published works include five books and more than 70 journal articles. He specializes in the measurement of advertising effects, and is an active consultant to many advertisers and advertising agencies in the United States and overseas. He has been the recipient of a number of professional awards, and is currently a member of the (U.S.) National Advertising Review Board.

Timothy Joyce (1933-1997), who was educated at Cambridge University, worked for J. Walter Thompson Company for 20 years, becoming Research Director of J. Walter Thompson, New York, and subsequently Media Director of J. Walter Thompson, London. A research innovator, he originated in Britain the pioneer system of syndicated single-source research that was subsequently copied in detail in the United States by the organization now known as Simmons Market Research Bureau. He left J. Walter Thompson and founded Mediamark Research Inc. in 1979. He subsequently worked as an Executive Consultant for A. C. Nielsen, and, until his death in September 1997, was Vice Chairman of the Starch Division of Roper Starch Worldwide. He is the author of many important papers on advertising and research topics.

Herbert E. Krugman started his career in the Psychological Branch, Office of the Air Surgeon, HQ, U.S. Army Air Force. He has been on the faculties of Yale, Princeton, and Columbia Universities. He served as Research Vice President, Raymond Leowy Associates, and at Marplan, before becoming Manager of Public Opinion Research at the General Electric Corporation (GE). It was at GE that he became a seminal contributor to the study of the psychological workings of advertising, and originator of the concepts of high and low involvement. He later became Principal of Herbert E. Krugman & Associates. He has been President of the American Association for Public Opinion Research, American Psychological

Association (Consumer Psychology), and the Market Research Council, and a member of the boards of several research organizations, including the Advertising Research Foundation, Marketing Science Institute, and Roper Institute. He has published 60 articles.

Josh McQueen (B.S., M.S., University of Illinois) joined Leo Burnett, Chicago, in 1974. He became Associate Research Director of Burnett's London office in 1978, Research Director of Burnett's Australia/Asia offices in 1980, and then returned to the United States in 1984 to become Burnett's Director of Research in 1985. He was named Executive Vice President in 1988, joined the Board of Directors in 1993, and became Global Head of Planning in 1996.

Scott D. Moore (Ph.D., University of Illinois) joined Leo Burnett, Chicago, in 1988 as Assistant Research Analyst. He then became, in turn, Research Analyst, Senior Research Analyst, Research Manager, Associate Research Director, and, in 1994, Director of Consumer Modeling. He has extensive experience with a broad range of clients.

Paula Pierce holds a B.A. in psychology and sociology from Fairleigh Dickinson University and has completed doctoral course work at the City University of New York Graduate Center. She is Vice President, Director of Qualitative Services for McCollum Spielman Worldwide (MSW). In addition, she is heavily involved in the development and direction of MSW's international, multicultural projects, qualitative, quantitative, and custom. With some 20 years in the business, her experience encompasses concept, strategy, copy, product, and packaging evaluation, as well as attitude/usage and customer satisfaction studies. She writes and edits MSW's newsletter, *Topline,* and has written many MSW white papers on topics such as celebrities, humor, and emotional and multicultural advertising. Her work has been published in the *Journal of Advertising Research, Quirk's,* and other industry journals, and she recently contributed chapters to marketing/advertising college textbooks edited by Larry Percy and Giep Franzen. She is a member of the Qualitative Research Consultants Association.

Alfred Politz (1902-1982) arrived in the United States in 1937 as a refugee from Nazi Germany. He had received a Ph.D. in physics and had already had a successful 8-year career in marketing and advertising research before his arrival in the United States. During the 1940s and 1950s he was the major figure in the American marketing and advertising research fields, providing counsel to most of the leading advertisers in the country. Arguably the most important figure the market research industry has ever produced, he will be particularly remembered for his development of random/probability sampling.

Jan S. Slater holds a B.A. from Hastings College in Hastings, Nebraska; an M.S. in advertising from the University of Illinois, Urbana-Champaign; and Ph.D. in mass communications from the Newhouse School of Public Communications at Syracuse University. Currently, she is Assistant Professor and Director of the Advertising Program in the Communication Arts Department at Xavier University in Cincinnati, Ohio. Previously, she was an instructor in advertising and public relations at the University of Nebraska at Omaha and at the Newhouse School at Syracuse University. In addition to her 10 years of teaching experience, she has had 20 years in the advertising business, working in both private industry and advertising agencies. Until 1990, she owned her own agency, J. Slater & Associates in Omaha, Nebraska.

Robert L. Steiner began an eclectic career after receiving an undergraduate degree from Dartmouth and an M.A. in economics from Columbia. It commenced with a 25-year stint as a consumer goods manufacturer in soap, soft drink concentrates, housewares, over-the-counter drugs, and toys, where he became president of Kenner Products Co. While teaching a graduate course in the history of marketing thought at the University of Cincinnati, he was asked to join the staff of the Federal Trade Commission, where he served for 5 years as a Senior Staff Economist. He has published widely in leading scholarly journals in economics, law, marketing, and advertising. The Steiner Effect and the Steiner Paradox are named after him. Currently, he is active as a business and economics consultant in Washington, D.C.

Alice K. Sylvester (B.S., M.S., DePaul University) spent 11 years with J. Walter Thompson, Chicago, ending as Senior Vice President/Media Research. From 1994 through 1997, she was with Leo Burnett, Chicago, first as Director of Brand Economics, where she explored the dynamics of brand accountability in all its aspects, then as Account Planner. In 1997, she joined Young & Rubicam in Chicago. She is Chair of the Board of Directors of the Advertising Research Foundation and serves on the Editorial Review Board of the *Journal of Advertising Research.*

Brian Wansink (Ph.D., Stanford University) has been a Marketing Professor at Dartmouth College (1990-1994), at the Vrije Universiteit in Amsterdam (1994-1995), and at the Wharton School at the University of Pennsylvania (1995-1997). Currently he is working at the University of Illinois, Urbana-Champaign, to establish a research program that focuses on brand revitalization—specifically to determine the types of advertising and packaging that increase the usage frequency and usage volume of mature packaged goods. His research has been sponsored by several Fortune 500 packaged goods companies, and it has won an award for its managerial relevance. His work has also been reported on the front pages of the *New York Times* and the *Wall Street Journal.* He is on the editorial boards of the *Journal of Marketing* and the *Journal of Advertising Research.*